Pan Africanism or Ne Colonialism?

Elenga M'buyinga

Pan Africanism or Neo-Colonialism?

The Bankruptcy of the O.A.U.

Elenga M'buyinga

Translated by Michael Pallis

Zed Press, 57 Caledonian Road,
London N1 9DN.

Union des Populations du Cameroun/
The Camerounian People's Union

887-253

Pan Africanism or Neo-Colonialism? was
first published in French by the Union des
Populations du Cameroun (U.P.C.) in 1975
under the title *PanAfricanisme et Neocolo-
nialisme*. First published in revised and
expanded edition in English by the U.P.C.
and Zed Press, 57 Caledonian Road, London
N1 9DN in 1982.

Facilitated by Amon Mukwedi

Typeset by Jenny Donald
Proofread by Penelope Fryxell
Cover design by Jan Brown Designs
Cover illustration by John Minnion
Printed by Redwood Burn, Trowbridge, Wiltshire

**British Library Cataloguing in
Publication Data**

M'buyinga, Elenga
    Pan-Africanism or neo-colonialism?
    1. Organisation of African Unity-
        History
    I. Title
    341.24'9   DT1.0754

    ISBN 0 86232 076 3
    ISBN 0 86232 013 5 Pbk

U.S. Distributor
Lawrence Hill and Co., 520 Riverside
Avenue, Westport, Conn. 06880, U.S.A.

Dedication

To all those who devoted their lives to a politically united
and genuinely independent Africa, especially Felix Moumie,
Patrice Lumumba, Kwame Nkrumah — pioneers of revolutionary Pan Africanism.

Contents

Really to understand what goes on in the world today, it is necessary to understand the economic influences and pressures that stand behind the political events.

Kwame Nkrumah
1965

Foreword to the English Edition

In this book, which is really more a book by our Party, the Cameroon Peoples' Union (U.P.C.) than simply by me, the author, we have tried to clarify the question of Pan-Africanism under the present neo-colonial conditions. During the course of more than 30 years of struggle, the U.P.C. in Cameroon, as well as on the African scene generally, has gained a rich political experience which has been set out in various pamphlets, and is brought together in this book.

What gives a certain importance to the present study is that it does not only focus on one or another aspect of the present neo-colonial situation in Africa, but, on the contrary, deals with neo-colonialism in our continent as a whole, and tries to find the fundamental roots of this policy being implemented by the present ruling classes in Africa.

The Scope of This Book

In Chapter 1, we give a summary, as briefly as possible, of the various ways Pan-Africanism has been conceived from the time the concept first appeared in 1900 to the May 1963 Conference which founded the Organization of African Unity (O.A.U.) in Addis Ababa.

Chapter 2 deals with the evolution of the African economy and of the imperialist nations' economies which determine that of our countries. This economic base is what can give us the keys to finding the answer to the question how to understand and explain the policies of the African ruling classes during the first 20 years of independence.

Chapter 3 develops our explanation of these policies, which we call the strategy of Pan-African Demagogy. This is the strategy being implemented by the emerging African neo-colonial bourgeoisies, who are telling mountains of lies to the African peoples and to world opinion about economic development, social integration and political unity.

Chapter 4 turns logically to the crucial political question: what is to be done? Here we try to define what it means to speak of Revolutionary Pan-Africanism today.

This is where the original (1975) edition of the book ended. But when our Party decided to publish a second French edition in late 1978 the bankruptcy of the O.A.U. had become a fact of common knowledge, beyond any doubt, and impossible to hide. It appeared impossible to avoid saying something about this problem. So Epilogue on the Bankruptcy of the O.A.U. was added.

The second edition was further enlarged by a Preface and a new Introduction which the reader will find here. Lastly, we should point out that the Appendix that appears here has its aim to criticize politically and ideologically the idea that certain opportunists — Cameroonians and others — are trying to spread amongst revolutionaries in our country as well as elsewhere in Africa.

The Central Questions Concerning Pan-Africanism

Briefly speaking, this whole study turns around two main problems. The first problem is as follows. Until the Ghana coup of 1966 which overthrew Kwame Nkrumah's regime, African revolutionary militants considered that the Pan-African Revolutionary Movement included three inseparable components: (1) the progressive independent African states, (2) the liberation movements fighting old-style colonialism, and (3) those revolutionary organizations struggling against African neo-colonial puppet regimes. Now, it has become necessary in our — the U.P.C. — view to pose the question whether these three components still form a coherent movement: i.e. do they still fight together in the same direction and with the same goals, or not?

The second problem involves the question: Does revolutionary Pan-Africanism, as the ideology of the Pan-African revolutionary movement, still have the same content in 1980 as it had in 1960? If so, why? And if not, what is its present content?

As soon as one looks at these two problems, one is led straight to face the following questions:
(1) What is Pan-Africanism, and, more precisely, Revolutionary Pan-Africanism? What does it mean and what are its contents?
(2) Why is it accurate today to claim that the policy of a large number of African ruling parties, which many people pretend is a revolutionary Pan-African policy, is not so at all? Or, in other words, what is this policy of Pan-African Demagogy?
(3) Are we currently undergoing a crisis or, more accurately, the bankruptcy of Pan-Africanism? Who is responsible for this bankruptcy?
(4) Does any link exist between imperialism, in its present form of neo-colonialism, and the victory that opportunism, using Pan-African rhetoric, has for the time being won over the Progressive Pan-African movement?
(5) In which ways are Pan-African Demagogy and the petty-bourgeois micro-nationalisms in Africa connected to each other?
(6) What is to be done?

These are the main questions we had in mind when this book was first published in 1975. And they are the questions this book has tried to tackle and solve without beating about the bush.

The Bogus Francophone/Anglophone Division

Our Party and its MANIDEM Movement* (the Popular United Front around
the U.P.C.) attach great importance to the publication of this English edition
of our book. Firstly, African peoples and specially African revolutionaries
are facing today a curious phenomenon — a sort of duality in every field,
which divides the Black African peoples into so-called *Francophones* and
English-speaking (or *Anglophones*). Despite some progress during recent years,
many persons, and especially intellectuals who are francophones, remain
ignorant about what is happening intellectually and politically in the
anglophone countries, and vice versa. Yet each group is well informed about
intellectual and other events in France and Britain. We are, therefore,
witnessing (and even participating in) a strange behaviour, which actually
perpetuates the divisions set up by the slavetraders' conference of 1884-85
in Berlin. Furthermore, it is quite obvious that, by accepting these empty
concepts of francophone and anglophone, we are weakening our own capacity
for liberation. We maintain a veritable Great Wall of China between two
groups of African freedom-fighters on the senseless ground that these groups
speak two different slavetraders' languages. Moreover, problems which are
common to all African peoples are usually not tackled by either group
from the correct basic point of view: *the African Peoples' one*. Instead they
often try to find solutions to African problems according to either the
British or the French way of thinking.

Secondly, this question of francophone and English-speaking African
countries highlights one aspect of the shameful political bankruptcy of the
Organization of African Unity: the language problem. No observer has failed
to take note of the fact that the O.A.U. has adopted only three languages
for its meetings and documents: English, French and Arabic! Of course, in
Africa, countries termed Arab do make up a population of some 70 million
people. It may therefore be quite right that their language be used as one of
the working languages of the O.A.U. On the other hand, nobody can argue
that there are really 50 million people in Africa who in practice use French as
their daily language, and the same remark holds for English. So, what about
Kiswahili, spoken by something like 100 million inhabitants in Africa, and
which is the most important Black African language today and one of the 10
major languages in the world? Had the O.A.U. adopted Kiswahili as one of
its languages, such a decision would have helped transform this pre-eminent
African mother tongue into a much more highly regarded, studied and spoken
tongue in the whole continent. It would have become a tool of communication, at least between African writers, no matter whether they were so-called
francophones or anglophones.

There is one important point which must be brought out. Every African
patriot is perfectly aware that countries like Kenya or Tanzania cannot
demand that Kiswahili be adopted as one of the working languages of the

* MANIDEM stands for 'MANIfesto for DEMocracy'.

O.A.U. The reason is quite simple: in view of their well-known puppet behaviour ever since the colonial period, people like Houphouet-Boigny of the Ivory Coast would develop their stupid 'theories' according to which this would be an attempt by Kenya and Tanzania to impose their own language on the O.A.U. And his colleagues in puppetism would also fight to defend their masters' language. Then, because of the well-known attitude within the O.A.U. ('we must, above all, avoid any risk of a split'), everybody would say: let us continue with English, French and Arabic. And the situation would remain unchanged!

This makes it very important that all African patriots and militants adopt a clear position on this language problem and, without any chauvinism, demand that Kiswahili (and even Hausa, the second most widely spoken language in Black Africa, spoken by something like 50 million people) be adopted by the O.A.U. as a working language. The question is so obviously important. Yet the O.A.U. which dares to pretend to be working for the liberation of Africa from foreign domination (including, presumably, cultural domination the destructive impact of which is notorious), has not found even a minute of time to solve it. No wonder we are justified in claiming that the failure of the O.A.U. on this language question is really an event of far-reaching significance.

Talking of francophones and anglophones in Africa today, trying to make the divisions between these two groups important, and failing to find African solutions to the question of lingua franca in Africa, is really a most shameful sell-out. By failing to solve this and similar problems the O.A.U. and those who support the already bankrupt Addis Ababa organization, are all contributing to keeping what are only secondary problems in the forefront of people's consciousness. *And by doing so, they are helping to hide what is the main emerging question in the present-day Africa: the deeper and deeper division of African society into classes and hence the class struggle which is the inevitable consequence of this division.* In creating such a diversion, they of course give great satisfaction to the African neo-colonial bourgeoisies who are shouting unceasingly that there exist no social classes — and no class struggles — in Africa today. But everyone is aware of the real facts.

Class as the Determinant of Africa's Future

Indeed, one of the central theses of this book is that what has happened in Africa during the past 20 years, as far as Pan-Africanism and African Unity are concerned, is fundamentally the consequence of the development of classes and class struggles in our continent. Every African who wants to fully understand the trend of events in the 1970s and 1980s must ask: How did Africans of the 1940s and the 1950s, like Jomo Kenyatta, Nnamdi Azikiwe, Julius Nyerere or Kwame Nkrumah in the anglophones' countries — or Sekou Toure, Houphouet-Boigny, Felix Moumie or Patrice Lumumba in francophones' countries — deal with Pan-Africanism and the problems of

African Unity? What were their conceptions of this matter? And what happened thereafter?

Some people try to behave as if History has never existed: this is the fundamental behaviour of the African ruling bourgeoisies today. This book, therefore, felt bound to recall some truths impossible to deny because they are registered in History. Using quotations from many of these African Heads of State, our Party intends to prove here that the various political theories and actions re Pan-Africanism and African Unity are rooted on class positions. Many people still try to explain what is happening in our countries in terms of the spitefulness of this or that leader. Some try to explain the total bankruptcy of the O.A.U. in terms of the inability of this or that president of the Organization. Our book, in contrast, tries to prove that, if somebody really intends to find the right explanation for the political *volte-faces* of leaders like Jomo Kenyatta or Sekou Toure (despite the latter's rhetoric), then one must, first of all, look at the development of the class structure of African societies since independence in the 1960s, rather than at individuals however apparently important their personal roles may be.

Within the Cameroonian revolutionary movement, the embodiment of which is now the MANIDEM led by the U.P.C., we believe that, if African leaders from such different countries as Kenya, Tunisia, Guinea etc. have failed during 20 years of office to achieve genuine liberation and authentic democratic and popular societies, then such a large and important phenomenon cannot be due to the personal defects of this or that individual. *It is basically due to social changes which have occurred during the long years of neo-colonialism our countries have undergone since 1960. It is due to the development of capitalism in Africa. And this has led the nationalistic petty bourgeoisie that existed at the end of the 1950s to become a turncoat and a neo-colonial bourgeoisie. Whatever mystifications and panaceas this class may continue to turn out, in attempts to mislead the African workers, poor peasants and radical youths, it is quite clear that the reactionaries will in the long run fail.*

Africa has entered a new phase in its history. From now on, there are only two alternatives: Neo-Colonialism or Socialism. But under present African and world conditions, *Socialism in our countries necessarily needs the political unity of African peoples and countries. A necessary (and we believe sufficient) condition for this to happen is that the African working class and poor peasantry take hold of the leadership of the revolutionary movement in each country and in the continent as a whole. They must build this movement in the form of a powerful African Peoples' Revolutionary Alliance (APRA), fighting clearly for a Union of African Socialist Republics.* This is our central argument.

Of course, we are not empty dreamers. We know that many people, hiding their interests behind plausible rhetoric, will find these ideas not at all realistic, even utopian. But we are sure that the ideas contained in this book and in analyses by other genuine African anti-imperialist militants and fighters will ultimately be proved correct by the direction of History.
Elenga M'buyinga, 1 May 1981.

5

Preface

In presenting this second enlarged edition of *Pan-Africanism and Neo-Colonialism* by our comrade Elenga M'buyinga, we feel that one question, above all others, calls for an answer: what course is now open to us; what is to be done?

What is to be Done?

The O.A.U. is bankrupt. We need a Revolutionary Pan-African Organization!
Raised around various issues, this slogan has been at the heart of all our party's work on Pan-Africanism and the prospects for an African Revolutionary Movement during the last five years. The bankruptcy of the Organization of African Unity (O.A.U.) is a plain and undeniable fact. Yet few people bother to point it out, for the simple reason that the present state of affairs suits the present rulers perfectly. But what is a Revolutionary Pan-African Organization? How can it be created? Why is it now, more than ever, an historical necessity? These questions demand a fuller explanation, especially today.

A Revolutionary United Front of the African Peoples

The creation of a Revolutionary United Front of all African Peoples has, in our opinion, become the most important and most urgent task facing progressive African militants. This task is not reducible to promoting a vague solidarity or even to adopting a common strategy of struggle. A Revolutionary United Front of African Peoples can only be viable and impose itself as the necessary historical alternative to the O.A.U. quagmire if it assigns itself, as its central goal, the task of establishing a Union of Socialist Republics of Africa.

In many respects, the African people enjoy fewer freedoms and civil rights in the era of the O.A.U. than they did under colonialism. But they have acquired considerable experience and reached a higher level of political consciousness: it has now become possible to create a Revolutionary United

Front of the African Peoples, just as, under colonialism, it was possible to launch the R.D.A. (*Rassemblement Democratique Africain*).*

Those who describe the call for a Union of Socialist Republics of Africa as utopian, and who do so while pretending to express the feelings of the African people are hardly trustworthy realists. Let us recall that, following the Second World War, it was exactly this kind of pseudo-representatives of the people, corrupt feudal chiefs and booklicking petty officials, who thought that independence was also so absurd as to be out of the question. Today, they have become the pillars of neo-colonialism.

The first step in understanding the importance and historical necessity of a Revolutionary United Front of the African Peoples is to get rid of a myth which is still widely taken as the starting point for every attempt at political analysis of events in our continent. This simplistic myth, wrapped around a neologism, is that East and West are struggling to 'destabilize' Africa. Most of the manipulation of public opinion and misleading analyses of African affairs are in some way connected with this myth.

It is a catch-all theory which lends itself well to the most reactionary propaganda uses. South African racists invoke it in their hysterical invective when they claim to be 'defending the West'. Arab reaction and all those who get embroiled in its strategy use it, and it is the basis for Mobutu's blatantly untrue claim that his army has captured Soviet soldiers.† The People's Republic of China also pretends to be resisting Soviet attempts at destabilization when it allies itself with the imperialists and other forces most hostile to the liberation struggles of the African peoples. One of the top African puppets of imperialism, Houphouet-Boigny, charged by his masters with the defence of imperialist military interventions in Africa, constantly proclaims that 'he who holds Africa will dominate the world'. It never occurs to this 'great African' that Africa might belong to itself rather than to someone else.

Nothing at all can be understood today about any African problem unless one starts from the realization that the one and only force which is 'destabilizing' Africa is the impoverished African peoples' rejection of the inhuman dictatorial regimes to which they are subordinated. This rejection cannot be either neutralized or diffused.

The Western countries are obviously not seeking to 'destabilize' Africa. Since formal independence has done virtually nothing to limit the domination, exercised by these countries over Africa, their policy is naturally one of consolidation and defence of the neo-colonial *status quo*. As in all Third

---

* The Rassemblement Democratique Africain (R.D.A.) was a united front of all the Black African French-dominated territories, launched just after World War Two. Its first Congress took place in Bamako (now the capital of Mali) in 1946. Houphouet-Boigny was elected President. But three years later he and his friends decided to surrender to French colonialism and, apart from its Cameroonian branch (the U.P.C.), the Rassemblement failed to carry on its fight for genuine independence.
†*Publisher's Note*: Mobutu made this propagandistic — and never validated — claim in order to whip up Western military support for his corrupt regime during the repeated risings in Shaba Province in the late 1970s.

World countries, this policy aims to keep the people in a constantly worsening state of destitution and oppression, by means of dictatorial puppet regimes.

The subversive actions directed by certain imperialist countries, such as France, against some African progressive regimes or even occasionally regimes merely putting up a show of anti-imperialism, are only tactical operations which fit into this broader overall strategy. Indeed, those regimes which have caved in under harassment and accepted the role of serving imperialist interests unconditionally are increasingly allowed by their appreciative masters to retain the use of a more or less radical rhetoric.

As for the socialist countries, they are certainly not seeking to 'destabilize' Africa either, as the instigators of the propaganda which presents these countries as fiery internationalists are well aware. The socialist countries' actions in Africa conform to the requirements of peaceful co-existence, their own self-interest and, often, to the best rules of realpolitik.

Inasmuch as they are Marxist, these countries take into account the historically irreversible character of the people's liberation movement and the popular revolt against inhuman social systems. Their active participation in the consolidation of what has been won by popular struggles in Africa thus fits into the normal framework of relations between states. It enables them to deploy an internationalist policy which, for all its limitations and whatever its motives, remains a precious and irreplaceable contribution to the process of liberating the African peoples.

How could it be otherwise, when the West shows such a total lack of imagination and bases its policy in Africa on crowning joke emperors and sending mercenaries to save utterly corrupt regimes?

Consequently, and happily, the struggles of the people themselves continue to be the determining factor in Africa's evolution, whatever outside interests may be involved. The future of Africa is no more in the hands of the imperialist West than in those of the socialist countries. The former offer no alternative to neo-colonialism, desperately shore up discredited regimes and strive in vain to conceal their alliance with the present racist South African rulers; their ship is sinking, and all they can do is patch a few holes. As for the socialist countries, they do not wish to smash the structure of co-existence; their support for popular struggles is selective and a function of their strategic and economic interests.

African revolutionary militants struggling against contemporary neo-colonialism must be fully aware of the immense potential and decisive role of popular struggles. Above all, they must rid themselves of a whole range of illusions about aid. Today, the most reactionary position *vis-a-vis* Africa's political problems is the one which denies the very existence of popular struggles and explains everything in terms of 'hegemonic interventions'.

It is quite obvious that Africa is one of the regions of the world whose future evolution will gradually modify the global strategic balance, even without a major crisis. But anybody who recognizes this obvious fact should be able to understand that this is precisely why nobody can (or intends to) 'systematically export revolution' to the continent, just as nobody can lastingly repress the revolutionary struggle of the masses. The French neo-colonialists, for instance, will find it increasingly difficult to use their legion-aires and mercenaries, and such operations will have more and more disastrous consequences for their perpetrators, as they provoke an ever more radical consciousness and anti-imperialist opposition amongst the African masses.

It is in this context that one can grasp why it is so important and necessary for African progressives to create a Revolutionary United Front of the African Peoples. Two kinds of factors underline this urgency: those which are to do with the difficulties faced by militants and organizations struggling against bourgeois neo-colonial dictatorships, and those which flow from the inexorable decadence and growing impotence of the so-called Organization of African Unity.

An increasing number of African revolutionary militants and leaders endorse the project of creating a Revolutionary United Front of the African Peoples. The complex interplay of state interests frequently leaves them with only two alternatives: either they can abandon the struggle, or they can concert their efforts to find concrete solutions to their concrete problems. Now that the neo-colonial bourgeoisie is operating quite openly on a continental scale, within the O.A.U. framework, the call to create a Revolutionary United Front brings home to every serious African revolutionary that the same continental scale of operation is just as relevant to the development of the struggle against the neo-colonial bourgeoisie.

The Bankruptcy of the O.A.U.

This book demonstrates the bankruptcy of the O.A.U. with scientific rigour. Its conclusions are constantly being borne out by current events in Africa. The O.A.U. can still waffle on about Southern Africa for a while, but it is already incapable of playing any real part in the major political problems and crises we face in Africa today. The O.A.U. has absolutely no perspective on Africa's fundamental contemporary problem, the problem of neo-colonialism, precisely because it is itself a product of neo-colonialism. It is no coincidence that the unification of Africa is so rarely on the agenda at the O.A.U.! The peoples of Africa cannot but react to such a betrayal of their aspirations.

Yet the O.A.U. is not short of champions. Indeed, there have never been so many people hurrying to defend it. This may at first seem mystifying, but if one stops to consider two simple facts, everything becomes clear. Firstly, those who defend the O.A.U. have little else in common. They certainly have different motivations. Secondly, and more crucially, none of the O.A.U.'s champions, beginning with its own members, is at all put out by its bankruptcy. On the contrary, an O.A.U. which dared to concern itself genuinely with African unification would immediately be viewed with suspicion, even hostility, by its own members, notably the lackeys of France, whom that country continues to summon to endless 'Franco-African

Conferences', just like in the good old days of the *Communaute*.*

In short, the O.A.U. is a Pan-Africanism without Pan-Africanists, the Pan-Africanism of the anti-Pan-Africanists. Everybody knows that the very idea of continental unification has always terrified most O.A.U. members. Even those who based their empty demagogy on the 'African Democratic Revolution' are now weary of the pretence.

What really appeals to most O.A.U. members is the splendour of its Summit meetings, which provide such a marvellous opportunity for mystification and propaganda. The O.A.U. is also the ideal diplomatic framework within which to cement the active solidarity of the neo-colonial state bourgeoisies and to clinch endless deals, to the greater detriment of the people of Africa and their struggles.

In its present form, the O.A.U. is perfectly suited to the role assigned to it by imperialism. No amount of hypocrisy can hide the fact that the imperialists were the real sponsors of the formula adopted, despite all Kwame Nkrumah's isolated efforts, in 1963 at Addis Ababa. How delighted these same imperialists must be with their creation, a faithful replica of the equally enfeebled Organization of American States, dominated by a substantial majority of dictators who reign by terror, who are manipulated by the Western powers and who are fiercely hostile to any notion of genuine African unification.

Although more surprising, the support which the socialist countries and certain parties anxious to demonstrate their 'statesmanship' give to the O.A.U. is no less logical. For the former, the defence of the O.A.U. seems to be the best way of showing respect for the 'young independent states' of Africa. Unfortunately, this attitude leads them to endorse the neo-colonial *status quo* blindly. For the latter, support for the O.A.U. is a manifestation of their will to act as serious patriots by defending the colonial interests of their own countries, even if these are not essentially proletarian. In this domain, as in many others, the Chinese have displayed an appalling cynicism, collaborating openly with the imperialists and the worst reactionaries. But they are not alone in behaving like an unscrupulous whore *vis-a-vis* the decrepit O.A.U.

There are those who think that even to point out the undeniable evidence that the O.A.U. is bankrupt is a manifestation of pure ultra-leftism. Our Party will shortly be publishing an analysis of the relations between the socialist countries and Africa. When some Communists are reduced to saying that they would not hesitate to work against the interests of the African peoples if in doing so they could intensify the co-operation between their government and the O.A.U. states, irrespective of the policy of those states, it is hardly surprising that anybody should be reluctant to investigate the true nature of the Organization.

Not long ago, the French social democrats declared themselves in

* *Publisher's Note:* The short-lived French Community was set up by de Gaulle after 1958 in an attempt to stave off demands for formal independence in France's African colonies.

favour of the African intervention force sponsored by President Giscard
and his neo-colonial collaborators. Yet their proclamations on the Third
World — especially concerning areas where the interests of French imperialism
were not at stake, of course — might have led one to believe that they were
well and truly cured of their old delusions, which in the past made them such
ardent political proponents of French colonialism.

So much esteem for the O.A.U. plunges the African petty bourgeoisie
into total disarray. On the one hand, they cannot ignore the undeniable and
blatant failure of this heads of state trade union. On the other, they are
seized with vertigo at the prospect of proposing an alternative. They thus
sink into a delirium of empty phrases about 'saving', 'reforming' or
'democratizing' the O.A.U., endowing it with endless new commissions, etc.

But if any possible reform could still save the O.A.U., in other words
give it even some meaning connected with the name that it bears, that reform
would paradoxically have to consist in creating a commission which would
(at last!) deal with the problem of unifying Africa.

Let it be said that those African progressives who automatically align
their opinions with the diplomacy of this or that socialist country flounder
about in equal confusion when it comes to the O.A.U.

Economic Co-operation: A Non-Solution

Could not a few progressive African states, within the O.A.U. or on the
margins of the inoperative structures of the Organization, open up some new
perspectives? Can we not advance towards genuine independence and a real
unification of Africa by establishing agreements on economic co-operation,
and notably by setting up an African Common Market? Unfortunately, the
answer is no, for the following reasons.

Current events in Africa do not just highlight the bankruptcy of the
O.A.U. They also bring home the collapse of Pan-African ideology in most
African states. All concrete proposals for unification have gone by the board
and nearly every state has opted unequivocally for narrowly nationalist
development strategies. At best, African states retain a cautious notion of
'solidarity'. All this represents a considerable step backwards compared to the
1960s.

It is now undeniable that the final elimination of the old colonialism
will in no way modify the way things are moving and will open up no new
perspectives, even for the limited number of relatively progressive states.

We can therefore state in all confidence that today — and indeed, ever
since the first O.A.U. Summit — African unity, the realization of Pan-African
ideology in the framework of a Union of Socialist Republics of Africa, will
be brought about by the peoples themselves, or it will never happen.

As for the disproportionate hopes certain people put in the virtues of
economic co-operation, it is worth recalling a few simple facts. We in Africa
are used to economistic arguments. The colonialists themselves once dreamed

of avoiding all mass struggle in the territories they dominated by paying their houseboys well and improving public sanitation. The Belgians, in particular, were firm advocates of colonial economism, although they were not alone in pushing stupidity to the extreme — remember the French Constantine Plan in Algeria.

Following the wave of formal independence in the 1960s, and notably at the first O.A.U. Summit in 1963, similar economistic illusions were wide-spread. A whole range of inconsistent theories were based on the naive belief that the great economic and social problems of Africa could be solved by purely economic measures and reforms.

As Comrade Elenga M'buyinga reminds us in this book, Kwame Nkrumah rightly denounced the erroneous neo-colonial economistic theories which claimed that the real independence and unification of Africa could be achieved or even furthered by invoking the miraculous virtues of an African Common Market or by means of economic agreements amongst neo-colonial states still under the economic and political yoke of international imperialism.

As long as we remain under the control of capitalist imperialism and its multinational companies — and in certain African states this control is almost total — no viable strategy for liberation and unification can be based on economistic theses. Let us be blunt: for 15 years the O.A.U. has done nothing but 'promote the real independence and unity of Africa' through economic agreements and co-operation. The result? Nil. This book, *Pan-Africanism or Neo-Colonialism*, makes this abundantly clear.

Of course, no serious African patriot will maintain that African states with different political orientations should necessarily live in a state of con-stant war. In Africa, as elsewhere in the world, economic relations between countries committed or leaning to different social systems are not necessarily reprehensible. It all depends on the political basis for such co-operation.

The progressively orientated African states are exposed to constant harassment from the imperialists, and as a matter of principle must develop policies which will ensure their own consolidation and the reduction of avoidable tensions. Even the newly emerged Soviet authorities, under the great Lenin, were forced to sign the Peace of Brest-Litovsk with capitalist Germany in 1918. But one should not underestimate the vigilance of the progressive militants and peoples of Africa by assuming that they are incapable of drawing a very clear distinction between this kind of policy and games of diplomatic poker in which awkward popular struggles are sacrificed.

It is certainly less utopian to work towards the creation of a Revolutionary United Front of the African Peoples and a Union of Socialist Republics of Africa than to hope that neo-colonial economistic theses will ever lead to the slightest concrete result. Let us not forget that the call for an African Common Market was launched 15 years ago by the Guinean, Sekou Toure. It was one of the main batteries used to shoot down Kwame Nkrumah's radical theses at the first O.A.U. Summit. Why have the protagon-ists of this plan conducted no serious political campaign to implement it during those 15 years? They never believed in it themselves, and now it is they who have lost all credibility.

The People's Republic of the Congo has been outspoken in its rejection of this call for an African Common Market and has denounced the reactionary and neo-colonialist character of such a scheme, given the present African context. In its 16-29 October 1978 issue, the journal, *Afrique Asie*, reported Congo-Brazzaville's head of state as saying:

> It is essential that the African countries should ensure that their, at present, still largely neo-colonial national economies should become independent, before we can even think of creating an African Common Market.
>
> Indeed, such a project could easily become a monster. We might end up with a vast institution which we could not master and which would thus become a powerful means whereby the old metropoles could perpetuate or even intensify their imperialist exploitation and recolonization of the continent.

The progressive stance taken by the People's Republic of the Congo over this suspect call for an African Common Market must be a heavy blow for the strategists of confusion, who no doubt hoped that the Congolese leaders would support them merely to be obliging. It is only to be regretted that the political courage of the Congolese Workers' Party leaders did not extend to recognizing the real problem for what it was.

For nearly 20 years, despite incessant proclamations about 'the struggle for economic independence', nearly all the O.A.U. regimes have proved totally incapable of making any progress whatever in this direction, or of providing for the most elementary needs of their populations!

It is now perfectly obvious that all the promises of future economic progress the O.A.U. regimes have made over the years to the starving and destitute African masses have done nothing and will do nothing to change the neo-colonial dependence of our countries and of the continent as a whole. Our peoples are uniquely qualified to know this: they have had long and painful experience of the verbal incantations and outright lies poured out by O.A.U. politicians whose only preoccupation is to hang on to power and fill their own pockets.

A Union of Socialist Republics of Africa — The Only Alternative

The real problem is that, in the present context, individual African states cannot implement any serious and exhaustive policy of economic independence and real development in every domain unless there emerges a great and powerful progressive black state, a Union of Socialist Republics of Africa. By turning their backs on the question of the political unification of Africa — under pressure from various sources — the O.A.U. regimes, including those who claim their allegiance is to socialism, condemn themselves to dependency and neo-colonialism.

The only hope for the African masses is thus to fight resolutely to establish a Union of Socialist Republics of Africa. The Revolutionary United Front of the African Peoples must be at the heart of the struggle.

The neo-colonial context of the O.A.U. will make the creation of this Revolutionary United Front a vital issue for all patriots who struggle against the African neo-colonial dictatorships. After 15 years of 'building socialism' in Africa, the balance sheet makes sad reading; African patriots and the masses of Africa as a whole have no choice but to turn to the creation of a Union of Socialist Republics of Africa as their only hope.

There is a fundamental difference between Revolutionary Pan-Africanism and the tendency to undertake commitments to build socialism only in national frameworks. The consequences of this divergence for the future of Africa may be serious indeed. Given the prevailing level of underdevelopment throughout Africa, a multitude of relatively small, even if sometimes fairly rich African countries, heading off one after the other along the road to socialism, would inevitably be condemned to objective dependence on the existing socialist countries in nearly every domain.

Only socialist development within the framework of a large African state organized on a continental or semi-continental scale can ensure an adequate economic equilibrium and forestall all dangers of this kind. As we see it, such a state is also a *sine qua non* for the real elimination of racial domination and racist crimes against black people.

Only a large state of this sort would not be tempted to invoke fear of 'Communist domination' as an excuse for opening itself up to international capital. Indeed, it is quite possible that some socialist countries might encourage such an opening up to international capital, with its investments and markets, even though such a course in an underdeveloped country can mean only a deadlock for socialist construction.

The question of a Union of Socialist Republics of Africa confronts the socialist countries with a simple choice: they can either genuinely contribute to building socialism in Africa, or they can try to create a set of more or less socialistic African client states, which would form a new type of neo-colonial zone.

A Revolutionary United Front of the African Peoples would in no way handicap any individual national struggle. On the contrary, it would constantly open up new approaches. It must, therefore, never be allowed to sink into a morass of mere 'solidarity', which in this context would mean its death.

Solidarity presupposes distinct objectives, limited co-operation, occasional exchanges. By definition, solidarity cannot mean the fusion of forces in a single struggle. It must be limited to mutual aid and constantly has to be adapted to cope with the chauvinistic selfishness, weaknesses and organizational or political errors of this or that group. In contrast, a Revolutionary United Front of the African Peoples must spring from a resolutely united, critical and self-critical desire to create the conditions for the most effective mobilization against neo-colonialism in Africa.

The Revolutionary United Front can, therefore, only be viable if it is conceived of and instituted as a means of combat which will unify, lead and co-ordinate the struggles of vanguard Marxist-Leninist national organizations, national popular fronts and all other relevant forces in the various countries.

The so-called Organization of African Unity illustrates its own bankruptcy in every sphere, including the cultural; it is constantly multiplying its 'working languages' but has still not adopted a single African tongue. The Revolutionary United Front of the African Peoples will need to adopt a clear policy on linguistic matters. The issue is fundamental.

Throughout the world, thousands of Negro-African intellectuals and thousands of black revolutionary militants have a perfect mastery of the languages our peoples encountered in the course of the terrible sufferings imposed upon them by the slave trade and colonialism. Why should they not now undertake to learn the foremost Negro language, Kiswahili, which is spoken by more than 100 million men and women in Africa and which figures among the ten foremost languages of the world? What better way to expose the hypocrites who claim to be singing the praises of *Negritude* while serving imperialism and Arab reaction?

It is highly desirable that Kiswahili should become the main language of the Revolutionary United Front of the African Peoples and that the Front's militants and cadres should learn to conduct their activities in the African languages spoken by the African masses.

African patriots must have the courage to define their own line of conduct, and assume the responsibility — which is theirs alone — of mapping out the course of the African revolutionary movement. This duty is not a matter of posing as super-revolutionaries, as our detractors would have it. It is fundamental to the very existence of our struggle. Only one kind of 'revolutionary movement', only one kind of 'patriot' can decide not to say anything which might displease somebody: the kind whose struggle no longer has any real meaning.

We must thus assume full responsibility for our own political and ideological identity. This is all the more crucial in an Africa where hypocrisy and confusion reign. Those who condemn us for 'attacking everybody' or 'running before we can walk' completely miss the point. Show us the 'model revolutionaries' who have obtained real results in their struggle against neo-colonialism without attacking anybody and we will gladly follow their example.

This edition of this book should encourage further and more precise debate concerning the creation of a Revolutionary United Front of the African Peoples. We have only advanced a few propositions to stimulate action and thought. The task of building the organization itself belongs, by definition, to the patriots of the different African countries. We hope that an ever increasing number of African patriots will find in Comrade Elenga M'buyinga's analyses a new source of inspiration, new motives to break with resignation, discord and petty quarrels.

To create such a front and to fight resolutely for the inauguration of a Union of Socialist Republics of Africa is the task to which we should all devote our modest efforts. It is the path by which we can build a genuinely socialist Africa, a people's Africa in which Africans will be truly free and masters of their own destiny.

Woungly-Massaga
Member of the Revolutionary Committee of the Union des Populations du Cameroun
November 1978

Introduction to the Second French Edition

When our Party first published *Pan-Africanism and Neo-Colonialism* in French, 15 years had elapsed since the majority of African countries started winning their independence in 1960. But because it came out in 1975, the book could not take into account the most important event to take place in Africa during the 1970s, namely the recovery of national independence by the old Portuguese colonies — Angola, Guinea-Bissau, Mozambique and Sao Tome. Much of the text was originally written during 1974. The book was not concerned with speculation but rather strove to highlight the essential features which characterize the development of contemporary African society, so it could only base itself on what had actually happened.

Since 1975, the situation in Africa has evolved considerably. Even those who like to bury their heads in the sand have to admit that the recently acquired independence of Mozambique and Angola has had a decisive influence on Southern Africa. Similarly, the significant changes in Madagascar, leading to the emergence of a progressive African country in the Indian Ocean, and the admittedly tortuous development of the anti-feudal and anti-imperialist revolution in Ethiopia have brought about a substantial modification of the balance of forces in Africa as a whole. Despite the notorious impotence of the O.A.U. — an impotence which is only denied out of cynical self-interest by forces both inside and outside the continent — this modification is noticeable even in the decisions which the O.A.U. takes and does not take.

China's Position On Africa: A Brief Critical Analysis

This Second Edition has therefore striven to integrate these new factors. To save space we have had to leave aside the systematic and painstaking analysis of another remarkable event of the last few years, namely the People's Republic of China's shift to a reactionary African policy. Given this omission, we feel obliged to say a few words on the subject here, so that people will at least have an idea of what revolutionary members of the U.P.C. think of China's present policy in Africa. After all, this policy is now an integral part of the African political landscape. Apart from the politically blind or venal, nobody can afford to treat this major development as merely incidental.

In 1974, the world was told by 'the cat which is satisfied with catching mice', that there was no longer a socialist camp and that the fundamental aspect of the international scene was no longer the basic class opposition between the forces of capitalism and those of socialism; instead, we were told to believe in the 'Three Worlds' theory. Since then, the African policy of China has moved steadily to the right, timidly at first and then more and more arrogantly.

China's support for the ultra-corrupt regime of Joseph Mobutu, a man who murdered Lumumba, Okito, M'polo, Mulele and thousands of Congolese patriots, and who is an open agent of the C.I.A. and the Belgian secret service, has completely exposed the essentially counter-revolutionary character of China's policy in Africa over the last few years.

The breathtaking cynicism and dishonesty of China's vociferous approval of France's armed neo-colonial interventions in Africa eliminated all possible doubt in the matter. China's support for France's official policy in Africa comes at a time when this imperialist country seems determined to replace Britain as the greatest black-slaving nation in history, as is clear from France's 20-year political, military, economic and cultural love affair with racist South Africa and from the development of blatantly anti-black and more generally anti-African racism in France itself over the last few years. The daily murders of Algerian immigrants may go unpunished in France, but they are noted in the rest of the world.

By asking Africans to raise their fists and cry 'Long live our alliance with the French, English and German imperialists, who are all part of the Second World and who oppose Soviet hegemonism', the Chinese Three Worlds theory has set the seal on China's anti-African alliance with the West European imperialists. The latter, of course, remain hand in glove with the United States, the African people's worst enemy.

It would be comic, if it were not so tragic, to see so-called patriotic and anti-imperialist Africans from countries like Gabon, where every square metre is dominated by French imperialism, waste so much energy denouncing so-called Soviet social imperialism whose threat to their country is as fictitious as the claims of Ahidjo, Bongo, Bokassa, Mobutu, Senghor, Houphouet-Boigny and Hassan II to a non-aligned progressive position.

The theoreticians of the People's Republic of China, who so carefully gloss over issues of class composition when they claim that the 'Third World' has displaced the forces of socialism as the fundamental agent in the struggle against imperialism, are in fact rejecting that which unites all those who recognize themselves in scientific socialism. Thus, it is not so surprising to find the revolutionary China of yesterday arm in arm with people like Mobutu, Bongo, Ahidjo, Bokassa, the Shah or Pinochet. Of course, all this is done in the name of the 'non-alignment and unity of the great family of the non-aligned countries of the Third World, in their struggle against hegemonism, dominationism and colonialism'. No mention of neo-colonialism, naturally. Neo-colonialism as a theme would require some analysis of concrete cases:

Cameroon under Ahidjo, Congo-Kinshasa under Mobutu, Gabon under Bongo, and so on.

It is now legitimate to ask whether China still considers itself to be a socialist country or not? If not, then it should first of all say so clearly, so that everybody could see the attempts by the People's Republic of China to infiltrate the Third World for what they would then be, a ruse to seize the leadership of a vast body of relatively weak nations, with the aim of struggling against the two other countries with human and geographical resources comparable to China's. But if the answer is no; if, as our Party still believes, China sees itself as socialist, then its persistence in declaring that the socialist camp is dead and buried and that China is an integral part of some politically and socially heterogenous 'Third World' can only be a ruse geared to attaining hegemony over this 'Third World'. It is not a matter of good or bad intentions.[1] It is just that there is simply no substitute for a careful analysis of classes and the balance of forces. Even a summary analysis of this kind would bring out the following key fact: China's position in this Third World that its theoreticians have cobbled together by disregarding the most elementary laws of Marxism-Leninism is a position of potential hegemony. Whether China is socialist or not, its aim is clearly to mislead the African peoples as to who their friends and enemies really are.

Socialist China has even had the affrontery to ask African revolutionaries to compromise with the Pretoria nazis. The People's Republic's insistence in 1975 on the need for an alliance in Angola between the MPLA and Savimbi's UNITA (an organization then being run entirely under the trusteeship of the Pretoria nazis) amounts to precisely that: a compromise between racist settlers and African revolutionaries! If an independent and internationally respected China chooses to forget its own historical experience with Japan and other imperialists, that is its own affair. But for China to try to convince the African peoples to forget 500 years of slavery, exploitation, oppression and racism, all in the name of the 'struggle against Soviet hegemonism', is quite outrageous, even if it would suit Chinese foreign policy.

Let us be clear. African revolutionary militants have always felt a deep comradely friendship for China, as for all the socialist countries, including the U.S.S.R. But the days when the Africans could be treated as cretins are over.

European Social Democracy: Its Collaboration With Imperialism in Africa

At one stage, one might have thought that the various social democratic forces in Europe had disavowed their infamous colonial past and were prepared to approach the African peoples in a spirit of true friendship. But, since 1975, an offensive led by British social democracy (which implements the policy of 'its' bourgeoisie better than that bourgeoisie itself) and German social democracy (which Rosa Luxemburg described as a 'stinking corpse' as far back as 1914) has been underway, with the aim of implanting this kind of social democracy in Africa.[2] Faithful to their own traditions, the leaders of the French Socialist Party have reintegrated Senghor, who is now 'reconciled' with socialism. In this context, the history of Senghor's resignation from the Socialist Federation of French West Africa in 1948, on the grounds that it was a dictatorial organization, is particularly illuminating.[3]

The *Rassemblement Democratique Africain* (R.D.A.) was founded immediately after the Second World War. It was a federation of Territorial Sections operating in the various black African countries under French colonial domination. As such, the R.D.A. played an effectively progressive role in promoting the emancipation of the African peoples from its foundation in 1946 up to late 1950, and quickly attracted enthusiastic mass support. The Cameroonian section of the R.D.A. was the *Union des Populations du Cameroun* (U.P.C.). The call for national reunification and independence launched by the U.P.C. from the moment it was founded (10 April 1948) expressed the aspirations of the Cameroonian people so accurately that in a very short time the organization was extraordinarily well implanted in the country. But the R.D.A.'s success in Cameroon was enough to frighten the French bourgeoisie, who immediately began putting obstacles in the R.D.A.'s path. The French bourgeoisie was not alone in its efforts:

> One of the most characteristic manifestations of the opposition to the R.D.A. mounted by the major French parties, the M.R.P. and S.F.I.O.,[4] with the help of the French Overseas Administration, is the way the latter has supported or even created parties which reject the R.D.A. With a few rare exceptions, these parties, unlike the R.D.A. sections, have no real constituency amongst the population; their occasional electoral successes are entirely due to the backing of the Administrator or his faithful traditional Chiefs.
>
> In 1948, the M.R.P. promoted the formation of an Independent Overseas Parliamentary Group, with Mr. Senghor as its most prominent member. . . . Mr. Senghor had resigned from the A.O.F. Socialist Federation in September 1948.[5]

Shortly after he resigned from the S.F.I.O., in order to start a Senegalese branch of the 'Overseas Independents' (independent of the R.D.A. and the Communist group in the French Parliament, but dependent on the colonialists), Senghor founded his *Bloc Democratique Senegalais* (B.D.S.). In 1949, he was rewarded by George Bidault, who appointed him Secretary of State for French Overseas Territories, or Junior Minister for the colonies if you prefer. In Cameroon, the equivalent of Senghor's B.D.S. was the *Bloc Democratique Camerounais* (B.D.C.). This body was founded by a former settler from Algeria, Louis Paul Aujoulat, and his associate Andre Marie Mbida. They later recruited Ahidjo. The B.D.C. was the Cameroonian Section of the 'Overseas Independents' (I.O.M.). As Mamadou Dia said at the time:

> The I.O.M. movement is not really a popular grouping; rather, it is an attempt to co-ordinate different parties, to integrate them from above. From this point of view it is a step backwards compared to the R.D.A., which has built up its superstructure from the popular masses.[6]

Mamadou Dia is being tactful. From his account, one might believe that the main difference between the I.O.M. and the R.D.A. was that the former merely co-ordinated 'from above' parties which in fact had little real existence. He does not say that the two parties diverged on the main issue: national independence. At the time, the French Socialist Party did not accept the idea of independence for the colonies (which were seen as an integral part of the French national heritage). But Senghor's resignation from the S.F.I.O. was no move towards political forces favourable to independence for colonized Africa. On the contrary, he shifted towards the M.R.P., which had set up the anti-independence I.O.M. movement. *Senghor was in fact expressing his opposition to national independence.* As for those who seek today to whitewash Senghor, one might ask who they supported at the time.

Another illustration of the function of the I.O.M. is documented by Claude Gerard, an observer whom not even the imperialists could accuse of being biased in favour of Communists.

> In Cameroon, Ruben Um Nyobe's U.P.C., which had called for independence and national reunification from the moment it was founded on 10 April 1948, responded to increasing repression with more and more intense resistance, despite having no allies or supporters in the metropole apart from the P.C.F. [French Communist Party].
>
> Unlike the Togolese nationalists, the U.P.C. was not granted a U.N. supervised referendum. Tension grew, till in May 1955, armed struggle broke out. Although localized in the south of the Cameroons [incorrect, E.M.], the U.P.C. was the major political force in the country, in both numbers and influence.
>
> Alongside the U.P.C., there were several other parties, the most important of which was the *Bloc Democratique Camerounais* led by Dr. Louis Aujoulat (I.O.M.), Mr. Duala Manga, a parliamentary deputy, and Ahmadou Ahidjo, councillor to the *Union Francaise*, who rallied to this I.O.M. tendency.[7]

And what was the function of these groups which existed 'alongside' the U.P.C.? Quite simply, to fight against the very idea of national independence. Even an author as far from being a Communist as Claude Gerard comes to the same conclusion. 'The aims of the U.P.C., namely national independence and reunification, were achieved on 1 January 1960 and 1 September 1961, by the non-U.P.C. political forces which had originally opposed these concepts and had thus enjoyed the support of the administration.'[8] Unfortunately, the author fails to tell us how this miraculous substitution took place. But it is none the less clear from her account that, when Senghor and Ahidjo present themselves as 'Fathers of the Nation', 'Apostles of Independence', etc., they are cynically falsifying history, even though many of the original actors are still alive.

Knowing this background, the young people and revolutionaries of our continent have a duty to grasp and explain the exact nature of the present social democratic offensive directed at Africa. A few recent examples should help.

During the last popular uprising against Mobutu's corrupt and much detested regime in Congo-Kinshasa in 1978, the American and West European imperialists held several meetings, notably in Paris and Brussels, in an effort to save the Kinshasa dictator and his clique, and to decide matters for Africa generally. Once again, it was back to Berlin 1884.

At the first meeting, on 6 June 1978 in Paris, the 'socialist' (i.e. social democratic) governments of Britain and West Germany sat side by side with the proudly imperialist governments of the U.S., France and Belgium. At the second meeting, on 13 and 14 June 1978 in Brussels, the same 'socialist' governments, plus the Dutch Government, conferred with the imperialist pirates from the U.S., France, Belgium, Japan, Canada and Italy, along with the ultra-reactionary monarchist cliques (those proud defenders of human rights) of Iran and Saudi Arabia.

A year before, in 1977, another popular rising against Mobutu had only been smashed thanks to the intervention of a French-Egyptian-Moroccan expeditionary force.

Given that the underlying causes of these popular uprisings against Mobutu, and indeed against all the present-day neo-colonial bourgeois dictatorships, remained unchanged, the imperialist governments suggested to the bourgeois African regimes of Senghor, Houphouet, Bongo, Bokassa, etc., that they set up a permanent police force capable of flying to the rescue of any African dictatorship threatened by its people. During May 1978, when the French imperialist slave traders held their fifth neo-colonial 'Franco-African' conference, this intervention force was again in fact the most important item on the agenda.

Given the French, German and British socialist parties' unfailing attachment to the principles of democracy, freedom and human rights, in Latin America, in Asia, in the Communist bloc, in Papua-New Guinea, among baby seals and at the North Pole, indeed everywhere except ex-colonial Africa, no African militant was surprised to learn that Mr. Charles Hernu, the French Socialist Party's defence spokesman, had fully endorsed this African intervention force. Having been plied with wine and caviar at the Chateau de Versailles, Mr. Hernu told the press that he found the idea an 'attractive' one. A few of the other prominent French Socialist Party figures were not quite so accommodating, but their protests did not go very far.

On 11 June 1978, the First Secretary of the French Socialist Party spoke up:

Whilst I am quite convinced that the Cubans have no business in Africa,

I feel that their influence in the continent has been exaggerated. In any case, it is not by imitating the Cubans that France can play an appropriate role. Rather than arguing about the Cubans, it would be better to discuss the stability of Africa with the Soviet Union. Why are such talks not already underway?

Surely it is time to open negotiations, especially as it is legitimate to ask whether the Soviets and the Communist world have really gained so much ground in Africa over the last few years, or whether they have lost some.[9]

It is thus clear that the French Socialist leader believes that Africa's problems should be settled by negotiations amongst superpowers, for example, the U.S.S.R. and the imperialist countries. Not so different from Berlin in 1884, after all. Paternalism (at best) remains one of the cornerstones of social democratic policy in Africa.

The French Socialist leader's suggestion was so much in keeping with the ideas of the neo-colonial lobby and was so much 'in accord with the interests of the nation' that it was put into effect barely two months later. Indeed:

> A delegation led by Mr. Guy Georgy, the Ministry of Foreign Affairs' Director of African Affairs, held talks with their Soviet counterparts in Moscow from 9 to 10 August [1978]. The Soviet chief representative was Mr. Leonid Illitchev, Vice-Minister for Foreign Affairs, assisted by the Directors of the Africa Section. The two parties outlined their respective — and contradictory — viewpoints concerning Soviet-Cuban and Western interventions in Africa.[10]

The social democratic offensive in Africa has recently been manifest in two ways. First, there has been an attempt (which will no doubt continue) to bring together parties such as the U.S.F.P. (*Union Socialiste des Forces Populaires*), Istiqlal of Morocco, the Tunisian Destour, the Arab Socialist Unions of Sudan, Egypt and even Libya, Senghor's party and Ahidjo's C.N.U. Second, during the congress of the Socialist International in Vancouver, Canada, Willy Brandt (that defender of human rights who delivered Louis Metangmo to Ahidjo) and his friends tried to draw in the M.P.L.A., FRELIMO and the P.A.I.G.C. by inviting them to the social democratic assembly.

It is common knowledge that Sadat's 'socialist' Egypt fought alongside Morocco and the French against the patriots in the Congo. In Morocco, the U.S.F.P. strove to be even more chauvinistic than the bourgeois Istiqlal on the question of the Western Sahara. These parties, and the Moroccan Communist Party, remained shamefully silent during the Moroccan interventions in the Congo. Under such conditions, it seems obvious that European social democracy, having fought for 30 years to preserve colonialism, is now busily organizing all these parties into an African 'social democracy',

with the aim of maintaining neo-colonial domination over the peoples of
Africa. It is well known that the finance for this 'African' social democracy
will come from the S.P.D. and its subsidiaries, such as the Friedrich Ebert
Foundation, the outfit which co-ordinates all the German social democrats'
dealings with dominated countries, as was recently confirmed by the Swiss
sociologist Jean Ziegler.

It is the duty of every African revolutionary to check this vast enterprise
which aims, quite simply, to keep our continent under capitalist slavery.

On A Divergence within the African Revolutionary Movement

The complete independence of the African revolutionary movement is today
the absolute precondition of any revolutionary struggle in Africa. As long as
the African revolutionary movement as a whole has not resolved to work
out and determine, autonomously and responsibly, its own stance, in
accordance with the interests and aspirations of the workers and poor peasants
of Africa (which in no way excludes militant internationalism, on the
contrary), every political force in the world will treat Africa as a backyard to
play in. Objective observers will not argue that this is a chauvinistic position
on our part, especially if they take into account the remarkable discretion
with which world progressive forces approach the subject of African political
unity. Yet everybody knows that, as long as Africa remains as split up as it
has been since the European slave traders' conference in Berlin in 1884, the
African countries will always be likely to become client states of this or that
major power, whether they wish to or not. But, although this is generally
accepted, the moment it comes to drawing the relevant political conclusion,
a lethargy develops which can have only one explanation: the awareness that
the present fragmentation of Africa is in one way or another extremely
profitable to a wide variety of forces, who have no interest in seeing a political
unification of Africa or the emergence of a Union of Socialist Republics of
Africa.

Our Party recently became aware of a document produced during a
meeting of African revolutionary parties. Certain African Communist Parties
met and drew up a programme for the African revolutionary movement as a
whole in the coming years. To our astonishment, this long document does not
contain a single clear sentence on the crucial subject of African political
unification.[11] To be blunt, we smelled a rat. Our Party fully intends to contribute, as is our duty, to the debate as to the most appropriate programme
and most urgent tasks for African revolutionaries today. This is, therefore,
not the place for a critique of the programme put forward by the three
African Communist Parties in question, especially as the document is full of
highly contestable statements. Its immediate endorsement by the
'International Communist Movement' expresses an arrogance which is not
without dangers even for the most elementary kind of solidarity amongst
African revolutionary patriots, not to mention the need for autonomy from

the foreign policy of this or that socialist country. We will therefore content ourselves with answering these African Communist Parties' arguments about those who wish to 'destroy the O.A.U.'.

For at least five years, as we recalled in the Preface, our Party has been pointing to the shameful political bankruptcy of the O.A.U. The epilogue to this volume completes the demonstration. We have not been reticent to say that the O.A.U. is a politically discredited lie-factory which misleads the African people, to the great delight of imperialists, reactionaries and opportunists of all sorts. Without boasting, we can say that the U.P.C. is the only *political party* in Africa to have taken such a clear stance publicly. We know that our position is fully shared by many African patriots, especially those who struggle against the neo-colonial bourgeois dictatorships in Africa. And we have never resorted to allusion in order to make our point.

We were, therefore, amused to find the following sentence in the document so painstakingly produced by the three above-mentioned African Communist Parties:

> The Marxist-Leninists and all the other progressive forces support the O.A.U. while reserving the right to constructive criticism of irresolute actions or actions which are not appropriate to the historical situation: all are opposed to any attempt to destroy the organization.[12]

So who are these wreckers? Surely clarity demands that they be identified.

To our knowledge, no African state seeks to 'destroy the O.A.U.', since it suits them all well enough. Individuals hardly constitute a major threat to an organization of over 50 states. So the African Communist Parties must be thinking of certain specific political parties and organizations.

Everybody knows that, while we in the U.P.C. do not support the O.A.U., we do not call on the progressive African states to quit the organization.[13] But we do think, and believe we have proved, that the O.A.U. is a political con-trick as far as its contribution to African unity goes. Every informed person is aware that the U.P.C. bases its thought and action on scientific socialism, i.e. on Marxism-Leninism, so it is quite wrong to claim that all (African) 'Marxist-Leninists support the O.A.U.'. A pious wish it may be, a fact it is not. But a Communist Party should not base its approach on pious wishes. Furthermore, is it not naive — or ingenuous — to behave as if one was unaware that one has to work out what it means to be an African Communist and who is in a position to decide what is an African Communist Party? African revolutionaries who have been in exile in the socialist countries for decades only court ridicule when they speak derisively of 'middle-class democratic revolutionaries' — just barely good enough to carry out the 'National Democratic and Popular Revolution' — and pose as paragons of African Communism. The peremptory affirmation that (African) 'Marxist-Leninists support the O.A.U.', without any Marxist-Leninist analysis of what the O.A.U. actually is, implies something quite different, namely that the Marxist-Leninist stance in Africa must follow blindly the diplomatic policy of this or that socialist country, which certifies who is a Communist in Africa and who is not. This amounts to an excommunication of all those who do not support the O.A.U., and who, therefore, in the pontifical opinion of our three 'African Communist Parties', do not qualify as true 'Marxist-Leninists'.

Given the notable divergences which exist between all the various political forces which claim allegiance to Marxism-Leninism in the world, and given the resulting tendency for some of them to consider themselves as the only true Marxist-Leninists, one might, at a pinch, have understood if the comrades who drew up the document had classified the U.P.C. amongst 'the other progressive African forces', the 'revolutionary democrats'. That much, at least, must be granted us by anybody who is not interested only in the wildest subjectivism. So it is quite wrong to claim that 'the Marxist-Leninists and all the other progressive forces support the O.A.U.'. The document's total lack of a Marxist-Leninist analysis of the O.A.U. and its strangely unexplicit distinction between 'communists' and 'Marxist-Leninists' is bad enough. We want to make it absolutely clear here and now that the U.P.C. does not support the O.A.U.

The problem which the O.A.U. poses for militant Africa is too serious to be dealt with without a systematic and thorough enquiry. Those who claim allegiance to scientific socialism cannot be content with 'political games', or with a simple reiteration of this or that socialist country's position on Africa and the African revolution.

Since a debate is called for, every African revolutionary organization owes it to the revolution to set out its point of view clearly and explicitly. As Marx and Engels said in the *Communist Manifesto*, 'Communists do not stoop to hiding their opinions and their projects'.

Like many other African patriots, we in the U.P.C. are certain that Africa will be free. She will be freed with the help of all the progressive forces in the world, and especially of those who are the most reliable the moment it is a question of solidarity with the peoples' struggle against imperialism, namely the socialist countries, the Communist Parties and the other Marxist-Leninist forces everywhere. But Africa will be liberated, above all, by the African revolutionaries themselves. The latter have a duty to work out their own ideas, in an internationalist perspective of course, but also as people who are responsible for their own destiny and for the socialist revolution in Africa. The development of these ideas demands an open, frank and healthy debate on the problems our revolution faces, with an eye to that which will promote the common struggle of all African workers.

Our party, the U.P.C., has long been committed to this approach. It is to this end that we have published this book.

Elenga M'buyinga
29 December 1978

Notes

1. See Karl Marx and Friedrich Engels, *The German Ideology*, Part I.
2. German social democracy remained shamefully silent in August 1914, when the German imperialists assassinated the great Cameroonian patriots, Duala Manga, Martin Samba and Ngosso Din. More recently, Willy Brandt, that champion of 'human rights', was Chancellor when the Bonn government handed the Cameroonian patriot Louis Metangmo over to Ahidjo. His opinions were his only crime; he was eventually murdered.
3. See Claude Gerard, *Les Pionniers de l'Independence*, 1975, p. 33.
4. M.R.P.: Mouvement du Rassemblement Populaire, a French bourgeois party. S.F.I.O.: French section of the Worker's International, now part of the French Socialist Party.
5. Claude Gerard, op. cit., p. 33.
6. Quoted in ibid.
7. Ibid, pp. 37-8.
8. Ibid, p. 38.
9. *Le Monde*, 13 June 1978, p. 6.
10. Ibid, 13 August 1978, p. 18.
11. The document in question is entitled *Pour la liberte, la renaissance nationale et le progres social des peuples d'Afrique tropicale et australe*, The version published in *Badolo Bi* was signed by the Senegalese African Independence Party and by the Communist Parties of Sudan and South Africa. It was published in late 1978.
12. Ibid.
13. 'The U.P.C. believes that African revolutionaries have no right to demand that those revolutionary militants active within the OAU should pull out of that organization'. See *'l'OUA et l'Afrique australe'* in *Cahiers Upecistes*, No. 10, April 1977, p.34.

1. Pan Africanism: A Brief Historical Overview

Pan-Africanism is generally taken to mean that set of political ideas asserting that Africa is a single entity which must unite. All the peoples of the continent are fundamentally similar. They all bore the yoke of colonialism, not to mention slavery, just as today they all suffer the exactions of neo-colonialism. The peoples of Africa have a common struggle against a common enemy which dominates and exploits them all: imperialism. Also, there is in Africa a profound cultural unity, which, thanks to Pan-Africanism, proves that the African peoples share a common destiny.

However, the fact that the first theoreticians of Pan-Africanism were North American blacks, labouring under a system of exploitation of black workers, gives the concept a particular historical and social dimension which such a sketchy definition cannot convey.

We must place the whole question in its socio-historic context, examine the evolution of Pan-Africanism over time and see how its meaning has changed during different historical periods. Only then will we be able to determine what it means today. Even so, the history of Pan-Africanism is not our main concern in this book. Our real aim is to describe where Pan-Africanism stands right now.

Pan-African ideas overseas before 1945

The Initial Idea – Solidarity Among People of African Descent

In his book, *Pan-Africanism or Communism?*, published in 1955, George Padmore,[1] one of the main historians of Pan-Africanism, explains that:

> The idea of Pan-Africanism first arose as a manifestation of fraternal solidarity among Africans and peoples of African descent. It was originally conceived by a West Indian barrister, Mr. Henry Sylvester-Williams of Trinidad, who practised at the English bar at the end of the 19th Century, and beginning of the present. It appears that during his undergraduate days and after, Mr. Sylvester-Williams established relations with West Africans in Britain and later acted as legal adviser to several African chiefs who visited the United Kingdom on political

missions to the Colonial Office . . . .

To combat the aggressive policies of British imperialists, Mr. Sylvester-Williams took the initiative in convening a Pan-African Conference in London in 1900 . . . . This meeting attracted attention, putting the word 'Pan-Africanism' in the dictionaries for the first time . . . .

Today, Pan-Africanism is becoming part and parcel of emergent African nationalism, serving as a beacon light in the struggle for self-determination, the pre-requisite to regional federations of self-governing African communities which may one day evolve into a Pan-African Federation of United States.[2]

It is thus quite clear that Pan-Africanism emerged from the African peoples' struggle against imperialism. Explicitly or not, it was, in practice and right from the start, a set of ideas geared to 'combat the aggressive policies of imperialists' in Africa.

However, the 'Black problem', the fact that populations of African origin were scattered all over the world by the Slave Trade, which was itself linked to the development of capitalism, as has been amply documented elsewhere,[3] combined with the double exploitation of Blacks in America, both as workers and as Black workers, gave the original Pan-Africanism a definite 'racial' dimension.

Garvey and the Back to Africa Movement

Certain historians of Pan-Africanism have spoken, rather inaccurately, of a Black Zionism. The movement they refer to, which called for a mass return of emigrant Blacks to Africa, was founded by the Black Jamaican, Marcus Garvey. His ideas are summed up in the questions he asks in his book, *Philosophy and Opinions*:

I asked: Where is the black man's government? Where is his King and his kingdom? Where is his President, his country, and his ambassador, his army, his navy, his men of big affairs? I could not find them and then I declared: I will help make them.[4]

Garvey's ideology was manifestly racist, which no doubt contributed considerably to the failure of his endeavours. He first founded a Universal Association for the Progress of Black People, then an Imperial League of African Communities, which was supposed to organize the emigrants' return to Africa. Then, in 1920, he founded a Black Empire in New York, and on 1 August 1920 assembled his first Parliament. This international gathering of Blacks enthusiastically approved his call to 'work for a single but glorious goal: A free and powerful nation. Let Africa become a brilliant star in the constellation of the nations.' Garvey, 33 years old at the time, was unanimously elected Provisional President of Africa.

One historically important point is that, although Garvey was a fierce opponent of imperialist domination over Africa, he detested it especially inasmuch as it was domination by whites. He asked:

> Why should not Africa give to the world its black Rockefeller,
> Rothschild and Henry Ford? Now is the opportunity. Now is the
> chance for every Negro to make every effort towards a commercial,
> industrial standard that will make us comparable with the successful
> businessmen of other races.[5]

Further on, he added that capitalism was necessary to progress and that those who opposed it opposed progress. To be fair to Garvey, one must point out that he intended to prevent any individual from investing more than one million dollars, or any company from controlling more than five million, beyond which sum the state would take over the business concerned. Clearly, Garvey had no precise ideas of the fundamental laws of capitalism. None the less, it is worth stressing that he was very much aware of the need for active and militant solidarity amongst all oppressed and dominated peoples. For instance, he sent messages of solidarity to Abd-el-Krim, the leader of the rebellion in 'Spanish' Morocco, who was President of the Rif Republic for some years in the 1920s. He also called for a union of all 'coloured' peoples in the Caribbean, in Africa, in India, in China and in Japan.

The questions Garvey posed have, by now, generally received affirmative answers. But the problem of liberating the African peoples from foreign domination remains practically unchanged. In fact, a new aspect of the problem has emerged, namely the domination and exploitation of the majority of Africans by a tiny minority of fellow Africans allied to foreign imperialists.

DuBois: Pan-Africanism as Anti-Colonialism

Pan-Africanist ideas obviously change with historical circumstance. Not surprisingly, Garvey's Pan-Africanism was eventually superseded by a more adequate conception. The first careful systematization of Pan-Africanist ideas, notably involving the exclusion of the racist aspects of Garvey's theory, is due to Dr. William E. B. DuBois, who is usually cast as the 'Father of Pan-Africanism'. Padmore knew DuBois right from the early Pan-African Congresses held in Europe between the two World Wars, and met him again in Ghana, under Nkrumah, where DuBois finally died in 1964. He gives the following account of DuBois' conception.

> During the period when Marcus Aurelius Garvey was at the zenith of
> his power, his chief antagonist, William Edward Burghardt DuBois,
> was expounding ideas of Pan-Africanism which were to have a more
> permanent effect on African political awakening.
> Pan-Africanism differed from Garveyism in that it was never
> conceived as a Back to Africa Movement, but rather as a dynamic
> political philosophy and guide to action for Africans in Africa who
> were laying the foundations of national liberation organizations . . . .
> Pan-Africanism was intended as a stimulant to anti-colonialism . . . .

Dr. DuBois was not only firmly against transporting American Negroes to Africa but was a staunch advocate of complete self-government for Africans in Africa organized on a basis of socialism and co-operative economy which would leave no room for millionaires, black or white. National self-determination, individual liberty and democratic socialism constituted the essential elements of Pan-Africanism as expounded by Dubois. . . . [6]

DuBois naturally opposed Garvey's utopianism. He, like most American Negroes, considered America to be their true native land. But . . . he was equally interested in helping forward the emancipation of Africa. Where DuBois differed from Garvey was in his conception of *the Pan-African movement as an aid to the promotion of national self-determination among Africans under African leadership, for the benefit of Africans themselves.*[7]

To the extent that *Negritude* means the exaltation of some kind of Black specificity (whether in general or in purely cultural terms), it is clearly not to be confused with Pan-Africanism. Furthermore, it was only when Pan-Africanism managed to do away with *Negritude* that it asserted itself clearly as a theory of revolution in Africa, designed to serve Africans – or at least so it claimed. The African revolution was then understood as the struggle of the African people for national independence and African unity, all of which was supposedly in the best interest of the Africans themselves. African unity itself came to mean the constitution of a political grouping of African states, who would gradually form themselves into a United States of Africa.

The Early Pan-African Congresses
In the pursuit of these aims, Dr. DuBois called four Pan-African Congresses between the two World Wars. Pan-Africanism was slowly becoming a much clearer conception. The First Pan-African Congress met in Paris in 1919, thanks to the support given to DuBois by Blaise Diagne, a Senegalese representative in the French Parliament. Most of the delegates came from the Antilles colonies and the United States. The French Prime Minister, Clemenceau, had authorized Diagne to organize the conference in Paris in recognition of Diagne's distinguished services to France during the war, notably organizing the recruitment of 80,000 African soldiers from Senegal, most of whom participated in the decisive Battle of the Marne in July 1918, which permitted the French to defeat the Germans.

The First Congress's resolutions embraced a variety of themes, but one emerged particularly clearly. *The delegates insisted, above all, on the right of the colonized peoples of Africa to self-determination, their right to own their own lands, their right not to be exploited by investment capital.* The Congress demanded that the German ex-colonies in Africa be placed under international control, a demand which was later distorted by the League of Nations when it imposed its system of mandates on countries such as Cameroon, Namibia, Tanganyika and Togo.

The Second Pan-African Congress opened in London on 28 August 1921. This time, 41 out of the 130 delegates were from Africa. Most of them came as individuals rather than as representatives of an organization. The Congress adopted a World Declaration, drawn up by DuBois, which reiterated the contents of the resolutions passed at the First Congress. At the time, as DuBois himself pointed out in 1923, 'Pan-Africanism was (still) more of an idea than a fact'. Therefore:

> After the Second Pan-African Congress, Dr. DuBois conceived the idea of establishing a permanent secretariat in order to maintain regular contact between the representatives who had attended the various conferences. He hoped that, in so doing, the Pan-African idea would be kept alive until such time as political parties emerged and nationalism took deeper roots in African soil.[8]

At the Third Pan-African Congress, which met in London during the summer of 1923, the political content of the Pan-Africanist demands emerged with still greater clarity. The Congress notably demanded that Africans be granted:

1) A voice in their own governments.
2) The development of Africa for the benefit of Africans and not merely for the profit of Europeans.
3) World disarmament and the abolition of war; but failing this, and as long as white folk bear arms against black folk, the right of blacks to bear arms in their own defence.[9]

The Congress adopted a Manifesto denouncing apartheid in South Africa. Forced labour and slavery were still rife in the colonies, especially in the Portuguese ones, notably Angola. At the same time, a group of African intellectuals had emerged in Lisbon and were agitating for reforms. These intellectuals organized themselves into a group called the *Liga Africana*. To encourage them, DuBois decided to hold the second session of the Congress in Lisbon. This *Liga Africana* was, so to speak, the political ancestor of what was later to become the Committee of Nationalist Organizations in the Portuguese Colonies (C.O.N.C.P.), of which the P.A.I.G.C. of Guinea Bissau, the Angolan M.P.L.A. and Mozambique's FRELIMO were all members.[10]

Between the Third and Fourth Congresses Garvey's movement disappeared from the scene; and, with the birth of two new Pan-African organizations, Africans from Africa began to play a part, almost for the first time. The first of these, the International African Friends of Abyssinia (I.A.F.A.), was founded when the Italian fascists, led by Mussolini, launched their criminal aggression against Ethiopia. Its members included J. B. Danquah (Ghana), Jomo Kenyatta (Kenya) and Mohammed Said (Somalia).

The second organization, the International African Service Bureau, soon counted Wallace Johnson, the West African trade unionist, Chris Jones from Barbados, Jomo Kenyatta (at the time the official representative of the Kikuyu Central Association) and George Padmore of Trinidad amongst its principal officers. The entente between DuBois and the Bureau was to be historically significant, in that it promoted the implantation of Pan-Africanist ideas in Africa itself.

The Fourth Pan-African Congress met in New York in 1927. It confirmed the decisions and orientations adopted at previous congresses.

Then, in 1944, representatives of various black peoples' organizations in England got together in Manchester, to set up a United Pan-African Front. The result was the Pan-African Federation, which from then on functioned as the British section of the Pan-African Congress Movement. The Federation adopted a programme which extended the principles of the first four Congresses and stated them even more precisely. Its declared aims were:

1) To promote the well-being and unity of African peoples and peoples of African descent throughout the world.
2) To demand self-determination and independence for African peoples and other subject races from the domination of powers claiming sovereignty and trusteeship over them.
3) To secure equality of civil rights for African peoples and the total abolition of all forms of racial discrimination.
4) To strive to co-operate between African peoples and others who share our aspirations.[11]

The Federation tackled a wide range of issues, notably 'theoretical problems such as the methods and forms of organization to be adopted by colonial peoples; the tactics and strategy of the national freedom struggle; the applicability of Gandhian non-violent, non co-operative techniques to the African situation', which were 'all openly discussed and debated in the columns of the Federation's journal, *International African Opinion*'.[12]

The 1945 Congress and the Adoption of Marxist Socialism
The Pan-African Federation marked the end of Pan-Africanism's infancy. The Fifth Pan-African Congress, held in Manchester during March and October 1945, put the finishing touches to Pan-Africanism's evolution into a set of theoretical and practical political conceptions elaborate enough to meet the needs of the contemporary anti-colonialist struggle.

Some idea of the Fifth Pan-African Congress can be obtained from the account of one of its organizers, Kwame Nkrumah, to this day still the greatest African advocate and theoretician of Pan-Africanism:

Although this conference was the fifth of its kind that had taken place, it was quite distinct and different in tone, outlook and ideology from the four that had preceded it. While the four previous conferences were both promoted and supported mainly by middle-class intellectuals and bourgeois Negro reformists, this Fifth Pan-African Congress was attended by workers, trade unionists, farmers, co-operative societies and by African and other coloured students. As the preponderance of members attending the Congress were African, its ideology became African nationalism – a revolt by African nationalism against colonialism, racialism and imperialism in Africa – and it adopted Marxist socialism as its philosophy . . . .

Garvey's ideology was concerned with *black* nationalism as opposed to *African* nationalism. And it was this Fifth Pan-African Congress that provided an outlet for African nationalism and brought about the awakening of African political consciousness. It became, in fact, a mass movement of Africa for the Africans.[13]

The Fifth Congress was thus a turning-point for Pan-Africanism. Class struggle was recognized, in principle at least, as the driving force of history, including African history (albeit from 1945 onwards); in other words, 'Marxist socialism was adopted as a philosophy'. The Fifth Congress was equally explicit on the question of African unity. One resolution in particular stressed that 'the artificial divisions and territorial boundaries created by the imperialist powers are deliberate steps to obstruct the political unity of the West African peoples'.[14]

It was only after the Fifth Congress that Pan-Africanist ideas began to find widespread roots in Africa itself, usually in close association with the struggle for independence. The link between Africa's independence and its unity was thus made clearly apparent.

To sum up, it is fair to say that, right from the start, Pan-Africanism was in no way to be confused with a 'racial' alignment. It was certainly not concerned with *Negritude*. Rather, it set out to provide a set of political and philosophical ideas for the guidance of African peoples in their struggle for liberation, independence and unity, a struggle for independence within the unity of Africa. If by African revolution one means the struggle for national and social liberation of African peoples dominated by imperialism and its allies, then early Pan-Africanism emerges as the ideology of the African revolution. African unity, conceived of as a *political unity*, is clearly an integral part of the African revolution's programme. Compared to the Pan-Africanism of 1945, the contemporary inconsistent notions of 'economic unity' amount to a vast step backwards.

Pan-Africanism in Africa, 1945-62: The Two Currents

Shortly after the Fifth Pan-African Congress, just as African nationalism was beginning to emerge as quite distinct from a politically vague Pan-Negro movement, and soon after Pan-Africanism had recognized Marxism as the theory and conception of the world which would enable Pan-Africanist ideas to be realized, the historical conditions of the anti-colonialist struggle forced the Pan-Africanist movement to adopt tactics based on the quest for common action, on rather confused political grounds, with people such as Senghor, Apithy and Houphouet-Boigny.

Houphouet-Boigny Exposed: His Opposition to Independence and African Unity

Nkrumah, who had been nominated to run the National Secretariat of West Africa, founded a journal, the *New African*, which eventually failed for lack of funds. But:

> Before the paper folded, we were able to use it in order to call the first West African Conference in London. It was in this connection, in an effort to include in the conference Africans from the French territories of West Africa that I paid a visit to Paris. I went to meet the African members of the French National Assembly, Sourous Apithy, Leopold Senghor, Lamine Gueye, Houphouet-Boigny and others. We had long discussions and planned, among other things, a movement for *the Union of West African Socialist Republics.*[15]

The Conference in question was held in London from 30 August to 1 September 1946. As the Fifth Pan-African Congress took place between March and October 1945, it seems likely that Nkrumah's trip to Paris took place between these two dates. One would therefore expect some correspondence between the ideas outlined by Nkrumah and the projects sponsored by Houphouet-Boigny and friends in 1946, when they set up the *Rassemblement Democratique Africain* (R.D.A.), whose first conference was held that very year, in Bamako. But it is quite obvious that Houphouet-Boigny must have been indulging in pure demagogy during his talks with Nkrumah; Houphouet himself described ten years later how:

> At the Bamako Conference in 1946, the case for autonomy, for independence in other words, had prevailed against my own views. But I was being asked to become the Movement's President. As I could not bring myself to assume functions which would have forced me to apply decisions I did not agree with, the debate was reopened, my motion was carried by a very narrow margin [!] and I was able to assume the Presidency. . . . And so it was that we opted for membership of the French *Communaute* rather than for the struggle for independence. It is a great source of satisfaction to me today that, not only has this viewpoint remained that of the entire R.D.A., it is now also shared by all the other African parties. [!!?][16]

In the introduction to the latest edition of his book, *Les fondements economiques et culturels d'un etat federal d'Afrique Noire,* the Senegalese African historian Sheikh Anta Diop, indirectly but emphatically, confirms that these were Houphouet's opinions concerning African independence in the early 1950s. Diop says:

It was in February 1952, when I was Secretary-General of the R.D.A. Students, that we posed ourselves the problem of the Black Continent's political independence and the possibility of eventually creating a federal state. ('Vers une ideologie politique en Afrique Noire', published in *La Voix de l'Afrique Noire*, organ of the R.D.A. Students, Paris, February 1952).

It is undisputable that at the time, apart from the Malagasy delegates and the Cameroonian leader Ruben Um Nyobe, no franco-phone African politician dared to talk about African independence, African nations or even African culture. Current declarations on the subject verge on imposture and are usually outright lies.[17]

On the basis of these quotes, we can conclude that, from 1946 to 1957, Houphouet-Boigny was already against African independence. This does not prevent him proclaiming himself a Pan-Africanist and an advocate of African unity. After all, he is President of the R.D.A., a body which even Um Nyobe's U.P.C. recognizes, and designates itself the Cameroonian Branch.

Meanwhile, in May 1955, the situation in Cameroon was evolving rapidly. Faced with the U.P.C.'s demand for independence and immediate re-unification, the French colonialists chose to resort to violence. Houphouet and his associates, who had conducted their famous 'tactical retreat' as early as 1950, called a special session of the R.D.A. Co-ordination Committee in Conakry. The aim of the meeting was clear: to suppress the 'hate-filled slogans' demanding independence launched by the U.P.C. The meeting was held from 8 to 11 July 1955. And, as if by chance, on 13 July in Paris, the French Government (Edgar Faure was then President of the Council) decided to ban the U.P.C. in Cameroon.

During the Conakry meeting, Houphouet declared, among other things, that: 'There is no deep antagonism separating the Africans and the [European] settlers: there is only a barrier of futile prejudice and unfounded fears, which must be overcome for the common good.'[18] He went on to add that Africa could not but embrace 'the creation of a new and prosperous Africa within the bosom of a strong and fraternal French Union'.[19] On 28 April 1956, in Abidjan, Houphouet declared that, contrary to certain claims, 'there is no national problem in Black Africa'.[20] [!!!] And on 11 November 1957, probably to celebrate the 1918 armistice which confirmed 'his country's' victory over Germany, he specified that, from his point of view, the struggle for independence was no more than 'that spirit of vengeance against the one-time colonizers which was expressed at Bandung'.[21] The previous year, on 9 November 1956, he had already made the following outrageous statement about independence: 'To be quite frank, I have always thought that we would be betraying our own masses if we tried to lead them along what I can only describe as a hopeless road.'[22]

Not that any of this prevented Houphouet-Boigny from declaring, in a message to the nation on 31 December 1960, that the present independence of the Ivory Coast was, in fact, 'the result of 15 years of struggle and effort we have all participated in and which has led us, stage by stage, towards taking command of our own country's destiny'.[23] He even had the cheek to salute 'all those who have suffered pain, grief, humiliation or death along the way, so that we should live through these glorious days of our recovered independence'.[24]

The 'hopeless road' had suddenly become 'these glorious days of our recovered independence'. What a farce! Especially when one recalls that the Fifth Pan-African Congress in 1945 had already clearly indicated that: 'The Congress unanimously supported the members of the West African delegation in declaring that complete and absolute independence for the peoples of West Africa is the only solution to the existing problem.'[25]

Houphouet-Boigny and friends have indubitably distinguished themselves in the struggle *against* the independence of Africa. They have been truly consistent opponents. Referring to the 'vast fraternal whole' which Africa and France together should form, here is what Houphouet had to say about African integration and unity:

> We wish to stress that, as far as we are concerned, the most effective methods of attaining this end are, firstly, the elimination, as quickly as possible, of all intermediary bodies between the central federal authorities and the territories, and secondly, constantly reinforced affirmation of the territories' personality and autonomy.[26]

The 'intermediary bodies' referred to were the so-called Federal Governments of French Equatorial Africa and French West Africa; as for 'the central federal authorities', Houphouet was talking about Paris. He made the point even more explicitly on 15 March 1958, when De Gaulle sought to 'grant' independence to all the French-dominated African colonial territories. Houphouet peremptorily declared that: 'The Ivory Coast has made its own choice. Whatever happens, we will remain full members of the Franco-African *Communaute*. A federal executive is all very well, but in Paris, not in Dakar.'[27]

Shortly after, having fought his last battle against independence (at an R.D.A. Congress in September 1959), Houphouet learnt that De Gaulle had 'offered independence to anybody who wanted it' without even consulting him. Like a disillusioned lover, Houphouet turned away from the still-born *Communaute renovee* which had thus come into the world. 'I waited on the threshold with my wilted flowers . . . . The *Communaute renovee* has been elaborated without our participation, and against our wishes; what we wanted was a federal linkage [with France].'[28]

Houphouet-Boigny, the present 'Apostle of Independence' and 'Father of the Nation' was, like his friend Ahidjo in Cameroon, so opposed to independence that even his masters in Paris arranged for the transition to neo-colonial independence without telling him; he would have been quite capable of opposing even this kind of 'independence', so it had to be forced on him instead. If we have quoted Houphouet-Boigny at length, it is only as the leader of a certain political tendency which first carried the day at the Constituent Congress of the R.D.A. in Bamako in 1946. The historians of Pan-Africanism are, on the whole, still wondering what was the exact position taken by Sekou Toure during the famous July 1955 meeting of the R.D.A. Co-ordination Committee in Conakry, which illegally decided to expel the U.P.C. from the R.D.A. (an expulsion our Party has never recognized), thereby giving French colonialism a free hand to ban the U.P.C. in Cameroon itself. What is quite clear is that the Labe section of the Guinean Democratic Party was severely reprimanded for having expressed its disagreement over the expulsion of the U.P.C.

The Tactical Alliance Between Nkrumah and Reformists

Now that we have seen what Houphouet's position on independence and African unity amounted to, we can measure the gulf which separated him from Nkrumah's conception of African liberation. As early as 20 September 1956, Nkrumah had written that: 'African nationalism was not confined to the Gold Coast — the new Ghana. From now on it must be Pan-African nationalism, and the ideology of African political consciousness and African political emancipation must spread throughout the whole continent.'[29]

One can only conclude that it was simply the specific historical conditions of the anti-imperialist struggle in Africa between 1940 and 1950 which made an alliance such as the R.D.A. possible, an alliance between truly anti-imperialist militants like Nkrumah, on the one hand, and people like Senghor and Houphouet, on the other. These conditions can be summed up as a still embryonic class differentiation and the absence of a working class with a clear consciousness of its own interests. The first consequence of these conditions was the possibility of bringing all the social strata together in a vast anti-colonialist United Front, the bigger the better. Such a front seemed not only possible but indispensable.

If one does not take all this into account (as some astonishingly naive European political groups do not), then the alliance between Nkrumah, Senghor and Houphouet does indeed seem absurd. When Nkrumah returned from the U.S., he had already learnt to understand the social dialectic, and, as he says in the Preface to his *Consciencism*, he was already one of those African students who sought to approach Western culture as a free man. He was already an African intellectual who desired the independence and unification of Africa and who recognized historical materialism as the philosphy of struggle appropriate to this noble cause. Senghor, on the other hand, was an intellectual half-breed. On finishing his studies he taught at the *Ecole Coloniale*, where he helped the French imperialist bourgeoisie train its Governors and other colonial administrators. As for Houphouet-Boigny, he was simply a big Ivory Coast plantation owner. Short of some radical change, such an alliance could only lead to a dead end, just as the alliance within the R.D.A. between revolutionary militants and reformist representatives of Ivory Coast plantation owners and local Senegalese businessmen was bound to fail. Its failure was sealed in 1955 by the decisions taken in Cameroon in

May and in Conakry in July. Similarly, the failure of the alliance within the
C.P.C. (Convention People's Party) between Nkrumahist Pan-African
revolutionaries, bourgeois bureaucrats, landowners and micro-nationalist
Ashanti chiefs was sealed by the February 1966 coup which overthrew
Nkrumah.

Nkrumah, on his return from the U.S. at the end of the Second World
War and especially when he came to Paris to debate with Houphouet and his
cronies, was thus already far more than just an anti-imperialist intellectual.
His interlocutors, on the other hand, were well integrated into the French
imperialist system, as deputies in the French National Assembly. The tactical
meanderings of the African anti-imperialist movement of the period show
clearly that, to paraphrase Engels, the anti-imperialist militants of 1940-50,
like their predecessors, could not transcend the boundaries fixed by their
epoch.[30]

The 1958-61 Conferences: Compromise Takes Hold

From 1957-58, after independence had been achieved in Ghana, the Pan-
African struggle entered a new phase, marked by the Conferences of Independent African States and, from 1958 onwards, the Conferences of African
Peoples, in which representatives of peoples who had not as yet gained
independence also participated. The Conferences of Independent States were
always very different from the African Peoples Conferences. This point is
fairly fundamental, as any close examination of the decisions taken at the
one and the other will show.

When the first Conference of Independent States met in Accra, in April
1958, wars of liberation were raging in Cameroon and Algeria, yet it was
only after strenuous debate and several formal amendments that a resolution
of support, stemming from the original Egyptian-sponsored motion, was
passed.

A few months later, from 25 to 28 July 1958, the Constituent Congress
of the *Parti du Regroupement Africain* (P.R.A.) met in Conakry. The
participants were organizations (and not particularly revolutionary ones at
that) rather than independent states, yet even the French bourgeoisie was
forced to recognize that the Conference delegates

> laid much greater stress on the question of purely African *Communauté*
> than on that of the Franco-African *Communauté*; the two main watch-
> words unanimously endorsed by the Congress were 'immediate
> independence' and 'a United States of Africa'. Indeed the P.R.A.
> delegates demanded the abolition of all frontiers established following
> the 1885 Berlin Conference so that the Peoples of Africa might unite
> along 'complimentary' lines. During the closing session . . . Mr. Djibo
> Bakary, head of the Niger delegation and General Secretary of the
> P.R.A., was greeted with wild applause when he declared 'we want a
> united Africa, from Cairo to Johannesburg'.[31]

The first Conference of African Peoples (Accra, 5-13 December 1958) was attended by all the popular anti-colonialist African organizations. Not only were the Algerian delegates warmly applauded, but Algeria and Cameroon were the subject of special resolutions.[32] All the delegates were obviously very conscious of the anti-colonialist armed struggle being waged in those countries. It was only three months since French colonial troops had murdered the founder and General Secretary of the U.P.C., Ruben Um Nyobe (with the full agreement of their puppet, Ahidjo, whom France had installed as Prime Minister in February of that year). The Conference took several practical decisions, notably to set up a permanent Secretariat in Accra.[33] It is thus quite clear that, in keeping with the line of the pre-1946 Pan-African Congresses, the people of Africa understood that African unity could only be realized as a political unity.

When the Second Conference of Independent States met in Monrovia, from 4 to 8 August 1959, the spirit of compromise at any price was abroad once again. Even on the question of Algeria, which was perfectly straight-forward and had already been correctly analysed nine months before by the People's Conference, 'moderate' Liberia found reasons to oppose the Guinean resolution. As a result, the Provisional Government of the Algerian Republic (G.P.R.A.), which was then leading the Algerian people's anti-colonialist struggle under the aegis of the National Liberation Front, was not recognized, and an 'appeal for a political truce in Cameroon' was considered sufficient response to the situation there.

In January 1960, the Second African People's Conference met in Tunis. Among the participants was a large delegation from Cameroon, led by the President of the U.P.C., Comrade Felix-Roland Moumie. The Leadership Committee elected by the Conference included Ahmed Boumendjel (Algeria), Felix Moumie (Cameroon) and Patrice Lumumba (Congo), names which amply testify to the resolutely anti-imperialist spirit of the Conference. A political resolution explicitly condemned the Franco-African *Communaute*, so dear to Houphouet-Boigny, as a new form of imperialism. A special resolution on Algeria called for 'the recognition of the G.P.R.A. by all African states, the creation of a volunteer brigade, regular contributions from the budgets of African states and the withdrawal of all black troops committed to the Algerian conflict by the French Republic'.[34]

None of this prevented the Third Conference of Independent States, which met in June 1960 at Addis Ababa and to which our Party submitted a voluminous, detailed, precise and well-substantiated memorandum,[35] from accepting the presence in its ranks of a puppet delegation led by Charles Okala, the then Minister of Foreign Affairs of the French lackey, Ahidjo.

In Cairo, in March 1961, at the Third Conference of African Peoples, the delegates approved 'the use of force to eliminate imperialism'.[36] They carried a series of militant resolutions on Algeria, Cameroon, South Africa, the Congo-Kinshasa[37] and the Portuguese colonies. 'Support for the G.P.R.A. was unanimous' and demands were made for 'the withdrawal of all French and British troops stationed in Cameroon'. The delegates gave their support, and that of the African peoples, to the Stanleyville-based Lumumbist Government of Antoine Gizenga and denounced the U.N. machinations in the Congo. They also called for the independence of the Portuguese colonies.

Several points emerge clearly from this brief summary of the situation in Africa by 1961. The peoples of Africa were struggling against colonialism, seeking to recover their national independence and build the political unity of the continent. In the course of several continental conferences, they repeatedly stated that what they needed was the complete abolition of all the frontiers arbitrarily imposed by imperialism. Some independent states did already exist, but they were riven by pronounced divisions, much to the joy of the imperialists. A few of these states continued to struggle in one way or another against imperialism, both in its colonial form and in its newly emerging neo-colonialist aspect. But others, like those led by Houphouet-Boigny in the Ivory Coast and by Ahidjo in Cameroon, were simply imperialist puppets. Under such conditions, there was no fundamental basis of co-operation for Nkrumah's Ghana and a Cameroon on which imperialism had forcibly imposed Ahidjo. They manifestly did not share the same conceptions, either of the anti-imperialist struggle in general or of Pan-Africanism in particular, and it was clear that, as far as African unity was concerned, serious collaboration between them was quite out of the question. In fact, nobody even envisaged discussing such a project. The essentials of the situation were clear and the African states aligned themselves by political affinity.

Casablanca versus Monrovia: Revolutionary versus Demagogic Pan-Africanism
A conference attended by Egypt, Ghana, Guinea, Morocco, Tunisia and the G.P.R.A. was held in Casablanca from 3 to 7 January 1961. The participants endowed themselves with a Charter and emerged as the so-called Casablanca Group, which proved consistent in its support for African revolutionary anti-imperialist movements, especially in Algeria and Cameroon.

Five months later, from 8 to 12 May 1961, in Monrovia, Liberia, another conference was held. It was attended by 21 countries, including Ahidjo's puppet regime. The participants in the Casablanca Conference did not go to Monrovia. So what was decided at this new conference, called almost as a riposte to the one in Casablanca? The delegates adopted one fundamental resolution, insisting on 'non-interference in the internal affairs of other states', and expressed 'unreserved condemnation of any subversive action conducted from outside by adjoining states', finally concluding that: 'The unity we must achieve at the moment *is not the political integration of sovereign African states*, but [hold on tight! E.M.] a unity of aspiration and action, to promote African social solidarity [??] and political identity [??]. [My emphasis, E.M.]'[38]

One only has to compare this verbiage with the decisions of the Fifth Pan-African Congress in 1945 to see just how big a step backwards it represents for Pan-African thought. It is worth noting that the Monrovia Conference was attended by all those ex-French colonies of Black Africa (excepting Guinea) aligned together in the African and Malagasy Union

(U.A.M.) since the neo-colonial Brazzaville Conference (15-19 December 1960) who eventually became members of the supposedly renovated French *Communaute.*[39] Nigeria, at the time led by Nnamdi Azikiwe and Abubakar Tafewa Balewa, was also represented at Monrovia.[40]

The fundamental resolution adopted at Monrovia was crucially important. Two years later, the O.A.U. charter reasserted the same basic theses.

It should already be clear that, *throughout the period from 1945 to 1960-61, there were two distinct currents within Pan-Africanism, the one demagogic and the other revolutionary.*

Revolutionary Pan-Africanism's strength during these years was its just and popular cause, the independence and unification of Africa. This Pan-Africanism enjoyed the backing of progressive forces throughout the world and the support of the African masses, who were to a greater or lesser extent aware that independence would only come through unification. Its great weakness, however, was a lack of clarity and acuity, the absence of any coherent overall conception of African unity. The first major attempt to fill this lacuna, Nkrumah's book, *Africa Must Unite*, was only published in 1963. But the real cause of revolutionary Pan Africanism's downfall was that, instead of trying to achieve this unity through the efforts of those who had most to gain, the African workers and peasants, it put its hopes in heads of state. In other words, it tried to bring about African unity 'from above', despite the fact that many, indeed most, of these heads of state were notorious reformists, not to say outright reactionaries, linked in a thousand and one ways to international imperialism.

As for the merely demagogic current in Pan-Africanism, its main strength at the time was the international imperialist bourgeoisie, and the presence of that bourgeoisie's agents in the fairly confused ranks of Africa's progressive militants. Reformism and opportunism were by no means the exclusive prerogatives of heads of state.

How far could the struggle between these two tendencies go? Probably as far as the imperialist bourgeoisie was prepared to take the defence of its economic interests in Africa — in other words, all the way. It was not long before the two tendencies showed what they really stood for. The Congo provided the arena, and the events there laid bare the fundamental and irreducible contradiction between a revolutionary Pan-African wing expressing the interests of African workers and peasants and a Pan-Africanist demagogy expressing the interests of African and world reaction. The African revolution was left to fend for itself and had 'to count essentially on its own forces'. When Patrice Lumumba was murdered, the battle was already irretrievably lost.

Early Practical Attempts at Unification by Independent African States

From 1958 to 1962, there were numerous theoretical debates as to the best way of achieving the unification of Africa, but there were also some practical attempts to unite by independent African states. The importance of all these attempts, and of the lessons Pan-African revolutionaries can draw from their failure, should not be underestimated.

On 23 November 1958, Ghana and Guinea decided to unite and form the core of a future United States of Africa. Such a decision, taken less than two months after Guinea achieved independence (28 September), was of considerable importance for Africa as a whole. Yet it must be admitted that the decision was never put into practice, a fact which neither Nkrumah's stay in Conakry from 1966 on following the reactionary coup in Ghana nor the rigmarole of the co-presidency he was offered by the 'Great Strategist of the African Democratic Revolution' can ever obviate, (especially as Nkrumah was practically under house arrest during his stay in Guinea). The reality seems to be that no detailed study of the precise political content of unification was carried out before the decision was taken, even though there were very real historical and social difficulties, rooted in different patterns of colonization in the two countries concerned.

We have already seen how Houphouet-Boigny and the French imperialists torpedoed the old French West African and French Equatorial African Federations. Houphouet, the 'wise man of Africa', if one is to believe the infamous propaganda of the French, had decided that these federations were harmful, since, as he put it: 'The continued existence of the A.O.F. and A.E.F. federations might well have encouraged secession in African territories. [!!!] The establishment of a federal executive in Dakar would certainly have been contrary to the economic interests of the Ivory Coast.'[41] In short, Houphouet had the same programme as Moise Tshombe in Katanga.

Sometime after the formal Ghana-Guinea Union, representatives of Senegal, Dahomey, Sudan and Upper Volta met in Dakar and, on 17 January 1959, decided to unite these four countries in a Federation of Mali. French imperialism and Houphouet-Boigny immediately went into action, setting up their own project for a *Conseil de l'Entente*. The very close economic ties between the Ivory Coast and Upper Volta represented a particularly effective means by which Houphouet and his masters in Paris could blackmail the latter country. And indeed, it was not long before Dahomey and Upper Volta dropped out of the Mali Federation project, leaving only Senegal and French-dominated Sudan. But the Senegalese and Sudanese leaders — Senghor and Modibo Keita — could not reach agreement as to the precise political content of unity. As the previously quoted reactionary journalist says: 'Right from 18 June 1960, the day independence was achieved, the partisans of a flexible federal system clashed with the Bamako leaders, who upheld the principles of a unitary state.'[42]

As usual, Decraene gives a quite superficial explanation of these events.

In the light of what has been said above, it is quite clear that French imperialism could not possibly have approved a project which might well have set the ball of African unification rolling. Senghor's group, therefore, engineered a split on 20 August 1960, and all that remained of the Mali Federation was the territory of the ex-French Sudan. As for the *Conseil de l'Entente* it has done nothing whatsoever to promote integration in the region and is heard of less and less. All this only confirms what we already knew: the *Conseil de l'Entente* was launched with the sole purpose of sinking the Mali Federation as originally envisaged. Houphouet-Boigny's constant efforts to undermine African unity had paid off once again.

The Ghana-Guinea-Mali Union was another project which never really got much further than one or two meetings between those countries' heads of state. There was also the East African Common Market (E.A.C.M.), which served essentially as a free-trade zone. Lacking any political impetus, it failed to integrate the three countries concerned (Kenya, Tanzania and Uganda), as was amply confirmed by the noisy break-up of the association in 1977. As if the collapse of the E.A.C.M. was not enough, the highly dubious theory that African unity can be achieved through common markets and other economic agreements took another rude blow in 1978, when Idi Amin Dada attempted to 'adjust' Uganda's frontier with Tanzania. The people of Africa could not help noticing the crashing silence with which these events were greeted by nearly all the members of the O.A.U., the so-called guarantor of peace on the continent.

There remains the *Union Douaniere des Etats de L'Afrique Centrale* (U.D.E.A.C., or Central African States' Customs Union), which also functions purely as a free-trade zone involving Gabon, Cameroon, Congo-Brazzaville and the Central African 'Empire' (now Republic).

The Lessons to be Drawn

From all these attempts and others less significant,[43] we can plainly see that the concrete political content of unity is the touchstone of African unity. It should also be clear that the so-called divergences 'as to the ways and means to achieve African unity, the end to which we all aspire' (*sic!*) are anything but mere divergences about the best method to use.

In fact, just as there are two theoretical tendencies within Pan-Africanism, so there are two kinds of strategy and tactics within the Pan-African political struggle. That which corresponds to revolutionary Pan-Africanism is the truly unitary strategy which consists in striving for the *political unity* of existing countries, in order to win genuine social and economic freedom for the African peoples. And that which corresponds to Pan-Africanist demagogy is the pseudo-unitary strategy which relies on slogans such as 'sovereign states', 'non-interference in internal affairs' and the 'spirit of mutual tolerance'. *In other words, those who want nothing to do with African unity simply put forward methods of unification which lead nowhere.*

In 1962, Algeria won its independence after a bitter struggle which was supported by all the progressive forces in Africa. Revolutionary Pan-African militants throughout Africa waited expectantly to see whether they had gained a new and important ally.

The Creation of the O.A.U.

During 1962 and 1963, a broad movement aimed at bringing all African states into a single continental organization began to emerge. Naturally enough, this new tendency had opponents as well as supporters. The latter maintained that there was no point in preserving several different groups of independent states, since 'everybody is basically in agreement with the principle of African unity; the differences that do exist are essentially over questions of method, and can be overcome through discussion.' The opponents of this view on the other hand, asserted and demonstrated that 'caution is essential, since an emerging neo-colonialism threatens to spread throughout the Continent, especially if the Casablanca group accepts to play along with the current proposals'.

If we are to establish the truth of the matter and illustrate the genesis of the present O.A.U. and the general counter-revolutionary gangrene which prevails in Africa today, we must examine the ruling neo-colonial African bourgeoisies' close historical links with the interests of imperialism. The illusions of petty-bourgeois Pan-Africanism which led it into its bankruptcy have still not been dispelled and exposed; we shall try to do so.

Imperialism's View of African Unity

On 23 November 1958, when Ghana and Guinea jointly announced that they had decided to form the core of a United States of Africa, the British Embassy in Paris issued a communique, part of which read:

> British opinion, despite express reservations, has no desire to condemn *a priori* the first attempt at an *indigenous* African organization, even if French opinion, for equally good reasons of its own, receives the news of such an initiative with a measure of anxiety. British opinion is far more perturbed that Mr. Sekou Toure should see fit to sign a trade agreement with East Germany than that he should seek closer links with another African state which entertains the best possible relations with the West.[44]

The communique contains a mass of indications. Clearly 'the West' is very interested in any moves towards unity in Africa, and is indignant that the 'natives' should seek to reorganize Africa along lines different from those decided in 1885 in Berlin. But, at a pinch, such 'native' reorganization can be accepted, as long as it involves only African states — today the phrase would be 'without Soviet-Cuban interference' — preferably the more docile and pro-Western amongst them.[45] In other words, the imperialists are prepared to recognize, if only in the hypocritical verbiage of diplomacy, that the trend towards unification in Africa is as irresistible as the preceding trend towards independence. They, therefore, accept that their best option is not to oppose openly this tendency towards unity, but rather to ensure that any such unity should involve pro-imperialist African states. It is fair to say that, with their usual flair for imperialist pillage, the British actually created the O.A.U. as we know it today.

Sekou Toure Changes Tune

When the Monrovia Conference met in 1961, the Casablanca Group states were invited but refused to come. We have already outlined what was going on in Africa at the time: Patrice Lumumba had just been assassinated, and many of those present in Monrovia had manifestly been accomplices in that murder, as everybody in Africa well knew.[46] Sekou Toure, who had not yet promoted himself 'Great Strategist of the African Democratic Revolution' commented: 'Today Africa can quite unequivocally tell those who have worked for genuine decolonization from those who have deliberately compromised the historical process.'[47] Such a declaration implied, at the very least, that there were some heads of state who were genuinely working for African independence and unity, and others who were doing the opposite. Yet exactly a year later, the same orator could coolly declare:

> Just as there has never been a Trans-Saharan Africa and a Sub-Saharan Africa, so there are not today two antagonistic African blocs, for all the international press's parrotings about Casablanca Africa and Monrovia Africa. For us, as for all men of conscience throughout the world [*sic*], there is only one Africa, recently and only partially liberated from colonial domination, whose efforts are entirely bent towards the reconquest of its total liberty, the protection of its dignity and originality, the development of its personality and culture, the creation and consolidation of the material, social and moral bases of its peoples' wellbeing.[48]

It might seem incredible that such a speech could be made in the Africa of 1961-62, yet it indubitably was. One does not really have to look very far for the explanation. On 8 June 1961, after Sekou's first declaration, Houphouet-Boigny gave a press conference in Paris, where he was on an official visit to his masters. There he asserted that 'he too' was in favour of African unity, but wanted this unity to be 'realistic', 'based on reality'. Houphouet went on to elaborate: 'This reality amounts to a unity of constructive aspirations [??] *within an affirmation of each state's personality*.' [My emphasis, E.M.]

Senghor's Mystifications

In other words, Houphouet was still busily opposing any attempt at a political unification of Africa. His fundamental position had not changed one jot since the days when he had helped dismantle the A.O.F. and A.E.F.

federations. None the less, Sekou Toure was sufficiently impressed by these words to make the second speech, quoted above, on 1 May 1962. Houphouet's position was endorsed by his colleague Senghor in July 1963, shortly after Senghor had returned from the Addis Ababa Conference which had supposedly brought African heads of state together to plan the unification of Africa. Also in Paris, naturally, Senghor declared: 'My conception of African unity is similar to General de Gaulle's conception of Europe [but of course! E.M.] . *We must build an Africa of nations. We are too different from each other, as much in terms of race* [!!] *as of culture* [!] *and language* [!] '. [My emphasis, E.M.] [49]

On 16 February 1967, in Cairo, Senghor, the champion of *Negritude* and *Arabicity*, the Poet-President who had just been made Doctor *honoris causa* of Cairo University, had this to say about 'our future':

It can rest firmly only on values which are shared by all Africans, and which are permanent. It is precisely this set of values I call *Africanicity*.

My aim in this conference is to try to define these values. Essentially they are *cultural values* which, as everybody knows, are always conditioned by geography, history and ethnic, if not racial, factors. [N.B., E.M.]

I have often defined *Africanicity* as a symbiosis between the values of *Arabism* and of *Negritude*. But I have come to prefer the term *Arabicity*. [50]

Let us be clear: Senghor is talking about 'Africanicity'. Now, either there are no (or almost no) permanent values common to all Africans, since 'we are too different from each other', in which case the concept of Africanicity, as defined by Senghor, is completely hollow and good for nothing better than impressing naive students grateful for the opportunity to applaud a head of state in an auditorium. And, if so, then Senghor, as usual, is speaking simply for the pleasure of hearing his own voice. Or else, the concept is not hollow, which implies that the common, important and permanent values shared by all Africans cannot be dismissed as merely secondary. In that case, to use Senghor's own words, those values are 'cultural values', 'conditioned by . . . history and ethnic, if not racial, factors'. How can we at the same time be 'too different from each other, as much in terms of race as of culture', yet share permanent important values conditioned by race, history and geography? The only possible conclusion is that Senghor is a specialist in meaningless waffle, a political demagogue on a par with his friend Houphouet-Boigny.

Having seen what their 'theses' amount to, we can now turn to the positions taken by other African leaders, who are not known as outright vassals of imperialism; leaders who, on the contrary, enjoy a certain reputation as progressive men of good faith.

Nyerere Goes Along

In the January 1963 issue of the *Journal of Modern African Studies*, some
five months before the Addis Ababa Conference which set up the O.A.U.,
Julius Nyerere published a text which was subsequently translated into
French and issued as a pamphlet entitled *Des Etats Unis d'Afrique*.[51] In it
he says:

> For the sake of all African states, large or small, African unity must
> come and it must be real unity. Our goal must be a United States of
> Africa — only this can really give Africa the future her people deserve
> after centuries of economic uncertainty and social oppression. This
> goal must be achieved, and it does not matter whether this is done by
> one step or by many, or through economic, political or social develop-
> ment.[52]

If the Tanzanian President had stopped short of the last sentence quoted
above, we would have been entitled to understand him as saying that
Houphouet, Senghor and their fellow puppets in the Monrovia Group had
absolutely nothing to contribute to those who believed in African unity. But
that last sentence effectively cancels out what came previously. Of course,
it is good to hear a President enunciating the principle that African unity is
essential. It is even better when he says that this unity, in order to be a
genuine unity, must mean the setting up of a United States of Africa. But if
detailed and practical methods to achieve all this are not specified, the
principles remain mere word-play. Julius Nyerere cannot possibly be unaware
that the choice of a path towards one's goal is crucial, especially in the case
of a goal such as the one he is discussing. He knows full well that merely
formal proposals will lead strictly nowhere. It is not enough to say that,
after all, there is no *a priori* reason why this or that method cannot lead to
the creation of a United States of Africa. One must be quite sure that the
method *effectively* will lead to the result envisaged. Yet this essential point
is simply ignored by the Tanzanian leader, even though it is clear that there
is no substitute for a painstaking examination of each proposed method's
suitability. Putting one's 'trust' in a 'feeling of unity' is blatantly inadequate.
Nyerere himself points out that: 'The boundaries which divide African states
are so nonsensical, that without our sense of unity they would be a cause of
friction.'[53]

But he is surely aware that such a feeling cannot really provide us with
the means to resist the divisive manoeuvres of the imperialists and
reactionaries. Idi Amin's 1978 incursions on the Uganda-Tanzania border
have merely reinforced the point. As long as Africa remains balkanized, no
sensible person can dismiss the possibility of such frictions. Indeed, there
have been so many confrontations of that sort since 1963 that the O.A.U.
is tired of acting as a conciliator. Nyerere recognizes the problem when he
says:

As long as there remain separate African nations, there will also remain a danger that other states will exploit our differences for their own purposes. Only with unity can we ensure that Africa really governs Africa. Only with unity can we be sure that African resources will be used for the benefit of Africa.[54]

Having read the above quotes from Nyerere, the attentive reader might well conclude that, had the Tanzanian leader been consistent, given the clearly expressed positions outlined from 1946 onwards by Houphouet-Boigny, and Senghor, he could never have come to any agreement with them over the question of African unity, and the O.A.U. would never have been born. However, when Nyerere finally tackles the *practical issue* of whether or not the Monrovia and Casablanca groups should fuse, we find him writing:

The fact is that none of the conferences to which these names refer have abandoned the final aim; the differences between them lie in the ways of expressing the aim and the description of the path which must be followed to reach it. This can clearly be seen by a careful reading of the different communiques, which reveal much more common ground than differences. . . . This would obviate the danger of unnecessary suspicion being engendered.

There is really only one way for us to deal with this transitional problem. That is for us all to act now as if we already had unity. In any one country, members of the government do not always like each other or approve of each other's public phraseology. But this is not allowed to become public, the arguments are conducted in the Cabinet or the offices, not blazoned to the opposition. So it must be between African states now. And similarly, just as a Minister does not interfere with the political support of a colleague, African states must accept the decisions of the people in the different national units, as regards their own leaders.

This is very important. It means that any differences we have must be sorted out privately between ourselves. It means that we must avoid judging each other's internal policies, recognizing that each country has special problems which are its own concern, as well as problems which have inter-African repercussions . . . .

When we are genuinely concerned about the policies of another African state, the right people to address are the leaders of that state — and then in a brotherly spirit.[55]

This deliberately long quote is such a good summary of the philosophy which inspired the creators of the O.A.U. that commentary almost seems superfluous. So what if unity has not yet been achieved, provided we continue to desire it? We can just carry on as if it had already been won! This is more or less Nyerere's starting point. And then, since we are already united (!), we must not cause too much trouble for each other. Above all,

we must not judge each other. The African peoples of the various small states
have already 'freely chosen' their leaders, so there can be no justification for
disobliging remarks about any of them. Has Nyerere forgotten the history
of the African people's anti-colonialist struggle from 1945 to 1960? Unlikely.
Is he then deliberately ignoring this history? He tells us that we must not pass
judgement on the domestic politics of another state, yet he himself openly
disregarded this principle over Biafra, and was indeed one of the few African
heads of state to recognize Colonel Ojukwu's regime. Nyerere's whole position
is characteristic of politicians who are prepared to seek accommodation with
any established authority whatsoever, and whose judgements on this or that
individual or social group are usually based entirely on the public pronouncements they make. What is lacking is any consideration of what the individuals
or social groups concerned are actually doing. Reading pronouncements is
not going to tell us who is and who is not genuinely committed to the
creation of a United States of Africa. The only real way to find out is by
examining the policies and political practice of each group over the years.

Nkrumah and Revolutionary Pan-Africanism in the 1960s
President Kwame Nkrumah is still the only African head of state to have
elaborated a coherent theory of African unity based on the practical realities
of African society rather than on feelings and communiques. His theory
asserts that *African unity must necessarily take the form of a continent-wide
political unification. There will have to be a Continental Government charged
with the management of all essential functions, notably the economy, defence
and foreign affairs.* The thesis is outlined in his book *Africa Must Unite*, first
published just before the May 1963 Addis Ababa Conference which set up
the O.A.U. On 11 November 1963, he spelled out his position to the Pan-
African Conference of Journalists:

> If Africa does not set forth on the path to socialism, it will fall back
> instead of advancing. With any other system we will at best make only
> very slow progress. Our people may then become impatient. They want
> to see progress in action, and socialism is the only means to achieve it
> quickly.

In which case, one is entitled to ask why such a Pan-African programme
needed to secure the participation of patently neo-colonialist African
governments. In other words, why was this programme proposed to African
heads of state rather than to the African people themselves, who could then
have put it into practice? After all, leaders like Houphouet-Boigny had
openly exposed themselves as demagogues ever since 1946, and continued to
do so in 1960-61. The question is an important one, in that it allows us to
pinpoint at least some of the causes underlying the failure of Kwame
Nkrumah's political strategy, notably in Pan-African affairs, and the more
general failure of revolutionary Pan-Africanism throughout the 1960s.
  First, let us consider the positions adopted at the time by the various

revolutionary groups when faced with this problem. Even today, some Cameroonian opportunists find a variety of equally fallacious pretexts for carrying on as if the U.P.C. had never said anything about the O.A.U., even before it was set up.

In May 1962, a Conference of African Nationalist Organizations was held in Accra, Ghana. The U.P.C. delegation presented a declaration which the Party subsequently published as a 16-page pamphlet entitled *Unite Africaine ou Neo-Colonialisme* (and dated 30 May 1962, exactly one year before the O.A.U. was set up in Addis Ababa). The pamphlet notably points out that:

> In Africa, the imperialists now intend to bring about a union between the Africa of the Casablanca Charter and the reformist Africa comprising the U.A.M. and the Monrovia Group states. Their hope is that their lackeys within such a body will enable them to orient the whole union towards acceptance of subordination and neo-colonialist oppression . . . . Imperialism's lackeys will enter the Union with the aim of turning it into a counter-revolutionary organization. (p.10)
>
> The road to genuine African unity does not pass through a fusion of the Brazzaville, Monrovia, Lagos and Casablanca groups of states. Such a fusion would only lead to a confusion from which neo-colonialism and imperialism would be the sole beneficiaries. African leaders would find themselves being pushed into relegating the fundamental problem, the struggle against neo-colonialism, into the background. (p.11)
>
> The sincerely anti-imperialist independent African states must resolutely undertake actions which keep the Casablanca Charter alive and bring the realization of its aims closer . . . by giving concrete assistance to nationalist movements struggling against colonialism and neo-colonialism [and] . . . by avoiding the trap set by neo-colonialism, *the trap of unity with the counter-revolutionary camp* as embodied in the Afro-Malagasy Union, the Monrovia Group and the Lagos Group. (p.16)

This was the position of the U.P.C. before the birth of the O.A.U. In this period, two fundamentally divergent conceptions met in open conflict. One of these was clearly reactionary and firmly opposed to any political unification of Africa along the lines which had been put forward even before independence by the Pan-African Conferences.[56] The supporters of this conception stood for an 'Africa of Nations', but, as good demagogues, declared themselves 'willing to co-operate' provided their conditions were met. In practice, they were demanding that African revolutionaries renege on any commitment to revolutionary Pan-Africanism. The 1958 British communique issued in Paris had suggested something very similar.

The second conception based itself on the need for revolution and for a political unification of the African continent. Only such a unification would enable Africa to overcome its many pressing problems and prepare the ground for rapid economic development. But even among the advocates of this thesis, there were those who thought unification could be achieved diplomatically through the offices of a Continental Union of Heads of Independent States; others, including our Party, believed that only the revolutionary action of the African masses could lead to a solution. The U.P.C. argued at the time that any form of unity with the local reactionaries who had taken power in countries still dominated by the imperialists would be disastrous, since these reactionaries were actually opposed to any genuine form of African unity (political unity). Any such fake unity would directly benefit imperialism and neo-colonialism by forcing all African governments, including the progressive ones, to give up the struggle against neo-colonialism. Although the contrast between the two positions could not have been starker, some people managed to procrastinate right up to the real moment of choice, when they opted decisively for reaction.

Divergent Views Papered Over at the 1963 Conference

On 24 May 1963, just one day before the Addis Ababa Conference came to a close, the *Spark*, an Accra paper, published an article by the Secretary-General of the Nigeria Action Group, Samuel G. Ikoku, writing under the pseudonym of Julius Sago. The author outlined the three main divergent theses being put forward at the Conference. The first, advanced by a group of Anglo-American puppets led by Haile Selassie, Tubman of Liberia and Tafewa Balewa of Nigeria, claimed that what Africa needed was a limited body of inter-African institutions. The second thesis, based on the idea of regional groupings, was defended by agents of French imperialism, including Houphouet-Boigny, Fulbert Youlou (who was to be ousted from power in Brazzaville a few months later), Senghor, Yameogo of Upper Volta and, naturally, Ahmadou Ahidjo. After keeping silent on the subject for the next ten years, Houphouet and Ahidjo trotted out the same nonsense in 1973. And the role played by the O.A.U. during the latest French interventions in Africa, in 1977 and 1978, seems very much in keeping with what they had in mind. Finally, there was a third group, which called for the political unification of the continent. It included Nasser, Nkrumah, Modibo Keita of Mali, Nyerere and others. Ikoku called it the 'radical nationalist' group.[57]

French imperialism, having successfully set up the puppet African and Malagasy Union, clearly had nothing to gain from allowing it to fuse with a new continental organization which could easily fall under the control of its more powerful rival, Anglo-American imperialism. The fact that the projected charter for the new organization was based mainly on the Charter of the U.S.-dominated Organization of American States and on the decisions of the May 1961 Monrovia Conference did nothing to reassure the French. Such inter-imperialist rivalries explain the divergences which emerged among those who opposed political unification; each group of puppets was firmly committed to the specific interests of its masters.

Of all the puppets of French neo-colonialism who attended the conference. Ahidjo was probably the most outspoken. As one of the advocates of the Monrovia Charter he must have been constantly aware of the precariousness of his own position in Cameroon at that time as he constantly insisted that: 'Present African realities force us to accept one another as we are and demand that we make efforts to understand one another.'[58] And again, in the same speech:

> If all this is to be feasible, we must agree on certain fundamental principles. We must accept each other as we are. We must accept that each and every one of our states, whatever its size or population, is equal to the others. We have to recognize each state's sovereignty, its absolute right to exist as a sovereign state in keeping with the aspirations of its inhabitants. This implies complete respect for our neighbours, abstention from any intervention in their domestic affairs and a commitment not to provide open or covert support for subversion.[59]

But the real surprise of the conference was Sekou Toure's support for the American and Ethiopian sponsored Charter. In plenary session, he practically defined African unity as a policy by which African *states* could simply 'co-ordinate their activities in the pursuit of freely chosen goals expressing our common desire for democratic progress and social justice'.[60] He even asserted that the African states had already made 'identical choices':

> To a greater or lesser extent, all the African states have opted for the complete emancipation of the African people. Since the purpose of their actions is the same and all seek to give their development the same character, it is quite understandable that the mission we have set ourselves has found such widespread response in all our states. [Obvious lies and verbiage, E.M.]
> The creation of an African Common Market [N.B., E.M.], the industrialization of Africa, the sharing of its resources, the harmonization and rationalization of our actions in order to avoid contradiction and unnecessary duplication of tasks are all direct consequences of the identical choices our states have made, choices which call for an honest and realistic attitude on the part of our government.[61]

As the experience of the last 15 years has shown, Sekou's Guinea, Houphouet's Ivory Coast and Senghor's Senegal do indeed make, unmake and remake 'identical choices' of the sort the Guinean President has in mind.[62]

Nkrumah had spoken just before Sekou Toure. In his speech, he asked the Conference:

> What are we trying to achieve? Are we trying to draw up a Charter rather like that of the United Nations, whose resolutions, as we have seen for ourselves, are sometimes ignored by certain member states? ...

Or do we intend to turn Africa into some sort of Organization of American States? . . . Is that the kind of association we want for the United Africa we have all been talking about so vehemently and emotionally?[63]

African unity is, above all, a political realm which can only be won by political means. Africa's economic and social development will grow out of its political achievements, but the formula is not reversible.[64]

Unless we achieve African unity now, we who sit here today will become the victims and martyrs of neo-colonialism.[65]

Only a United Africa, with a Union Government, can seriously mobilize the material and moral resources of our individual states and apply them with the efficacity and energy which is indispensable if we are to improve the living conditions of our peoples quickly.

Without necessarily sacrificing sovereignty, great and small alike can here and now forge a political union based on common defence policies, common diplomacy and diplomatic representation, common citizenship, an African currency, an African monetary zone and an African central bank. We must unite to bring about the complete liberation of our Continent. We need a common system of defence, with an African High Command.[66]

To which Sekou Toure replied:

The goal of emancipation our states have committed themselves to is just, legitimate and achievable. The firm, loyal and faithful attitude with which our governments will apply the decisions this Conference has enabled us to take, combined with the quality of the new structure we must set up if we are to promote direct co-operation between our sister nations, will be the basis for our success in accomplishing the common task we have undertaken in the name and interests of our peoples.

This Conference must draw up and adopt a Charter, specify its fundamental principles and aims, and create an Executive Secretariat charged with co-ordinating the activities of our states.[67]

As for Houphouet-Boigny, secure in the knowledge that his friends and masters were manoeuvring in the wings, he was able to blackmail the Conference with the threat of failure, thereby forcing everybody to compromise. Throughout, he was exultantly confident that the American-Ethiopian sponsored Charter would be adopted. At one stage, he declared:

History already has its 4th of August.[68] Let us now give it the 22nd of May, a new flower in Addis Ababa's month of flowers, the birthday of a new Africa, a fraternally United Africa.

How? By unanimously acclaiming the Charter project our Ministers are working on so competently . . . a simple, supple Charter which will consecrate the union of all our groups on the altar of African Unity, providing us with a framework we can fill in gradually . . . . And once we have adopted this project, let us, above all, strive to apply it honestly.[69]

Of course, after so many speeches, a decision had to be taken. When the time came, history records that Nkrumah found himself alone in defending the thesis of continental political unification to the very end. Nyerere remained a prisoner of the logic exemplified by the passage quoted previously. He turned his back on radical political unification and, as if to reproach Nkrumah for intransigence, declared: 'History will not record that the Addis Ababa Conference would have been a success had it not been for Tanganyika's stubbornness and lack of co-operation.'[70]

Barely a few months later, Africa's revolutionary militants had the nauseating pleasure of hearing Sekou Toure declare:

Nothing prevents us creating a Continental State of Africa apart from personal selfishness, political disloyalty and the insufficiently high level of African consciousness. If we were really determined to turn Africa into a Continental State, we could do so immediately.[71]

If it was the 'insufficiently high level of African consciousness' which held back the creation of a Continental African State — the most developed, not to say the only real form of African unity — how could Sekou Toure go on to say:

African Unity, which some people confuse with the O.A.U., does exist; it exists amongst the peoples of Africa and is, at that level, more real, more profound and more historically rooted than the present O.A.U., which is after all only the organic and structural extension of that consciousness.[72]

But the question is precisely whether the O.A.U. has ever been, or will ever be 'the organic and structural extension' of that African unity which the African peoples of the entire continent dream about.

Africa Under the O.A.U.

Now that we know under what conditions the O.A.U. was born, the question of its record can be dealt with. In later chapters we will try to bring out what the facts suggest about its present and future capacities.

The Nature of the O.A.U.
As far as its record to date is concerned, we have just seen that, from the very start, the O.A.U. was nothing more than the practical expression of the

desires of neo-colonialist imperialism and the African bourgeoisie, who sought to prevent the development of a revolutionary wing of independent African states opposed to neo-colonialism. The aim was to sap the ideological and practical unity of the independent African states and revolutionary organizations who were struggling against classical colonialism or neo-colonialism. The reactionaries' tactical objective was to bring about a compromise between the anti-imperialist Casablanca Group states and the reactionary African puppets of international imperialism. Their overall strategy, the effects of which we can still see today, was to eliminate any African revolution which corresponded to the interests of African workers. The political unification of Africa, the genuine liberation of our continent and a commitment to socialist economic and social development policies, were essential to those interests then, and are even more so today.[73]

Houphouet-Boigny and the Right Take Hold
At the second O.A.U. Summit Conference (Cairo, 1964), Philippe Yace, then Houphouet's mouthpiece and deputy, outlined the O.A.U. credo on solidarity between African states:

> It is obvious that this solidarity can only work if it is practised within a general atmosphere of peace and trust, by states which have confidence in themselves and in their neighbours. African solidarity and unity cannot be produced simply by adding together a set of national units [the man probably does not even know what his deceitful nonsense means, E.M.] since our young states provide a framework and a body of values which it would be foolish to ignore and wasteful not to use. We, therefore, conclude that any interference by one country in the internal affairs of another should be formally condemned and treated as an affront to our ideal of African unity.[74]

Three years later, Nigeria, one of those 'young states' referred to by Yace, was in the midst of civil war. Biafra had seceded with the encouragement of French imperialists drawn by the smell of oil. At the request of his masters in Paris, Houphouet-Boigny completely forgot what Yace had said on his behalf in 1964: he was one of the few African heads of state to recognize Biafra as an independent state, thereby grossly infringing the principle of the inviolability of frontiers inherited from the colonialists, a principle which is one of the pillars of the O.A.U. Reactionaries are invariably willing to make a nonsense of their own words whenever it suits them.

The Third O.A.U. Summit Conference had been set for 1965 in Accra, Ghana. Shortly before the meeting, Houphouet-Boigny and his fellow French puppets in U.A.M./O.C.A.M. arrogantly made it a condition of their attendance that Nkrumah expel all African political refugees in Ghana — in the name of the principle of 'non-interference in internal affairs' enshrined in the O.A.U. Charter. The President of Upper Volta, Yameogo, hysterically declared that: 'As far as we are concerned, all those who support Mr.

Nkrumah's policies are enemies of Africa. We will do everything in our power to neutralize him.' And on 8 May, Houphouet added bluntly, 'Nkrumah is finished.'

The O.A.U. was set up partly as a result of imperialism's desire to stabilize its still shaky neo-colonial system. Any moderately progressive African state had to be duped into thinking that an organization of independent states along with major political compromises was the best way of *moving towards* African unity, never mind achieving it. Right from May 1962 the U.P.C. and others warned that this was an enormous con-trick and that the best watchword for revolutionaries was 'Form Popular Associations to provide dynamic support for the Casablanca Charter'.[75] The major compromise involved was acceptance of the principle of 'non-interference in internal affairs', which broke the unity of revolutionary Pan-Africanism and prevented it pursuing its struggle against neo-colonialism. Imperialism and its African puppets thereby succeeded in forcing the progressive states to accept *the de facto balkanization of Africa.* The emerging but already reactionary African bourgeoisie found its own interests and those of imperialism were in this respect well matched.

Nonetheless, it is also true that the O.A.U. was born out of the political illusions of the African petty bourgeoisie, the class which was leading the progressive states at the time. One cannot avoid the fact that Nkrumah was the only head of state to oppose what was happening.[76] These illusions are still rampant and find periodic expression in, for example, Sekou Toure's recurrent vacillations. We find him embracing Houphouet and Senghor one day, cursing them the next, only to embrace them again a little later. It is illusions like these which explain why, although Houphouet and all the other puppets had shown themselves for what they were long before 1960, and blatantly continued to be faithful servants of imperialism thereafter, the progressive regimes still believed that it was possible to build African unity through an organization of heads of state.

The struggle of the African peoples has thus only confirmed the historical truth which tells us that the petty bourgeoisie's commitment to revolutionary principles is never lasting.

Revolutionary Pan-Africanism in Retreat

How has Africa evolved politically since the O.A.U. was set up? We will examine this crucial question in detail, in subsequent chapters, but it seems useful to give a brief outline right away.

Even after 1963, some African countries such as Algeria and Ghana (till Nkrumah fell) continued to provide considerable support to revolutionary anti-colonialist organizations and African militants struggling against neo-colonialism. Since 1975, Mozambique, Angola and countries like Tanzania have given a great deal of assistance to the anti-colonialist guerrillas in Southern Africa. But one cannot avoid the fact that, after 1963, the Pan-Africanist revolutionary current of the period 1958-62 was forced on to the defensive. The African countries which had once been part of that current seemed to have lost their way completely. Revolutionary Pan-Africanism was beating a retreat throughout the continent, in Egypt, in Guinea, even in Algeria. Then, in 1966, neo-colonialism won what was probably its greatest victory in Africa for 13 years: a *coup d'etat* in Ghana overthrew Nkrumah. By comparison, the fall of the already seriously discredited Sudanese Union-R.D.A. regime in Mali was secondary (for Africa as a whole, of course, not in terms of the specific situation of the people of Mali). The retreat of Pan-Africanism in African official circles reached appalling proportions during the 1970s, to the point where there is not a single African head of state who still refers explicitly to the political unity of Africa.

At the moment, organizations struggling against neo-colonialism receive almost no militant support from any African state; the few exceptions are mainly motivated by self-interest and a desire to control the revolution in question. Worse still, *within the O.A.U. itself, there are ever more pronounced and co-ordinated attempts to reduce such revolutionary organizations to silence.* One concrete example of this tendency is the notorious O.A.U. Charter on political refugees, which lumps them together with bandits and mercenaries. This Charter defines mercenaries as 'any persons with no national ties to the African country in which they exercise their activities'. The definition is so badly phrased and vague as to encompass the external activities of parties such as our own. The O.A.U. seeks to build an integrated Africa on the basis of a Charter which begins by recognizing the principle of non-interference in internal affairs and goes on to insist that the frontiers inherited from colonialism must never be altered. Many of these frontiers are ridiculously arbitrary, and there are good reasons to believe that it is their preservation rather than their elimination which will eventually be seen as a fanciful Utopia. As for the so-called principle of non-interference, it has turned out to be a piece of reactionary hypocrisy which serves to unite the reactionaries in the battle against revolutionaries. And, of course, the reactionaries do not themselves hesitate to interfere openly or covertly in the internal affairs of any even slightly progressive state.

We now find ourselves faced with the question of what the events of the last 15 years mean. What does revolutionary Pan-Africanism mean today and what does it rest on? What has demagogic Pan-Africanism become, and why? Only an opportunist would seek to avoid these questions, which must be answered if we are not to deceive ourselves and others.

With all that we know about Ahidjo, we can safely say that, when he starts declaring that O.C.A.M. (*Organisation Commune Africaine et Mauricienne*) is now useless and applauding the U.D.E.A.C. (*Central African Customs Union*), his actions are not to be explained in terms of some 'philosophy' of non-alignment but rather by reference to changes in the African economy. Even Houphouet-Boigny's peers in the 'moderate' O.A.U. condemn his more or less secret friendly discussions with the South African racists. So when this gentleman suddenly announced that what we in Africa need are 'large independent economic zones' (*sic!*) based on regional and sub-regional groupings, the most likely explanation is that in the Ivory Coast, or even in the whole of Africa, 'either the system of production or the mechanisms of exchange [perhaps both] have been secretly modified.'

Since the 19th Century, historical materialism has been teaching revolutionaries that in the last instance this is always the right way to explain social facts and modifications which underlie sudden changes of heart on the part of statesmen.

Notes

1. Padmore was born in Trinidad in 1903. His book first appeared in English, in London, in 1955.
2. G. Padmore, *Pan Africanism or Communism*, (London, Dobson, 1955), pp. 117-18. The reader will note that in this formulation, Pan-Africanism, self-determination and African unity are already inseparable.
3. The role of the Slave Trade in the primitive accumulation of capital in Europe and America from the 16th Century onwards is highlighted by several authors, notably Eric Williams in his *Capitalism and Slavery* (London, Deutsch, 1964). Marx brings out this decisive role in the chapters of *Capital* dealing with primitive accumulation and in his famous *Letter to Annenkov*, in which he attacks Proudhon's nonsense.
4. Quoted in Padmore, op. cit., p. 88.
5. Ibid., p. 105.
6. Ibid., pp. 105-6.
7. Ibid., p. 128.
8. Ibid., p. 137.
9. Ibid., p. 140.
10. C.O.N.C.P. naturally ceased to exist once the Portuguese colonies had won their independence.
11. Padmore, op. cit., p. 149.
12. Ibid., p. 150.
13. Nkrumah, *Ghana* (London, Nelson, 1956), p. 53. This is the real origin of the watchword 'Africa for the Africans'. The plagiarism of various contemporary 'experts' is all the more shameful in that they usually change the precise content of what they are plagiarizing.
14. Padmore, op. cit., p. 164.
15. Nkrumah, op. cit., p. 57.
16. Interview with Houphouet-Boigny by Andre Blanchet published in *Le Monde*, 4 October 1957. Since 1960, Houphouet has naturally become one of the original 'Apostles of Independence'.
17. Shaikh Anta Diop, *Les fondements economiques et culturels d'un etat federal d'Afrique Noire* (Paris, Editions Presence Africaine, 1974), p. 6. Contrary to general opinion, the youth of Africa is very ill informed in these matters, and needs to be reminded often. For instance, in Cameroon, from 1952 to 1955, Ahidjo and his gang were so opposed to the idea of independence that they sent telegrams to the U.N.O., calling on it not to listen to Um Nyobe who had come to demand independence for our country. Nowadays, all this is covered up.
18. Quoted by J. Ndong-Obiang in *l'O.U.A. et la lutte pour l'independance*, (Paris, D.E.S., Political Science, 1972), p. 39. See also F. Wodie in *Le*

P.D.C.I., for contemporary versions of this approach to apartheid.
19. Ndong-Obiang, op. cit., p. 39.
20. Ibid., p. 40.
21. Interview with Houphouet-Boigny by Andre Blanchet, *Le Monde*, 11 November 1957.
22. J. Ndong-Obiang, op. cit., p. 41.
23. See Ivory Coast Government paper, *Fraternite Matin*, 6 January 1961.
24. Ibid.
25. Padmore, op. cit., p. 165.
26. Houphouet-Boigny, *Rapport moral au Congres de Bamako*.
27. See *Afrique Nouvelle*, 18 April 1958.
28. See *Paris Normandie*, 13 August 1960. These two declarations were widely noted; indeed when the Malagasy, Tsiranana, heard that Ivory Coast was about to become independent, he said: 'If even my friend Houphouet-Boigny is taking it, I will take it too.'
29. Nkrumah, op. cit., p. 290.
30. F. Engels, *Anti-Duhring*, (various editions).
31. Philippe Decraene, *Le Panafricanisme, Que Sais-Je?* (Paris, PUF), pp. 47-8.
32. Ibid., pp. 50-52.
33. 'The aims of this body [were to] accelerate the liberation of Africa and the development of "a feeling of Pan-African solidarity", to "pave the way for the eventual creation of the United States of Africa".' P. Decraene, op. cit., p. 52.
34. Ibid., pp. 53-4.
35. See *L'U.P.C. a la Conference d'Addis-Abeba* (U.P.C., June-August 1960).
36. Quoted in P. Decraene, op. cit., p. 55.
37. Patrice Lumumba had just been assassinated by the Mobutu-Tshombe-Kasavubu clique, at the order of their imperialist masters. Since Mobutu became Sese Seko Kuku, etc., this agent of the C.I.A. and Belgian Secret Service has tried to pose as a progressive. He thus sits alongside Ahidjo in the non-aligned movement and enjoys the support of the People's Republic of China, in keeping with China's new political line in Africa.
38. Quoted in Yves Benot, *Ideologies des Independances Africains*, (Paris, Maspero, 1972), p. 154.
39. U.A.M. became OCAM and then OCAMM, when Mauritius joined; finally, it reverted to calling itself OCAM, when Madagascar pulled out after 1975.
40. Azikiwe's affection for his pompous title 'Governor-General of Nigeria', seems to have pushed aside the relatively Pan-African and patriotic conceptions he once held. See his 1943 Memorandum, ' The Atlantic Charter and British West Africa'.
41. P. Decraene, op. cit., p. 70.
42. Ibid., p. 73.
43. In one of his fits of delirium, Mobutu launched a project for a Union of Central African States, made up of the Congo and Chad. The project was still-born, despite Ngarta Tombalbaye's adoption of a variant on Mobutu's 'authenticity' theme.
44. Translated from Yves Benot, op. cit., p. 143.
45. The authors of the communique would, of course, have had their own

views on Ghana's relations with 'the West'.

46. Notably Ahidjo's great friends in Brazzaville led by the French puppet, Fulbert Youlou.
47. See *Horoya* (Conakry), 9 May 1961.
48. Ibid., 1 May 1962.
49. See the *Bulletin de l'Association pour l'etude des problemes d'Outre-Mer*, No. 183, July 1963. No wonder Senghor feels he has more in common with his masters than with the African people . . . . If only stupidity was a fatal ailment . . . .
50. Leopold S. Senghor, *Les fondements de l'Africanite ou Negritude et Arabite*, (Paris, Presence Africaine), p. 10. Is Senghor simply unaware of Cheikh Anta Diop's work on the *Cultural Unity of Black Africa*?
51. J. K. Nyerere, 'A United States of Africa', *Journal of Modern African Studies*, January 1963.
52. Ibid., p. 1.
53. Ibid., p. 2.
54. Ibid., p. 2.
55. Ibid., p. 4.
56. The O.A.U.'s very name is misleading. Originally, it was due to be called the Organization of African States. However, Algeria would have nothing to do with an organization which bore the same acronym (O.A.S.) as the *Organization de l'Armee Secrete*, the ultra-colonialist terrorist organization which had opposed Algerian independence so fiercely. 'Unity' was the second choice.
57. In the light of the above quotes, it would seem that Ikoku's characterization of Nyerere as a radical is open to some doubt.
58. See *Addis Abeba, Mai 1963: Conference au Sommet des Pays Independants Africains*, (Paris, Presence Africaine, 1964), p. 46.
59. Ibid., p. 48.
60. Ibid., p. 116.
61. Ibid., pp. 117-18.
62. In August 1973, Sekou in a letter to Houphouet spoke of the 'friendly and open ties between our two countries'. In September, he was accusing Senghor and Houphouet of treason, of being puppets of imperialism, and of having planned to co-operate with those who had sought to assassinate him and seize power. In 1978, the 'three brothers' were once again congratulating themselves on having made 'identical choices'.
63. *Addis-Abeba, Mai 1963 . . .*, op. cit., p. 106.
64. Ibid., p. 94.
65. Ibid., p. 96, Nkrumah was sadly prophetic.
66. Ibid., p. 101.
67. Ibid., pp. 118-19.
68. A reference to the events on 4 August 1789, during the French Revolution.
69. *Addis-Abeba, Mai 1963 . . .*, op. cit., p. 82.
70. Ibid., p. 225.
71. Sekou Toure, *L'Afrique et la Revolution*, (Paris, Presence Africaine), pp. 280-81.
72. Ibid., p. 284.
73. In July 1965, Ahidjo had the gall to announce: 'We are moving towards socialism, but Cameroonian socialism, not African socialism.' Demagogy

knows no bounds.

74. See Yves Benot, op. cit., p. 183.
75. *Unite Africaine ou Neo-Colonialisme*, p. 16.
76. Nkrumah cannot be judged purely, or even mainly, in terms of how we see the problem today. As Lenin says: 'Historical services are not judged by the contributions historical personalities *did not make* in respect of modern requirements, but by the new contributions they did make, as compared with their predecessors.' (V.I. Lenin, *A Characterization of Economic Romanticism*, Collected Works, Vol II, (Moscow, Progress, 1963), p. 185.

2. Africa's Economy and World Capitalism since 1960

How To Analyse The Problem

As we have just seen, the fundamental problem facing any revolutionary who seeks to understand the evolution of the African states over the last 20 years is to identify the socio-economic factors which can, in the last instance, explain the political evolution discussed in the latter part of the last chapter. What are these factors and how have they operated?

In order to determine these factors, we must turn to the best contemporary economic studies and draw on any data which promise to shed some light on the essential lines of force within Africa's economic evolution over the last two decades, and for the years to come.

The most cursory examination reveals that the world is not simply divided into two juxtaposed and self-contained economic blocs, with the so-called developed countries, on the one hand, and the so-called developing or underdeveloped countries, on the other. The reality is rather that all countries are enmeshed in a web of economic and political relations which form a world system.

But this world system is by no means a homogenous whole. The industrialized and technologically highly developed capitalist countries such as the U.S., Japan and Western Europe determine its overall evolution. These countries form what is often referred to as the centre of the world system. As for the other countries, their real influence on the course of events and on the economic evolution of the system remains quite marginal. They form the system's periphery.

To the extent that the system's overall evolution is determined by the industrialized capitalist and imperialist countries, one can say that this world system is simply the world *capitalist* system. In other words, it is the system of the world capitalist economy.[1] The study of this global economy is essentially the study of the relations between the various elements of the world capitalist system. And the study of underdevelopment, particularly the underdeveloped African economy, is — above all — the study of relations between the centre of the system and its periphery, although this does not mean that one can neglect the specific and intrinsic traits of given dominated economies.[2]

The first fundamental thesis in this approach is that one cannot study underdevelopment seriously without examining its genesis. And this genesis is to be found in the relations between the centre of the world capitalist system and its periphery. The development of relations between these two poles, inasmuch as it is a development of capitalism, consists essentially of the *accumulation of capital*. What is true of underdevelopment, in general, is naturally also true of underdevelopment in Africa.

The second, complementary, thesis suggests that, within this world capitalist system, relations between centre and periphery are not at all relations between equal partners. These relations are characterized by the economically developed centre's domination over the economically underdeveloped periphery. This domination is based on the economy but influences every other domain; the centre organizes the system as a whole in the light of its own needs and moulds the periphery accordingly. In other words, the evolution of capitalism in Africa (and in the periphery generally) is profoundly conditioned, one might even say determined, by its evolution at the centre of the system.

One of the congenital failings of bourgeois studies and theories on underdevelopment is that they never even begin to examine the genesis of underdevelopment. They deliberately ignore the question of where under-development comes from, and it is hard to believe that the desire to hide the fact of international imperialism's responsibility for the situation does not play a major part in this wilful blindness.

The two theses outlined above, backed as they are by the most elementary common sense, indicate that any would-be serious and comprehensive analysis of Africa's specific economic evolution must bear in mind the broad tendencies of the capitalist economy at the centre of the world capitalist system.

We will therefore begin by recalling, as briefly as possible, those tendencies within the evolution of the central capitalist economy which have decisively influenced the evolution of Africa's economy. As we shall see, these tendencies are closely interlinked, forming a network which is both coherent and contradictory.

Capitalism's Tendencies at the Centre Influencing Africa's Economies

Tendency to Expand the Foreign Market

As Marx and Lenin have already shown, this tendency is an inherent feature of the capitalist mode. During the imperialist phase, it manifests itself as the need to dominate new economic territories.[3] And today, this tendency finds its expression in the monopolistic character of the imperialist stage of capitalism. The contemporary form taken by these monopolies is the multi-national corporation, and the tendency itself is nowadays realized through export of capital and the internationalization of commodities.

In the present neo-colonialist phase, the need to dominate new economic territories takes a new form. It is no longer necessary physically to occupy such territories, as it was during the classical period of direct colonialism. *Domination is now disguised as 'capital investment' within a framework of 'aid' and 'co-operation'. The form of domination may have changed but the basis remains the same.* It is quite clear that such domination is no less efficacious, for all that it is less visible; this is apparent from the history of U.S. control over Latin America during 150 long years.

To the extent that it now manifests itself as capital exports geared to secure exorbitant profits (a point to which we shall return), it is clear that this tendency to expand the foreign market is closely linked with world trade and the need for international exchange. To show that world trade has played a decisive role in the development of capitalism right from its earliest days is to expose the giant con-trick inherent in theories which seek to convince the dominated countries that they obtain any genuine benefit whatsoever from this trade. Many economic studies have established beyond doubt that the role of world trade is to confer a constant and definite advantage on one of the countries involved in the exchange, in this case on the more economically developed capitalist countries of the centre.[4] It has long been clear that: 'Two nations may exchange according to the law of profit in such a way that both gain but one is always defrauded.'[5]

Two nations can indeed both gain from an exchange, in the sense that it is, in some ways, in the interest of countries such as Gabon and Congo-Brazzaville to sell their oil, in exchange for other products. But under what conditions does French imperialism obtain this oil? The reality is that, given the present relations between these two countries and France, out and out pillage is the rule, as the leaders of the two African countries have confirmed, and as the French imperialists themselves admit, with disarming cynicism, in the newspaper *Le Monde* (13 February 1979). Consequently, we may conclude that the benefits an African country can draw from world trade depend essentially on the *precise conditions* of exchange.[6]

One of the reasons why the imperialists and their ideologues refuse to recognize this obvious fact is that they will not admit the difference between the concepts of use value and exchange value. In the type of exchange which takes place between an African country and 'its' imperialist metropole, one of the key aspects of the process is that the African country increases its consumption of use values by importing a great deal of merchandise it does not produce itself. This is one of the ways in which it allegedly benefits from the exchange (we will deal with the point more extensively when we cover the whole question of unequal exchange). But in terms of exchange values, as will be amply demonstrated later, the African country concerned is forced to export far more labour than it imports, and is thus clearly the loser in the exchange. This has been well established ever since the 19th Century, yet the bourgeois economists, the whole apparatus of imperialist propaganda and those who have swallowed that propaganda hook, line and sinker all endlessly regurgitate variations on David Ricardo's supposed law of comparative and absolute costs in an attempt to convince the people of Africa that they should stay within the world capitalist market. As we shall see, the export of capital has become a vital necessity for imperialist capitalism. The extension of world trade is as necessary to it as air and water are to a human being. It is thus easy to understand why it does everything it can to encourage trade and promote a trade-oriented approach which seems to be gaining new converts throughout the world at the moment.[7]

This tendency to export capital is also linked, on a fundamental level at least, with developed capitalism's need to overcome another of its inherent tendencies, which we now turn to.

Tendency for the Rate of Profit to Fall at the Centre

The law of the tendency of the rate of profit to fall is an essential aspect of the capitalist mode of production.[8] It provides the fundamental explanation for developed capitalism's efforts at the centre to export capital and develop international trade. We have long known that: 'Since foreign trade partly cheapens the elements of constant capital, and partly the necessities of life for which the variable capital is exchanged, it tends to raise the rate of profit,[9] by increasing the rate of surplus value and lowering the value of constant capital.'[10]

So it is clear that, when the developed imperialist countries export their capital — *and they cannot do otherwise* — notably in the form of 'aid', it is essentially in order to fight against the tendency of the rate of profit to fall at the centre of the world capitalist system.[11]

We can go on to ask whether the general rate of profit is raised by the higher rate of profit realized by capital invested in foreign trade and especially in colonial trade. Marx answers that:

> Capitals invested in foreign trade can yield a higher rate of profit because, in the first place, there is competition with commodities produced in other countries with inferior production facilities, so that the more advanced country sells its goods above their value even though cheaper than the competing countries. In so far as the labour of the more advanced countries is here realized as labour of a higher specific weight, the rate of profit rises . . . . As concerns capitals invested in colonies, etc., they may yield higher rates of profit for the simple reason that the rate of profit is higher there due to backward development, and likewise the exploitation of labour, because of the use of slaves, coolies, etc.[12] Why should not these higher rates of profit, realized by capitals invested in certain lines and sent home by them, enter into the equalization of the general rate of profit and thus tend, *pro tanto* [proportionally] to raise it, unless it is the monopolies that stand in the way? There is so much less reason for it, since these spheres of investment of capital are subject to the laws of free competition.[13]

To the extent that it serves to compensate for the tendency for the rate of profit to fall in the centre of the world capitalist system, the export of capital is one of the basic features of this system today.

The superprofits realized in the dominated, or 'developing' countries, to use the hypocritical terminology of the dominant ideology, are so enormous as to defy belief. However, they are unfortunately all too real. To give only one example:

> Mr. Morton, an American Senator, has revealed that between 1950 and 1960 the U.S. invested some $8 billion in the underdeveloped countries . . . . This $8 billion investment provided the U.S. with a return of $25 billion in profits.
>
> These figures are less astonishing when one considers that the Firestone Tire and Rubber Company alone, and in a single year, made some $50 million in profits from Liberian rubber, *three times the complete budgetary resources of the whole country.* [My emphasis, E.M.][14]

The following table illustrates the growth of private investment abroad, that is to say the increasing amounts of capital exported with the aim of realizing capitalist superprofits by the U.S., France and Britain from the beginning of the century up to the 1950s.[15]

Amounts of Private Capital Abroad ($ million)

Year	France	Britain	U.S.
1900	600	1,200	500
1930	7,000	19,000	17,000
1949	2,000	12,000	19,000*

* This figure does not include the $14 billion invested by the U.S. Government.

The period immediately before and after the First World War (1914-18) was characterized by a bitter struggle between the various imperialisms to invest abroad; in other words, to export capital in order to make exorbitant profits. The economies of the three main imperialist countries boomed, but competition also became more and more frenetic, eventually culminating in the 1914 War.[16]

Following the Second World War (1939-45), French imperialism was back-broken, the British were on the defensive, and the U.S. emerged as the clear leaders of world capitalism. By 1964, the U.S. Trade Secretary could proudly announce that U.S. 'assets and private investments' abroad amounted to some $60 billion, and had increased by more than $3 billion during the first six months of the previous year. Between 1938 and 1948, U.S. trade

with Africa increased from $150 million to $1,200 million, annually.
Furthermore:

> Direct private investment in Africa increased between 1945 and 1958
> from $110 million to $789 million, most of it drawn from profits.
> Of the increase of $679 million, United States profits from these
> investments, including reinvestment of surplus, being estimated at
> $704 million. As a result, African countries sustained losses of $555
> million. If allowance is made for grants for 'non-military purposes',
> estimated then by the U.S. Congress at $136 million, Africa's net total
> losses still reached $419 million. American official statistics evaluate
> the gross profits realized in Africa by the American monopolies from
> 1955 to 1959 at $1,234 million, although other estimates put the
> figure as high as $1,500 million. Whichever way you look at it, you do
> not need to be a mathematical genius to see that U.S. investments
> in Africa bring in profits of about 100%.[17]

As for West Germany, its private investments in Africa reached
DM1,473.3 million on 31 December 1971 and DM1,767.7 million on 31
December 1972, an increase of 20% over a single year.[18]

Anybody who cares to look at this evidence and draw the obvious
conclusion will immediately understand that imperialism will carry on
imposing the present system of international trade, be it 'aid' (whatever the
'beneficiaries' may say on the subject) or 'mutually advantageous trade'.
The only real solution for the dominated countries is to launch
revolutionary liberation struggles which force the imperialists to put an end
to their bare-faced pillage. The crucial underlying question is whether Africa
can attain genuine liberation while remaining within the present world
capitalist market, as we shall see later.

Contradiction Between Capacity to Produce and Capacity to Consume
This contradiction can also be expressed as the problem of how to absorb
surplus economic production. Marx has indicated that the capitalist mode of
production cannot overcome this inherent contradiction. 'The ultimate
reason for all real crises always remains the poverty and restricted consumption
of the masses as opposed to the drive of capitalist production to develop the
productive forces as though the absolute consuming power of society
constituted their limit.'[19]

Various Marxist authors, notably Paul Baran and Paul Sweezy, have
shown how this contradiction operates within specifically monopolistic
capitalism, under which it becomes even more important. The problem of
absorbing the economic surplus is, in fact, linked to two key problems in
capitalist society, namely economic and social waste and the whole question
of capital and commodity exports. Before we can approach the question
seriously, we must have a correct analysis of the notion of economic surplus
itself. Baran gives the following useful definition:

Actual economic surplus is the difference between society's *actual* current output and its *actual* current consumption. *Potential* economic surplus is the difference between the output that could be produced in a given natural and technological environment with the help of employable productive resources, and what might be regarded as essential consumption.[20]

Developed capitalism may seize upon the export of capital as a solution to this contradiction between an ever increasing level of production and the working people's ability to consume, which is still deliberately blocked, despite all the talk about 'abundance' in the liberal democracies. This blocking of mass consumption inevitably leads to various forms of economic wastefulness in these countries. But the 'solution' only apparently resolves the problem; the reality is that society remains stuck in a permanent contradiction. The mechanisms by which the dominated countries are pillaged, the massive transfer of profits out of those countries where they are realized, and the lop-sided structure of international trade automatically produce a reflux of the exported capital, which then becomes part of the same vicious circle. This is one reason why imperialism has been described as a vain attempt to resolve the contradictions of monopoly capitalism by 'exporting its problems'.

The export of capital serves is a means of maintaining the present system of international economic exchange, in other words, world trade as we know it. This export of capital, therefore, serves to maintain the imperialist capitalist countries' domination over African and other peripheral countries. In the present neo-colonialist stage, this domination, unlike classical colonialism which required direct political means of domination, is essentially economic in both form and appearance.[21] The export of capital, with its corollary, the impossibility of any significant accumulation of local capital in African countries, is then presented by both the imperialist and African bourgeoisies as the one and only road towards the development of Africa. It may be true that the ideologues and economists of African bourgeois neo-colonial regimes are genuinely ignorant of the real nature and role of the hidden mechanisms behind the export of imperialist capital to Africa. But for the African bourgeoisie itself, this ideological viewpoint is simply an expression of the fact that their interests coincide with those of the imperialism they are almost completely dependent upon. We are thus presented with the spectacle of African bourgeoisies pontificating about their resolve to fight against 'foreign economic domination', whilst simultaneously whining for foreign imperialist investors to import yet more capital into our countries.

The African bourgeoisie, faced with the impossibility of any significant accumulation of local capital, falls back on rhetoric about the struggle for so-called 'economic independence', and tries to convince its audience that Africa can be effectively liberated by 'economic ways and means' and by an 'economic struggle'. The complete futility and indeed hypocrisy of this so-called struggle should by now be apparent. We will come back to this point when we examine whether the African bourgeoisie is in any way capable of liberating the continent from the yoke of imperialism. Suffice it to say here that, if the neo-colonial bourgeoisie really could make some sort of genuine contribution to the overthrow of neo-colonialism, they would by now surely have given some indication of the fact, seeing as 20 years have passed since they came to power.

Contradiction Between Growth of MNCs and Organization along National Lines

Capitalism, in its monopolistic stage, exports capital massively, extends itself throughout the world and subjugates the entire planet. The internationalization of capital, in the form of giant multinational corporations, has already attained a prodigious level of development.

But despite this internationalization of capital, the bourgeois states survive and to some extent constitute a brake on the tendency which pushes capital to cross frontiers in the quest for the highest possible profits. The example of the European Common Market is particularly eloquent. It is now quite clear that the struggles within that body between the supporters and opponents of greater integration (within Europe) and expansion (incorporation of new countries) are the political manifestation of a silent battle being waged by monopoly capital in its pursuit of the greatest possible integration of Western Europe as a whole under American leadership – that is to say under the leadership of the giant multinational corporations. The present political struggle between two fractions of the French bourgeoisie is, in fact, the struggle for the relatively autonomous survival of that section of French capital which finds itself threatened by the encroachment of giant U.S. and West German corporations. Naturally, this threatened fraction of the French bourgeoisie finds it easy to present itself as the flag-bearer of 'French national interests in Europe', despite incessant vacillations which express its real motivations all too clearly. Anybody who is capable of discerning the class interests at work behind political proclamations will realize that the motives of this fraction of the French bourgeoisie have nothing whatsoever to do with the interests of the French workers. The defence of these interests is left practically entirely to the Communist Party and a few relatively marginal groups.

As Bukharin noted:

> The great stimulus to the formation of an international capitalist
> trust is given by the internationalization of capitalist interests as
> described in the first section of our work (participation in and financing
> of international enterprises, international cartels, trusts, etc.).
> Significant as this process may be in itself, it is, however, counteracted
> by a still stronger tendency of capital towards nationalization and
> towards remaining secluded within state boundaries.[22]

Even if 60 years later the tendency to remain secluded within state boundaries is no longer 'stronger', the contradiction is manifestly still with us.

As far as the African countries are concerned, this contradiction operates as follows. On the one hand, there is a tendency for the various imperialisms to band together in consortiums and multinational corporations in order to exploit the African countries jointly. But, on the other hand, each imperialism seeks to seize the lion's share of the spoils resulting from any such ventures. For example, it seems that many European countries, including West Germany, objected to the high cost to them of an 'association' between African countries and the E.E.C. involving mostly ex-French colonies, from which France drew most of the benefit. But, following the Lome Convention, most of the other African states also aligned themselves with this policy of association. So there is reason to believe that the situation has evolved somewhat, although inter-imperialist conflicts do persist. However, the emergence of a socialist camp — with the threat that poses to the capitalist system as a whole — has meant that these inter-imperialist conflicts never go beyond a certain point, that point being defined in terms of the community of interests of international monopoly capital as an entity and by the requirements of the world struggle between capitalism and socialism.[23]

Tendency to Develop Trade Within the Centre and Marginalize Trade With Dominated Countries of the Periphery

The present crucial phase of the crisis of international capitalism, which began in the early 1970s, seems to favour the imperialist countries' tendency to seek out foreign markets, including those in the 'underdeveloped' countries. But even though this tendency may be growing, the statistics on world trade put the matter very much in perspective. It is still true that:

> Whereas the advanced countries do about 80% of their trade amongst themselves and only 20% with the underdeveloped countries, the proposition is inverse for the countries of the periphery, which do 80% of their trade with the advanced countries.[24]
> The proportion of internal exchanges within the developed group of countries, which was around 46% of world trade in 1928, had increased to 62% in 1965 while, correspondingly, the proportion represented by exchanges between the centre and the periphery decreased from 22% to 17%.[25]

Furthermore, the volume of exchange between the underdeveloped countries themselves is ridiculously low, less than 3% of total world trade. As for inter-African trade, it represented only 7.5% of total African trade in 1967, 60% of which was with Europe alone. Inter-African trade was actually diminishing as a proportion of the world total at the time, from 0.5% in 1958 to 0.4% in 1964, for example.[26]

Consequently, it is fair to say that, although in absolute terms the pillage of Africa by the imperialist countries is important, trade with Africa is more or less marginal as a proportion of world trade as a whole. The imperialist countries 'do not trade enough' with Africa. In other words, the markets of these countries are more closed to African products than to the products of one another. In fact, the earnings derived from this trade by the African countries are actually quite limited. This situation, nevertheless, contributes to economistic illusions about searching out capitalist markets in the centre, breaking into new markets and the possibility of resolving the great problems of African liberation by economic means. The African nationalist petty bourgeoisie has fallen hook, line and sinker for these theses, much to the delight of the neo-colonialists and African reactionaries who 'ask for nothing better than to trade and do business'.

Tendency to Transfer Certain Industries from Centre to Periphery

Having pretended for decades that specialization in agriculture was the African countries' 'best pathway to development', the imperialists are now noisily bubbling about the industrialization of Africa. An entire fashionable body of literature has grown up around the theme of the 'transfer of technology'. The underlying reality is that the extraordinary development of science and technology over the last 50 years has now culminated in a genuine technical and scientific revolution, as a result of which many 18th, 19th and even early 20th Century industries have ceased to be profitable for the European imperialists. As everybody knows – though some occasionally wish to forget – the quest for the highest possible profit is the driving force of capitalism.[27] Unprofitable activity, as determined by the capitalists, must be eliminated. Developed capitalism is therefore casting off old industries which are not proving profitable enough, and the imperialists find themselves faced with two options. They can either transfer these outdated industries to African and other dominated countries, thereby fuelling the present process of (distorted) industrialization in Africa; or they can simply ship in more cheap labour from the African countries to man these antiquated industries. (Cheap because these workers are forced to accept the lowest salaries and are denied access to trade unions.) This imported workforce makes it possible for capitalism to continue operating, at a lower cost, those sectors of industry which do not require a high level of scientific and technical training. The training of this labour force, thus, does not cost the imperialists a penny; it is the African countries which have paid to make it possible for the workers involved, even if they are unskilled, to produce in the first place.

Certain imperialists have even suggested that the imperialist countries should sell the African countries factory plant that is over 60 years old and hence unprofitable in the imperialist centre. They argue that, given Africa's technological backwardness, such equipment would be most suitable. This manoeuvre is clearly an attempt to kill two birds with one stone: imperialism would make profits out of outdated European factories and also prevent Africa from gaining access to more advanced highly productive technology. Leopold Senghor, France's puppet in Senegal, rather gave the game away in an interview with a reactionary journalist. The neo-colonialist press gave the following account of the President's views:

As a supporter of greater economic integration between Europe, Africa and the Middle East, President Senghor suggests that 'a possible aspect of this conjoined economic development' [of Africa and the Middle East] would be the transfer to the underdeveloped countries of the so-called 'polluting' industries, which an overcrowded Europe now finds unacceptable.

The Poet-President's reflections on the subject can be found in the French neo-colonial weekly, *Marches Tropicaux et Mediteranneens*, 11 January 1974, where Senghor's interview with *Le Point*, also a paper of the French neo-colonial lobby, is quoted at length.[28]

Even when the need to maximise profits forces imperialist capitalism to allow industries to be set up in Africa, it still tries to ensure that, as much as possible, those industries will only produce consumer goods. Alternatively, industries are set up, such as those by Pechiney-Ugine-Kuhlmann in Edea (Cameroon) and Fria (Guinea), which do nothing at all to help the country industrialize, in that they have no knock-on effect on the economy of the countries concerned.[29] These factories are the very prototype of 'non-industrializing industry', confirming the view that 'the Alucam factory was not a Cameroonian problem solved by Pechiney but rather a Pechiney problem solved by Cameroon'. Pechiney's problem in this case was to find the cheapest electricity in the world — and Edea could provide it.

Unequal Exchange — Basic Mechanism by which Capitalist Countries at Centre Exploit Dominated Countries

The present growing awareness of the phenomenon of unequal exchange[30] is probably due to the increasing seriousness of its effect, the deterioration in the terms of trade, as the phenomenon operates ever more favourably for the industrialized countries and massively disadvantageously for the least developed, least industrialized countries. It is now almost unanimously recognized that, for example:

A Senegalese peasant gets barely a seventh of what he used to get less than a century ago, in terms of the value contained in the products exchanged. Were it not for this growing inequality in exchange, which amounts to a constant devaluation of Senegalese labour, the terms of trade for goods would have shifted considerably in Senegal's favour and groundnut producers would be paid a price six times higher in real terms — that is to say in terms of purchasing power — than that which they now get for their produce. Unshelled groundnuts would be purchased from the producer at 100 francs rather that 17 francs, delivered to the oil manufacturers for 105 francs (since transport and marketing costs 4.25 francs) rather than 32 francs, and the price of groundnut oil would be 2.5 times higher; groundnuts would account for 65% of the price of the oil, and the other costs (assuming no changes in wages, gross profits, etc.) for 35%. This readjustment would simply bring the price of groundnut oil into line with that of olive oil and palm oil.

Can differences in the use values of these three cooking oils explain the present enormous difference in their price? We are told that such must indeed be the case; if consumers are willing to pay these different prices, then obviously the value of the products is different . . . . This tautological argument ignores the fact that in the 19th Century, for instance, French consumers used palm oil; they only became 'used to' groundnut oil because it could be obtained more cheaply, from Africa, where the peasants could be made to work for less. The consumers were told that there was nothing to match groundnut oil, just as today they are being persuaded that olive oil is much better! The only real reason that the latter is more expensive is because the work of European producers has to be paid for at a higher rate than that of the African peasants.

The transfer of revenue from Senegalese peasants to France, which this deterioration implies, is on such a scale that the moment one makes an attempt, however crude, to quantify it, one realizes to what extent the 'mechanism of the world market' is a synonym for pillage. Given that the current production of groundnuts represents a gross income of about 15 billion CFA francs for the producers, then over the last 80 years Senegal will have lost about 1,800 billion CFA francs at current values, the difference between what it did receive and what it would have received had the terms of exchange been modified to compensate for the evolution of disparities in the productivity of labour.[31]

Given that this deterioration in the terms of trade could only occur in the process of international trade, the expression 'unequal exchange' is particularly apt. It implies that in international economic exchange there is an imbalance in the values exchanged between the dominated countries and the dominant countries. Consequently, this kind of exchange eventually translates into a cumulative transfer of value to the centre of the world capitalist system. The question which immediately springs to mind is how this phenomenon comes about.

It has long been clear that:

If we want to examine the situation of two countries at different stages of capitalist development which none the less exchange their products . . . the Marxist theory of prices is a useful tool. The mass of surplus value produced in the two countries is determined by the surplus value supplied by the workers of the countries concerned. But the question is how this surplus value is shared out amongst each country's respective capitalists.

The capital of the more developed country will have a higher organic composition,[32] so a given quantity of the labour fund (variable capital) will correspond to a higher quantity of fixed capital than in

the less developed country . . . . Because of the tendency towards
equalization of the general rate of profit, instead of the workers of each
of the two countries producing surplus value for their own capitalists,
the sum of the surplus value produced by the workers in both countries
will be shared amongst the capitalists of both countries, and it will be
shared in proportion to the quantity of capital invested by each group
of capitalists, not in terms of the quantity of labour each country has
put into producing the goods. Since in the more developed country a
greater quantity of capital corresponds to a given quantity of labour,
that country will appropriate a greater share of the surplus value than
the one which corresponds to the quantity of labour it has supplied.
Everything happens as if the surplus value produced in the two
countries was first piled up in a heap and then shared between the
capitalists according to the size of their capital. So the capitalists of
the developed countries not only exploit their own workers, they also
appropriate part of the surplus value produced in the less developed
countries.[33]

Although the above analysis was based on a comparison between the
(developed) German regions of Austria and the (underdeveloped) Czech
regions of Bohemia, it can unquestionably also be applied to, say, France
today on the one hand, Cameroon and Gabon on the other. In our opinion,
the main defect of Bauer's argument is rather the following. It leads one
to believe that differences in the productivity of labour are the decisive, not
to say the only, cause of unequal exchange, since the countries where the
productivity of labour is low are precisely those in which the organic composition of capital is relatively low, while the industrialized, imperialist countries,
where the level of productivity is high, are those in which the organic
composition of capital is the highest. The point is particularly important as
it seems that other, more recent, Marxist economists are nowadays presenting
a point of view very much in line with Bauer's. For instance Christian Palloix
asserts that:

If, on the international level, three days of work in the underdeveloped
country are exchanged for one day of work in the developed country,
it is because the productivity of labour in the first country is very low.
International differences in the productivity of labour seem to be
intimately linked to the dominant economies' extraction of surplus
from the dominated economies.[34]

If we turn to Marx, however, we find him arguing thus:

First, if the English 10-hour working day is, on account of its higher
intensity, equal to an Austrian working day of 14 hours, then, dividing
the working day equally in both instances, 5 hours of English surplus
labour may represent a greater value than 7 hours of Austrian surplus

labour. Second, a larger portion of the English working day than of the Austrian working day may represent surplus labour.[35]

Marx is saying that, in exchanges between two countries with an uneven level of capitalist development, it is not only differences in the productivity of labour which come into play, but also differences in salaries, that is to say the different ways the working day is broken down into its component fractions (necessary labour time and surplus labour time).

The various purely ideological arguments put forward today by some theoreticians, including even a few Marxists, are simply an attempt to camouflage an all too obvious truth. Such arguments express mainly the political chauvinism of their authors. If we compare the productivity of labour in the oil fields of the North Sea with that in similar fields offshore from Gabon, Nigeria or Cameroon, nobody can possibly claim that they differ substantially, given that the techniques used are practically identical. Furthermore, it is well known that, in value terms, such extractive industries provide a substantial proportion of the income of the dominated countries. Given that the productivity of workers in this sector is roughly the same worldwide it really requires considerable stubbornness to avoid the conclusion that the enormous differences in wages which exist between the workers in these countries (dominant and dominated) do in fact play a considerable part in making exchanges between the countries unequal. One does not have to be a 'Third Worldist' to see the obvious, whatever certain European far-left so-called revolutionary Marxists may think.[36] Without seeking to close the debate, it seems fair to say that unequal exchange appears when 'the difference between the productivity of the labour involved in producing two products which are exchanged is less than the difference between the wages paid for their production'.[37]

As A. Emmanuel puts it:

> While one may be able to find reasons, whether good or bad, to explain the difference between the wages of an American metal worker who controls a power press worth a million dollars and those of a worker on a Brazilian coffee plantation who uses only a simple machete, it is much harder to explain why a building worker who puts up a bungalow in the suburbs of New York has to be paid 30 times as much as his counterpart in the Lebanon, though both use the same tools and perform exactly the same movements as their Assyrian fellow worker of 4,000 years ago.[38]

The above is obviously not just true of building workers. We could equally well compare the wages of iron miners in, say, Mauritania and the Ruhr or those of the workers employed by Pechiney-Ugine-Kuhlmann in Cameroon, on the one hand, and in the U.S., Canada and Southern France, on the other. Generally, given the same tools, the productivity of a worker in the dominated countries is said to be about 40-50% lower than that of a worker in the developed countries. These estimates are provided by the big capitalist firms themselves and are then taken up by the U.N.; there is, thus, nothing to suggest that they are particularly biased in favour of African workers, to say the least. Nonetheless, they will do as a starting hypothesis. Anybody who has bothered to investigate the living conditions of African workers knows perfectly well that their average wage is considerably less than £20 a month. Let us now compare this with the wages of their European or North American counterparts. No one will deny that in the developed West a wage of £250 a month is considered well below average.[39] The wages ratio between African and West European workers is thus about 12.5 to 1; but that is not the end of the story. We have so far only considered nominal salaries and have left out the by no means insignificant 'social wage' characteristic of the developed countries.[40] True, this particular relative advantage was only won through bitter struggle against the bourgeoisies of the developed countries, but the fact remains that, unlike their Western fellows, African workers enjoy no such benefits. It would therefore seem that there is little exaggeration in Arghiri Emmanuel's claim that the real ratio between wages paid in the developed and underdeveloped worlds is of the order of 15 to 1. Authors such as Christian Palloix may even come closer to the truth when they assert that we should be talking about '20 to 1 or more'.[41] Yet, as we have seen, even according to the imperialists' own calculations, the corresponding ratio between productivities is only about 2 to 1. Under such conditions, it is clear that, when the goods produced by these workers are exchanged, *one country is robbing the other.*[42] This does not mean that the problem of the exploitation of the dominated countries can simply be resolved by a sudden general increase in wages. But the facts are undeniable.

Let us reconsider for a moment the theory which suggests that unequal exchange and international economic relations simply express differences in productivity and other 'mutual advantages'. Marx, criticizing the views of the British economist, Ricardo, had this to say: 'Even according to Ricardo's theory . . . three days of work in one country may be exchanged for a single day in another. In this case, the rich country exploits the poor country, even if the latter gains from the exchange, as Mill demonstrated in "Some Unsettled Questions".'[43]

In an effort to explain away the facts, the imperialists and those who objectively act as their allies in this matter[44] advance a whole range of inconsistent theories, including the suggestion that 'it is none the less in the interests of the underdeveloped countries to trade with the developed countries'; it is thus worth dwelling on Marx's phrase 'even if the latter gains from the exchange.'

The imperialists and their mercantilist allies all claim that if, hypothetically, they no longer (generously!?) accepted to exchange products which Africa is short of for the products we supply, then we Africans would be hard put to find a use for our 'exotic produce'. They conclude that it is obviously in the interest of the African countries to trade with them. But it is one thing to recognize that in some cases there is indeed a relative advantage in exchanging, say, bananas, coffee, copper, crude oil, copper or uranium for tractors, factories and inevitably the odd tank or fighter aircraft with which to terrorize the peasants, workers and young people of Africa. But it is quite another to accept that, even given this supposed relative advantage, the African countries are not being robbed in this process of exchange. On the contrary, we believe that, even granting the hypothesis most favourable to imperialism, the African countries are demonstrably being cheated. Let us illustrate this with two examples, one from Africa, the other from Latin America.

It is well known that African states like Chad and those in the Central African Customs Union supply the imperialist countries, notably France, with a wide range of products and raw materials. Let us assume that these African countries decided to stockpile their products and stopped exchanging them for goods manufactured in the imperialist countries. The mercantilists and their allies would immediately raise a hullaballoo and denounce this 'insanity'. Colombia, for example, is one of Latin America's biggest coffee producers, and exchanges most of its output for U.S.-made manufactured products. Colombia cannot decide not to sell its coffee to North America without arousing the condescending laughter of the international business community. The imperialists present the matter as an open and shut case, but let us none the less examine some of the details more closely.

Although the countries in question (Congo Brazzaville, Central African Republic, Cameroon, Gabon, Chad) are lamentably poor, as French bourgeois journalists never tire of pointing out, the fact remains that: 'The loss corresponding to the worsening in the terms of trade between 1955 and 1967 represented 174 billion CFA francs or 20% of the value of their current exports during that period.'[45] In other words, they have lost about 14.5 billion CFA francs a year!

In 1963, Colombia received a 'generous' $150 million in 'aid' under the provisions of the Alliance for Progress launched by the then U.S. President, John F. Kennedy. During the very same year, Colombia lost some $450 million due to the fall in the price of coffee *sold to the United States*. No mathematical wizardry is necessary to conclude that, in a single year, U.S. 'aid' to Colombia consisted of the theft of some $300 million from this little country, some two times what the U.S. had paid out in 'aid'.[46]

Even Senghor, France's puppet in Senegal, was forced to observe that:

> French investments in Africa are becoming relatively smaller and the profits repatriated are growing larger and larger. In a study of Senegal's economic situation, Professor Samir Amin mentions 20 billion CFA francs in yearly investments and a corresponding 20 billion CFA francs in visible transfers; naturally Senegal also ends up paying for all invisible transfers.[47]

What Senghor forgets to say is that it was he who signed the unequal treaties under which this pillage is carried out quite legally.[48]

It should be clear by now that unequal exchange, as a permanent mechanism for the transfer of values from the countries of the periphery (including the African countries) towards the countries at the centre of world capitalism, is one of the fundamental means whereby the presently underdeveloped countries are kept in their underdeveloped state. In fact, capitalist relations of production — and hence the mode of production itself — can only be reproduced and extended on a world scale thanks to the subdivision of this mode of production in this way. In other words, thanks to the inequalities in the development of the productive forces and the accumulation of capital, the transfer of surplus value from the periphery to the centre, and an international division of labour between industry and agriculture as well as between manual and intellectual labour; *there has to be a network of unequal metropoles and satellites if capitalist relations are to be reproduced and survive.*[49]

Brief Summary

For more than three-quarters of a century, the world capitalist economy has been in an imperialist monopoly stage. The most modern manifestation is the giant multinational corporation, which expresses the prodigious degree to which capital has become internationalized. Imperialism, in its struggle against the tendency of the rate of profit in the developed countries (the centre) to fall, exports capital with the aim of realizing exorbitant profits in the colonies and neo-colonies where the workers are exploited like beasts of burden and paid appallingly low wages. Imperialism has thereby enormously broadened the capitalist countries' foreign market, creating a genuine world market which is absolutely essential to contemporary capitalism. Imperialism would cease to be itself if it ceased to impose the present world market! Because of the unequal development it forces on colonies and neo-colonies which are kept in a state of technological backwardness, because of the ensuing differences in productivity between the industrialized countries and the dominated ones, because of the relations of domination thanks to which the bourgeoisie of the imperialist countries can impose pitiful salaries on the workers in the dominated countries, *relations within the world market engender a constant transfer of wealth from the dominated countries to the imperialist countries*, a transfer which benefits mainly the bourgeoisie of the imperialist countries and, to a lesser extent, their class allies. *This unequal exchange is the very essence of the present world trade system between the dominant imperialist countries and the dominated colonies or neo-colonies.* Such trade also provides monopoly capital with a palliative to its most flagrant contradictions, notably the contradiction between the capacity to produce and the capacity to consume, which is expressed in blatant waste at every level.

In their efforts to dominate the so-called underdeveloped countries, the various imperialist bourgeoisies both collaborate and compete amongst themselves. The resulting inter-imperialist contradictions are permanently manifest in the periphery, notably in Africa. Science and technology have permitted an unprecedented development of the forces of production which has consigned a variety of industries to the museum. These outdated industries are deemed too unprofitable by the imperialist bourgeoisie, although it is still true that key discoveries are sometimes kept locked away until profits from previous technical investments have been fully realized. It is, therefore, not surprising that the imperialist bourgeoisie, in its quest for maximum profits, should ship such outdated 'classical' industries out to the dominated regions, notably to Africa. Of course, this in no way modifies the relations of domination and exploitation which have existed for so long between this bourgeoisie and the peoples of Africa.

Finally, the imperialist countries' inability to absorb the economic surplus 'profitably' creates serious problems for them. They are, therefore, unable to absorb the present and, *a fortiori*, potential export capacity of the dominated countries. The result is a tendency to marginalize trade with the dominated countries. In early March 1975 in Lome, Togo, a Convention associating nearly all the countries of Africa with the capitalist West European Common Market was signed. Like its predecessor signed five years previously in Yaounde (Cameroon), this Convention, which was presented as a model of perfect harmony, was in fact an attempt by European imperialists to create the impression that they were struggling against this tendency towards the marginalization of economic trade relations with Africa. It was also obviously a moment in the internecine struggle between European, U.S. and Japanese imperialisms over who will appropriate Africa's wealth.

We have examined the essential tendencies of capitalism at the centre which fundamentally determine the development of Africa's economic base. We can now turn to the essential tendencies within the African economy itself.

Evolution of the African Economy Since Independence

Tendency Towards Expansion of the Market

It is only normal that this tendency, which is inherent in the capitalist mode of production in general, should emerge as part of the development of capitalism in Africa.

The fierce competition which African products, especially manufactured ones, have to face in the capitalist markets of the developed world leads a young and weak African capitalism to do everything in its power to find markets of its own, especially in Africa itself. The same is true for agricultural products, which are also subject to the onslaught of monopoly capital.

There has recently developed a still embryonic tendency towards the export of African capital within Africa itself, a sort of 'Pan-Africanization of capital'. Typical examples are the MIFERGUI consortium, which jointly exploits Guinea-Conakry's iron ore,[50] and the important role of Libyan capital in Mauritania, Niger and elsewhere. In many cases, however, the primary concern is more strategic than economic.

It might be objected that, unlike the export of imperialist capital ever since the beginning of the 20th Century, what we are dealing with here is essentially 'fraternal' or even 'socialist' co-operation between Africans to exploit African resources. The conclusion would be that the relations stemming from this kind of project could not possibly have anything to do with capitalism and its characteristics. But one only has to illustrate the real economic meaning of contemporary 'socialism' in Africa to refute this objection.

It is important to remember that this tendency to try and expand the African economy's market is closely conditioned by tendencies within the developed capitalism of the imperialist countries. (For the moment we are only concerned with the African domestic market. We shall look at the foreign market for African goods a little further on.)

We have already mentioned the tendency for the developed capitalist countries to trade mainly amongst themselves. This makes it more and more difficult to market the products of the African countries. Furthermore, these African countries have a very weak, almost non-existent, commercial infrastructure of their own; this is partly due to the relations of domination between imperialist and African countries.[51] If, on top of all this, inter-African trade is inadequate — in other words, if the African economy cannot find sufficient outlets in Africa itself — it is as a direct consequence of imperialist colonial policy, a policy which oriented the trade of each colony towards its imperialist metropole. The African bourgeoisie is beginning to complain openly about this situation and is increasingly trying to overcome it by developing trade relations between African countries, which gives rise to the second tendency described below.

Tendency Towards Unification of Markets, Notably the Labour Market
A number of recent policy decisions show that the ruling African bourgeoisies have launched a process which is geared to enable the African labour force to move from any given country to any other in Africa whenever the need arises. Notable amongst such measures are the following.

> On 22 December 1972, in Brazzaville, the Council of Heads of State of the Central African Economic and Customs Union adopted a Common Convention on the free circulation of individuals and the right to settle within U.D.E.A.C.
>
> The Convention lays down that the citizens of the member states can come and go freely between all the member states and settle in any of these states at will.
>
> The free circulation of workers implies the abolition of all discrimination as to employment, pay or other working conditions between the workers of the different member states. These arrangements do not apply to employment in the public sector — either local or national.
>
> The Secretariat of the Union is particularly concerned to examine as quickly as possible those activities in which the freedom

to settle will constitute an especially useful contribution to the development of production and trade.[52]

Not surprisingly, the bureaucratic bourgeoisie is careful to protect its own job opportunities. There is no question of, say, a Gabonese bureaucrat being allowed to come to Cameroon to compete with his local counterpart for employment as a public official. By contrast, the potential private sector competition for jobs between workers of the entire Union is an excellent basis on which to increase capitalist profits. For instance, should the workers of Gabon start expressing their discontent, their bosses can always call in the 'reserve' of unemployed workers from Douala, Bangui or Pointe-Noire.

> Mr. Gerard Kango Ouedraogo, Prime Minister of Upper Volta, left Libreville on 17 March, having completed a 7-day official visit to Gabon. The joint communique published on the occasion of this visit confirmed that the representative of Upper Volta had shown great interest in the Gabonese proposals concerning co-operation between the two countries in employment matters. It is well known that sparsely populated Gabon is ready to welcome a number of workers from Upper Volta. The communique goes on to say that, given the importance and complexity of the question, the two parties have decided to establish a Working Party to study the whole problem of drawing up a Convention on labour.[53]

Again:

> Many Senegalese already work in this country — Gabon (a thousand of them work in the building industry in Port-Gentil). President Bongo has once again called for skilled Senegalese workers. His latest appeal, for the construction of a Transgabonese railway, involves some 3,000 people.[54]

One could cite many other examples. It is worth noting that Omar Bongo's neo-colonial regime, which issued the above mentioned appeal for thousands of African workers, organized full-scale micro-nationalist demonstrations of chauvinism against the citizens of Benin residing in Gabon in 1978. While Bongo himself was President of the O.A.U. (which claims to be achieving African unity), he and his Government did not hesitate to issue hate-filled demagogic slogans directed against workers from Benin, nor to imitate outright reactionaries like Houphouet-Boigny and develop relations with the Nazis of Pretoria and Salisbury. In Cameroon, to take another example, many Nigerian citizens are employed as agricultural workers and in various other branches of production, especially in the south-west of the country. Similarly, many proletarianized peasants from Upper Volta are employed in the Ivory Coast.

As noted in the aforementioned journal, many African countries are 'short of' manpower (which does not prevent them from keeping hundreds of thousands of people unemployed, most of whom are less than 30 years old), while others have an 'excess' of it. Without going into the causes of this situation immediately, we can highlight what these Conventions imply. They are clearly socially analogous to legislation passed in Europe from the 16th Century onwards, when capitalism was emerging and laws were required to legalize the primitive accumulation of capital. The mechanisms and specially designed laws which make it possible to move an excess of manpower from certain regions of Africa to others, according to the requirements of capital's quest for maximum realization of surplus value, are fundamentally similar to the processes described by Marx in his studies of 16th-19th Century Europe.[55]

In Africa's present situation, it is all too clear just how contradictory this process is. In one sense, it promotes Pan-African integration, since the workers of one area of Africa can go to work in another. But in a second sense, the process constitutes the basis for 'inter-African oppositions', since this integration takes place in the context of what could be called 'unequal underdevelopment',[56] allowing for the emergence of two types of 'developing underdevelopment'.[57] In the case of Gabon and Upper Volta, for instance, the latter is gradually being relegated to the status of a mere reservoir of labour, a position which it already holds *vis-a-vis* the Ivory Coast. A similar relationship prevailed between Mobutu's Zaire and Angola under the Portuguese. Indeed, the contribution of Angolan emigrants displaced during the war of national liberation (notably by the dubiously 'nationalist' manoeuvres of the anti-MPLA UNITA and FNLA movements) played a considerable and perhaps even decisive role in the accumulation of capital in Zaire from 1960 to 1975.[58]

Accelerated and Intensified Proletarianization

The phenomenon of proletarianization in Africa is recognized as such by all serious observers. What concerns us here is to investigate its causes, and especially the mechanisms which organize it, deepen it and thereby provide the African bourgeoisies and their masters in Europe and America with a labour force whose lives they can sign away in the various Conventions which African states agree amongst themselves or with non-African countries.

Any attentive observer can see that the present abundance of available labour in Africa stems fundamentally from the fact that the African societies of today are made up of giant disintegrating rural human reserves. Everybody has noted the mass movement of rural populations towards the urban centres, the so-called rural exodus. The neo-colonial regimes claim to find this move-ment surprising and most of them blame it on the people's 'mentality'. They would have us believe that people flock to the towns simply because they no longer wish to work the fields. Yet it is not difficult to understand that this disintegration of rural society is due to mechanisms which are clearly linked to the primitive accumulation of capital. Such mechanisms have been and still are set up by capital in order to provide itself with an abundant supply of cheap labour. Three-quarters of a century ago, Lenin stressed that: 'It is the law of all developing commodity economy, and the more so for capitalist economy, that the industrial (i.e. non-agricultural) population grows faster than the agricultural and diverts an ever growing part of the population from agriculture to manufacturing industry.'[59] He went on to say:

> Can there be a capitalism under which the development of commerce and industry does not outpace agriculture? For the growth of capitalism is the growth of commodity economy, that is to say of a social division of labour which separates from agriculture one branch of the processing of raw materials after another, breaking up the *single* natural economy in which the production, processing and consumption of these raw materials were combined. That is why capitalism always and everywhere signifies a more rapid development of commerce and industry than of agriculture, a more rapid growth of the commercial and industrial population, a greater weight and importance of commerce and industry in the social economic system as a whole. Nor can it be otherwise.[60]

This phenomenon has been observed in every country, without exception, wherever capitalism has had to develop out of pre-capitalist systems. Lenin is right to say it cannot be otherwise; the facts confirm his observations with a law-like regularity. Indeed, the peasant populations of Africa are perfectly aware that sooner or later, if things carry on as they are now (in other words, if capitalism continues to develop in Africa), the broad masses will be forced to quit agriculture and become proletarians. The African masses are far more cognizant of all this than they are usually given credit for by intellectuals and 'experts'; real life is the best possible school. Some Cameroonian peasants recently pressed the point home to one of Ahidjo's bureaucrats:

> The local population expressed their anxieties and grievances to the Prefect of Mungo who was staying in Dibombari for a few days (21-24 February 1974). They were concerned, above all, with the problem of the rural exodus. All the young people were emigrating to Douala and there were practically no able-bodied men left to work in the fields and keep the village going. The people of Dibombari naturally wanted SOCAPALM to recruit most of its workers from the neighbourhood.
> The Prefect reassured the population about the indemnities due to them as a result of the installation of the SOCAPALM agro-industrial complex. The matter is being investigated.[61]

Under such conditions, if the African bourgeoisies and their masters want to develop capitalism in Africa, they will not be able to avoid a rural exodus, short of forcibly keeping the peasant masses in the countryside. This solution would, of course, provide the bourgeoisie with a reserve labour force, which could then be used to back up threats of mass sackings in the towns, thereby keeping salaries low, but it does seem an extremely unlikely possibility. If the bourgeoisie genuinely wishes to prevent the rural exodus, the only two real choices open to it are both absurd from a capitalist point of view: either it decides not to develop capitalism in Africa or it starts moving directly towards socialism.

The introduction of money was the decisive step in the disintegration of the pre-capitalist African economies. Monetarization enabled colonialism to ruin the local artisans, who could not compete with the products imported by the colonial trading houses. The ruined artisans had no option but to sell their labour power in the towns, to become proletarians. One should also not forget that many peasants have been expropriated outright, either by brutal direct coercion or by a systematic pauperization of the countryside, so that people end up by saying 'it can't be any worse elsewhere', leave the village and thereby become proletarians.

It has long been quite obvious that, to stop the rural exodus, what is required is not moralizing speeches but a harmonization of the living and working conditions in the town and the countryside, a task which the present African bourgeois regimes cannot possibly undertake. The only basis on which such a harmonization could be achieved is a gigantic development of the productive forces, an enormous increase in production and industrialization which, as we shall show later, these bourgeois regimes are quite incapable of promoting. No capitalist country has ever developed without its rural population gradually moving away from the countryside, or more exactly, moving from agriculture to industry. Given that industry is to the towns what agriculture is to the countryside, it really is deliberate stupidity to reduce the problem of the rural exodus to a subject for moralizing sermons. Karl Marx pointed out long ago that:

> It is in the nature of capitalist production continually to reduce the agricultural population as compared to the non-agricultural, because in industry (in the strict sense) the increase of constant capital in relation to variable capital goes hand in hand with an absolute increase, though relative decrease, in variable capital; on the other hand, in agriculture, the variable capital required for the exploitation of a certain plot of land decreases absolutely, it can thus only increase to the extent that new land is taken into cultivation, but this again requires as a prerequisite a still greater growth of the non-agricultural population.[62]

While Lenin, following in this many lucid bourgeois authors, noted in his observations on the development of capitalism in 19th Century Russia that: 'The formation of industrial centres, their numerical growth and the attraction of the population by them cannot but exert a most profound influence on the whole rural system.'[63] Who could deny that this applies just as much to present-day Africa, where the expropriation of the peasantry, a process initiated in various ways by the colonialists, is becoming more and more extensive before our very eyes?[64]

85

In Cameroon, a law requiring that all citizens between 15 and 55 years of age serve two years in a National Civic Participation in Development Service was passed on 9 July 1973. In practice, it applies mainly to young people. This National Service is supposedly geared to promote 'the development of the country'; it is, however, worth noting that, according to Article 8:

> Under the provisions of the present law, the Government is empowered to incorporate into the private domain of the state [*sic*!] any land, agricultural enterprise, farm or plantation which has been formally declared abandoned property. The state can also avail itself of any land of which it is decided, after due process, that it is not being put to productive use.

In certain regions of Cameroon, the bureaucratic or business bureaucracy has at its disposal a thousand and one ways of ensuring that any lands or plantations it chooses will be 'formally declared abandoned property'. Similarly, it is easy enough to categorize land as unproductive. All that is necessary is to arrange things so that the National Rural Development Fund (FONADER, the so-called peasant bank) issues most of its credits to the bourgeoisie, thereby making sure that the impoverished peasants will not have the means to put their land to productive ways. This is exactly what happens, and it is, therefore, hardly surprising that every objective commentator has declared FONADER and Ahidjo's Green Revolution a failure.[65] As far as abandoned lands are concerned, everybody who visited the Mungo area during the 1960s knows full well that most of the peasants found it impossible to work their plantations properly. The reason was that Ahidjo's armed forces, for once not busy fighting the A.L.N.K. (the National Liberation Army of Kamerun led by the U.P.C.), frequently massacred the innocent peasants in their fields. These crimes were always officially blamed on the A.L.N.K., that is whenever the civilian victims were not themselves presented as guerrillas. On such occasions, the official communiqués would triumphantly announce that 'today, near Lala, three terrorisms [*sic*] were eliminated'. Under such conditions, many peasants chose not to go to their fields, for fear of being eliminated. So, gradually, more and more land fell into disuse, especially the relatively small plantations far from the urban centres. It was then no problem 'legally' to appropriate these lands, and this has indeed been the practice over the last five years. Naturally, those who benefit from these appropriations and 'incorporations into the private domain of the state' are the dignitaries of Ahidjo's fascist party, the U.N.C. Mr. Jean Keutcha, Ahidjo's 1973 Minister of Agriculture, accidentally let the cat out of the bag during a press conference in September of that year, when he said:

> Traditional agricultural plots still account for most of the cultivated land in Cameroon. These plots, 916,000 in all, are very small, ranging from a little less than one hectare to two and a half hectares. Only 5%

of cultivated land is given over to modern farming. Given this situation, the creation of modern production sectors is the only way to ensure the success of the revolution in Cameroonian agriculture. These sectors must gradually replace the traditional sectors, although the latter will continue to be afforded assistance geared to increasing both the quantity and quality of production, through technical advice and the popularization of new ideas.

Having stressed the importance of training farmers and re-training cadres, the Minister went on to say that the law instituting the National Civic Participation in Development Service and the ordinances empowering the Government to intervene in matters of land usage would ensure that land will be available for dynamic rural producers.[66]

So, 'should the need arise', the lands legally confiscated by the state will be made available to 'dynamic rural producers'. But how to determine who is and who is not a dynamic rural producer? It is quite obvious that only those with access to considerable sums of money will qualify as sufficiently 'dynamic' to administer a large, modern, that is to say, capitalist, agricultural enterprise. In practice, these people will almost certainly be the business and administrative bourgeoisie or rich landowners. The whole subterfuge is gross. Assuming that some of the confiscated land will be administered under the auspices of the state, there will be a steady flow of public funds through the management structure and directly into the pockets of the bourgeoisie. Surplus value will accumulate particularly fast since the people who actually do the work on the lands in question will be providing 'National Civic Participation in Development Service'.

One only has to listen to declarations made by Ahidjo's Government to realize the extent to which this 'National Service' is a response to proletarianization in Cameroon. According to official (1975) statistics, there are between 1 and 1.2 million unemployed young people under 25 in the towns.[67] Despite this figure, enormous as it is for a country with a registered population of less than 8 million, Ahidjo's Third Five-Year Plan (1971-76) only envisaged the creation of 70,000 new jobs *at best*. Since the Fourth Plan (1976-81) did no better, two million is probably a reasonable estimate of the number of people who are unemployed in Cameroon today. And this figure only relates to young people of working age under 25.[68] The legislation itself implies quite clearly that unemployment is by no means restricted to this age group — which would have been surprising, not to say miraculous, in any case. Indeed, the purpose of the law, if we are to believe Tonye Mbog, Minister for Youth and Sport, was to find work for unemployed young men and women 'from 16 to 55 years old'![69]

Furthermore, the drought in the Sahel, which has now lasted for over ten years, also affects Northern Cameroon, a fact which the international press has conspicuously failed to mention, in keeping with their usual practice wherever Cameroon is concerned.[70] This drought has its advantages, of course;

the peasants who leave for the city, as a result, can easily be categorized as having 'abandoned' their lands.

Finally, the information campaign launched by Tonye Mbog's Ministry at Ahidjo's request stressed that 'National Civic Service is not forced labour'. One could not ask for a clearer indication that the programme was meeting resistance, to say the least. Indeed it is well known that even in the top echelons of the ruling U.N.C. caste, reservations were expressed.

Other forms of expropriation have been and still are used against the peasantry in Southern and Eastern Africa, notably the Bantustan system. This involves forcibily removing the peasants from the lands that belong to them and resettling them on arid land. Since the peasants cannot make a living from the land they have been dumped on, they are forced to seek work elsewhere, usually in the mines. Capital gains on both counts. The Republic of South Africa's policy of systematic apartheid is merely the most striking example.

The massive endemic unemployment in towns all over Africa is, in fact, a by-product of such policies.

Anybody who talks of proletarianization must also approach the issue quantitatively; in other words, it must be dealt with in terms of the quantitative distribution of the socially generated income of each country. The fact is that, in Africa today, the poor, the bulk of the population, are steadily getting poorer as more and more of them become proletarianized. A parallel process is the increasingly blatant and frenetic enrichment of a small handful of *arrivistes*, the new dominant African bourgeois classes. The falling living standard of the people is inseparably linked to imperialist domination and exploitation, operating through the mechanisms of unequal exchange characteristic of the world capitalist market. The power of foreign monopoly may prevent the African bourgeoisies from getting rich as quickly as they would like; it certainly does nothing to slow the pauperization of the African workers. Since local capital is very weak, it tends to be invested only in the sectors left aside by imperialist capital. Given these conditions, the two types of capital tend to complement rather than compete against one another. This complementarity outweighs any rivalry; their common exploitation of the African workers is reinforced.

Although the African bourgeoisie is itself dominated by the imperialist bourgeoisie which creams off the largest portion of the surplus value extorted from the African workers (surplus value is appropriated according to capital invested), this neo-colonial African bourgeoisie is not inclined to revolt; on the contrary, it prefers to make the impoverished peasant masses of Africa pay for the pillage imposed by the imperialists. One could almost say the African bourgeoisie takes out its frustration on the working class and peasantry of Africa.

The changes in wages paid to the African workers, contrasted with the changes in prices those workers have to pay for staple products, is as good a way as any of illustrating the living conditions of the African peoples, even if we take only the most recent period (1973 to 1978). Look, for example, at Cameroon.

On 28 August 1973, the Ahidjo regime sonorously announced 'a substantial rise' in wages, which were to be increased by 3%, supposedly both in the private and the public sectors. In practice, the imperialist monopolies, who employ most of the private sector workers in Cameroon, were free to ignore the decision if they so chose. In any case, it very rapidly emerged that, even if the decision had been enforced, the workers would not have felt better off for long. Soaring prices would have seen to that. The 26 September issue of the Cameroonian Catholic journal, *Effort Camerounais*, provides some painstakingly established figures on the subject. The journal took as its example a worker in the tertiary sector, ranking just above foreman; in other words, somebody whose position on the wage scale was relatively good. The results were as follows. Following the rise decreed by Ahidjo, the worker's monthly wage would have risen to 33,600 CFA francs (about £67); family allowances would add another 2,500 francs (£5).[71] In Cameroon this is an average salary for the urban petty bourgeoisie. Assuming an average family, with five children, the journal went on to say that, providing the worker's family restricted itself to a one-course meal (never mind what growing children need!), spent nothing on health care or looking after parents, in-laws and other relatives (we are talking about African families, remember) and never bought new clothes, its monthly expenditure would be 35,800 CFA francs (£71).[72] The journal concluded that sucha salary would ensure 'bare survival'. And even then, only in a manner of speaking, since nothing is set aside in case of illness. Health care is by no means free in Cameroon, so any moderately serious illness would be disastrous. It should be remembered that the wage in question is well above that of the average worker, let alone that of an unskilled labourer. Agricultural workers employed by the *Organisation Camerounaise de la Banane* (O.C.B.) work eight hours a day in all weathers for a monthly wage of only 5,000 CFA francs (about £10). Hardly surprising, then, that the workers of Douala, Yaounde and elsewhere greeted the wage rise with derision; it was hardly worth waiting ten years on frozen wages for that kind of joke.[73] Nothing will convince Cameroonian workers of the opposite, especially as prices have continued to rise ever since.[74]

The Guaranteed Minimum Industrial and Professional Wage (SMIG) at the time for workers on a 40-hour week in all parts of the country varied from 5,500 CFA francs to 8,000 francs a month. The Guaranteed Minimum Agricultural Wage (SMAG) for employees working on the 2,400-hours a year system (operative in agricultural and associated enterprises) was even lower — varying between 4,400 and 6,500 CFA francs a month. Such salaries are worse than ridiculous, especially if one bears in mind the Catholic journal's figures for minimum family expenditure. In July 1974, Ahidjo announced a further wage increase. Wages were to rise 14-18% according to area. As was shown quite conclusively in the September and November 1974 issues of the U.P.C. bulletin *Resistance*, these increases did not even compensate for the way prices had soared in the interim. The reality was that the working people had effectively lost part of their buying power.

One should bear in mind that these measures, ridiculous as they are, affect only wage-earners, who represent only a minute portion of the population. 78% of the people live in the countryside, and about 70% of them are not wage-earners at all and are thus left out of the reckoning. Victor Ayissi Mvodo, Minister of State, then National Political Secretary of the U.N.C. and specialist in 'prison reform', had this to say about this large popular sector: 'Given the economic situation in our country, the peasant populations cannot be granted any family allowances. The main reasons are the ever-growing number of children and the fact that small employers do not declare their employees to the tax authorities.'[75] But it is perfectly alright for Mr. Ayissi Mvodo to build himself a complete castle in Douala!

Despite these enormous disparities in wealth, Ahidjo and friends continue to churn out the same old cynical demagogy, especially when it comes to discussing the fate of the peasantry. 'The Government is very conscious of the preponderant role agriculture plays in the economy and has always laid great stress on the development of this vital sector. For instance, 1963 was made the "Year of the Peasant" and our Second Five-Year Plan was called the "Peasant's Plan".'[76]

At the time when Ahidjo was boasting of having 'substantially increased wages' in Cameroon, his colleague Houphouet-Boigny was playing the same tune in Ivory Coast. The increase in question brought the average monthly wage for agricultural workers up to between 4,500 CFA francs (£9) and 7,000 CFA francs (£14). The salaries of Ivory Coast's 24,000 state employees rose by 5%. The minimum urban wage rose by 25%, which does indeed seem impressive. The underlying reality, however, was that urban workers' wages were pegged at ten different hourly rates, ranging from 73 to 165 CFA francs an hour; in other words, working 40 hours a week, they would earn between 12,000 francs (£24) and 26,400 francs (£53) a month.[77] Since the cost of living in Abidjan and other Ivory Coast towns is as high if not higher than in Cameroon or any other major town in Europe or America, and given our observations above about the budget of a Cameroonian family with a higher income than the ones we are considering here, it is hardly surprising that workers of Ivory Coast were not overcome with gratitude. Indeed, a mere six months later, it was announced that:

> In order to improve the purchasing power of wage-earners, the Government has decided to revise all public and private sector salaries as from 1 February 1974. The SMIG will be raised by 20%. The most recent previous SMIG increase in Ivory Coast was granted on our national holiday, 7 August, last year. At the time it rose by 25% for all sectors, even the agricultural sector. The minimum hourly wage went up to 73 CFA francs.
>
> That increase was the first since 1 January 1970, despite the rise in prices on the basis of which the SMIG was originally calculated. This new increase, only six months after the previous one, testifies

to the seriousness of the problem.[78]

From February 1974 onwards the SMIG in Ivory Coast was thus set at 90 CFA francs per hour. This did not apply to the agricultural sector, which employs about 80% of the population, as elsewhere in Africa. In the sectors affected by the new SMIG monthly salaries now varied between 14,400 CFA francs (£29) and 31,680 CFA francs (£63). But as we saw earlier, when we considered the position of a foreman in Cameroon, a salary of 36,100 francs (£72) a month is only enough for bare survival. Houphouet-Boigny and his crew may be able to fool the people of Ivory Coast for a while longer, but eventually the facts themselves will condemn them.[79]

In Senegal, also in 1974, Senghor's neo-colonial regime announced with a great fanfare a new policy supposedly geared to benefit the workers. Its provisions included a revaluation of the SMIG which was to be increased by 32%, backdated to August 1973; an increase in the price of groundnuts, from 25.50 to 35 CFA francs a kilo plus a bonus of 4 francs a kilo back-dated to 1973; and finally, an increase in the price of cotton to 40 CFA francs, plus a promise of another backdated bonus.[80] The price of groundnuts had thus increased by slightly less than 40%, excluding the bonus. But when all this is compared to the increase in prices for the staple items consumed by the Senegalese working people, a different picture again emerges:

> In his speech to the Economic and Social Council . . . President Senghor was at pains to illustrate the problems increased prices have caused in the country . . . .
> From January 1973 to January 1974, pre-tax prices for various products unloaded at Port Dakar increased considerably: powdered sugar went up by 105%, sugar in lumps by 75.7%, sugar in loaves by 63.3%, wheat by 63.3%, rice by 327%.[81]

The Government authorized corresponding price increases on the Senegalese market as follows: +60% for powdered sugar, +66% for sugar in lumps, +47.3% for sugar in loaves, +37.7% for flour and +50% for rice.

The figures speak for themselves. One day the Senegalese workers will call Senghor and friends to account.

French neo-colonialism generally presents the three countries we have been looking at as models of stability and growth, for all that U.N. reports have placed Cameroon amongst the 24 poorest countries in the world. Imperialist propaganda never misses a chance to stress that these countries are among the few in Africa not to have undergone a series of those unpredictable *coup d'etats* which African countries are so prone to. It would, therefore, be fair to say that the facts we have examined above amount to an overwhelming indictment of the neo-colonial system imposed by France in countries she colonized 100 years ago or more. Nor should one assume that less prominent French neo-colonies have a better time. Take Upper Volta, for example:

On 7 March [1974] the Council of Ministers decided to increase the wages and benefits of state employees and to raise the SMIG and the SMAG. State employees' index linking will be geared up by 2% and the index will be raised by 10 points. Bus and lorry drivers will get rises ranging from 17.7% to 21%. Temporary staff's monthly salary will be raised by 3% + 2,000 CFA francs. Manual workers will get rises ranging from 11% to 38.2%. Office staff will get rises ranging from 10.7% to 36.8%. The SMIG will be raised by 38.2% and the SMAG by 42.08%.[82]

On the other hand, the prices of the staple foodstuffs consumed by the people of Upper Volta have moved as follows: 'Sugar goes up from 110 to 150 CFA francs a kilo. Flour (produced in Upper Volta) goes up from 60 to 85 CFA francs a kilo.'[83] In other words, the price of sugar rose by 36%, far more than the actual increase in the SMIG, an increase which on average was less than the 38.2% mentioned. The rise in the price of flour was of similar proportions.

So the President of Upper Volta decided to address the business community and on 19 March 1974 he called a press conference, at which he had this to say:

Profit for profit's sake, at any price, whatever the cost, should not be your only reference point . . . .[84] I firmly believe that Upper Volta done and continues to do a great deal for the business community, enough for that community to trust our country and be prepared to make a few sacrifices for it.

The Head of State thundered on, 'assuring the business community that it would continue to enjoy the utmost consideration from the state of Upper Volta' since, as he put it, 'the formula has not proved too disappointing'.[85]

Given such a situation, the African workers of Upper Volta, like their counterparts in other African countries, have little except further poverty to look forward to, unless they manage to bring down the dictatorship exercised at present by the neo-colonial African bourgeoisies.

Turning from the 'Francophone' countries to Kenya, we find the press full of news about price rises:

From December 1976 to December 1977 the retail price index relevant to middle and low income groups rose by 13.5% and 21% respectively. The rise continued during the first quarter of 1978 at a rate of 3.7% and 5.2%.

The increased cost of foodstuffs was particularly burdensome for the low income group: foodstuffs rose in price by 17.2% in 1977 and have already gone up by a further 6.6% in the first three months of this year.[86]

As for the African peasant, who is even poorer and finds himself inserted into a market economy practically without any monetary income of his own, commentary seems superfluous.

Alongside all this poverty, the bureaucratic bourgeoisie and its allies lead '*la dolce vita*', grant themselves the salaries of big industrialists and bureaucrats in Europe or America, and generally display the extremes of cynical greed.

To cap it all, the tendency towards a growing inequality in the distribution of national income in Africa is also increasing. Indeed studies have shown that:

> The evolution of the system in no way suggests that, by gradual expansion, the privileged stratum will extend to embrace the whole population. Even while the rate of growth of overall income is very high (between 7% and 10% *per annum*, for instance), the numerical growth of the privileged stratum remains small (increasing by 3-4% a year at most). In other words, the privileged stratum reaches a ceiling at some 20-25% of the population, irrespective of the time prospect, even if this be a century.[87]

For instance, in late 1974, public sector wage increases were announced in Nigeria. When many private firms refused to institute a parallel increase, there was a wave of strikes throughout the country. But what did these increases amount to?

> A great many workers at the bottom of the scale did not even earn 1 naira a day [1 naira is about £0.75]. This was especially true of unskilled factory hands, whose basic minimum salary was only 312 naira a year. Their annual wage was raised to 720 naira . . . . The corresponding new salary for a Permanent Secretary in the Civil Service, an Inspector-General in the police force, a High Court Judge, a University Vice-Chancellor or a Commissioner was set at 15,000 naira a year. A Nigerian engineer could expect to earn a similar amount in the oil industry, once he had proved himself. Most university graduates could hope to earn about 10,000 naira a year after about four years in private business.[88]

If people still have any illusions about the possibility of reforming the system and reducing the total incompatibility between the class interests of the workers and the bourgeoisie, they only have to look at the way the African bourgeoisie is developing, in Zaire for instance, to dispel their misconceptions. Because of the particular form of Belgian colonization, there was practically no local bureaucratic or business class ready to take over the reins when Zaire regained its independence in 1960. A doctoral thesis, published in Kinshasa in 1969 by B. Ryelandt, shows how the U.S. used its instrument, the International Monetary Fund (I.M.F.), deliberately to promote eight years of inflation in the Congo.[89] This inflation was

93

followed by a more stable period, but now 'marked by very considerable changes in relative prices and real incomes in Congo-Kinshasa as compared with the situation in 1960, reflecting a transfer of income from the peasants and lower-paid wage-earners [the real wages of the working class had been cut by half] to the new ruling class'.[90]

As can be seen in most African countries, the real consequence of such a policy is an increase in the importation of the consumer goods purchased by the new ruling class; the country's economy in no way benefits. In 1968, for instance, the new dominant class in Zaire had no qualms about pushing the income of small wage-earners down to the level it had been at eight years previously, in 1960. The interests and survival of Zairean businessmen were all that counted.[91]

Throughout present-day neo-colonial Africa the same picture emerges: destitution and unemployment prevails.[92]

The appallingly low salaries paid to African workers disprove the bourgeoisie's claim that the worker's standard of living cannot but rise as capitalism develops. The present wage levels of African workers expose the ineptitude of the leaders of the neo-colonial bourgeoisie, notably in Cameroon. Ahidjo's concept of a 'planned liberal economy' is simply nonsense. Not only does it ignore the appalling poverty which befell European workers as capitalism emerged in Europe, from the 17th to the 19th Century;[93] it also seeks to hide the fact that, since African economies are all oriented to the capitalist countries at the centre and most of the export income they produce is also accumulated abroad, the freezing of African workers' salaries at a low level need not have any detrimental effect on the operation of the existing neo-colonial system. No amount of speechifying by the African bourgeoisie and its petty-bourgeois agents about how the country is 'moving forward and getting richer' will change the simple truth, outlined long ago by Karl Marx, that in a capitalist regime 'the wealth of the nation and the poverty of the people are, by the very nature of things, inseparable'.[94] Lenin was right to add:

> The impoverishment of the mass of the people not only does not hinder the development of capitalism, but, on the contrary, is the expression of that development, is a condition of capitalism and strengthens it. Capitalism needs 'free labour' and impoverishment consists in the petty producers being converted into wage workers. The impoverishment of the masses is accompanied by the enrichment of a few exploiters.[95]

There is no reason to suppose that economic mechanisms alone will change — let alone destroy — the system. Only workers' action can do away with the present disastrous system. The fact that wages could be almost frozen for ten years, as in Cameroon (1960-70), proves the point. Even in Ivory Coast, that 'model country', that 'showcase for capitalism in West Africa', the present level of wages shows just how little change 'economic destiny' produces. The fact that it was only in 1979, after 20 years of independence and 'phenomenal growth' that the Minimum Wage (SMIG) rose to 30,000 CFA francs (£60) a month is particularly telling.[96]

As for Ahidjo, shamed as he was by his inability to raise the SMIG in Cameroon and resenting the possibility of unfavourable comparisons with other countries, he found a simple enough solution: he just abolished the SMIG, by decree. Meanwhile, even officially admitted minimum wages remain below £20 a month.

To sum up: for about many years there has been a very definite tendency towards the proletarianization of the popular masses in Africa, notably the peasantry. This tendency manifests itself both qualitatively and quantitatively. Furthermore, objective factors have developed which, as we noted, favour a Pan-Africanization of the African proletariat: the workers are increasingly inserted into the same economic space, the same labour market they may eventually be able to go from one part of the continent to another in the quest for work. This proletarianization develops along lines which are fundamentally analogous to the process of primitive accumulation of capital in Europe during the phase of emergent capitalism. This basic feature of present-day African evolution has, as its inevitable corollary, the increasingly acute class contradiction between the African proletariat and the dominant neo-colonial bourgeoisie.

Tendency Towards Industrialization and Commercial Takeovers: Some Contradictions
Nobody denies that Africa is now industrializing. The point to grasp is the orientation and real content of this tendency, to see what it actually means.

Industrialization in Africa Still Linked to the Export of Raw Materials
The first major aspect of the present process of industrialization in Africa is still the fact that this process remains linked to the export of raw materials. This tendency has an objective basis. Because local capital has never had any serious opportunity to engage in primitive accumulation, it is weak and cannot compete with foreign monopoly capital; thus, this monopoly capital determines the rules of the game. As we saw earlier, the main reason behind monopoly capital's drive to expand abroad is the need to counterbalance the falling rate of profit in the imperialist countries. In other words, foreign capital is after maximum profits within the shortest possible intervals. This is quite feasible in Africa, for two simple reasons. First, labour is cheap, as we have just seen. Second, imperialism has established specific relations of domination over its colonies and neo-colonies in Africa. The monopolies who invest in Africa and supposedly aim to 'industrialize the continent' are the very ones who export manufactured products from the imperialist countries to Africa at prices geared to maximize profits. Consequently, it is not surprising that in order to maximise the profitability of their overall activities, these companies prefer to limit their operations in Africa to extracting raw materials and exporting them to Europe. The recent tendency

— already noted — of transferring certain industries, even heavy industries, to African countries is only an adaptation, albeit a contradictory one, to the new international situation. The dominant aspect is still the one outlined above.

And as for local capital, it can only insert itself into those sectors not occupied by the monopolies. Consequently, the exports of African countries are forced to follow a rhythm dictated by the needs of the capitalist economies. As the income from these exports falls, the African bourgeoisies are constantly led to demand a larger slice of the cake, in the form of increased exports (both in terms of prices and volume), notably through guaranteed markets in the imperialist countries. The result is what Samir Amin describes as a contradiction between national development (in Africa) and the requirements of foreign capital's domination. For nearly 20 years the West European imperialists and the African neo-colonial bourgeoisies have been trying to resolve this particular contradiction, hence the periodic signing of yet another 'Convention of Association between the African States and the E.E.C.'. These conventions (two at Yaounde, one at Lome and the latest, Lome II) are, in practice, nooses around the necks of the African countries.

The main sectors into which local capital flows, in order to avoid unequal competition with foreign monopoly capital, are trade (mainly local but also some foreign trade), other tertiary activities, transport and speculation in buildings and land. Even in these restricted sectors, the tendency towards the concentration of capital (an inevitable feature of capitalism) cannot be avoided. Local capital thus tends to accumulate in fewer and fewer hands. A demand for new, broader areas of investment emerges, sharpening the contradiction between this local capital and imperialist high finance. But the forces are too unequal.

Objectively, as we have seen, imperialist capital can transfer certain industries which are relatively unprofitable in Europe or North America to the periphery, thereby overcoming this contradiction to some extent, at least for a while. By broadening out the areas of industry open to the African bourgeoisie, which thereby becomes more fully integrated into the network of world bourgeois relations (at the tail end, naturally), imperialist capital may win a breathing space. It can not only avoid any eventual revolt by its allies and puppets, but also, in some cases, even hope to defuse the deep popular discontent of the African peoples, a discontent which would otherwise cause enormous difficulties for imperialism's African lackeys. This kind of transfer could pave the way for a new international division of labour, a different but necessarily still unequal form of international specialization. Under this new unequal international specialization, the highly productive 'lead' industries would be kept in the imperialist countries, while other less productive industries would be set up in the dominated countries, notably in Africa. The overall operation of the world capitalist system would remain fundamentally unchanged. Africa would gain some extra industry, even heavy industry, but the pillage would continue since the mechanisms of unequal exchange, which are at the root of the pillage, would still be intact. Perhaps the African neo-colonial bourgeoisie will, to quote Senghor, 'win its second war of independence' (without ever having fought in the first), but it is clear that the third would break out immediately.

If the present relations of domination remain unchanged, the industrialization of Africa could even accentuate the pillage and exploitation of the African workers. It would steadily reduce the differences in productivity between the African and imperialist countries; if the discrepancies in wages between the two groups of countries nonetheless continued to grow (for instance, relative increases in Europe and North America while wages stagnate in Africa), unequal exchange would actually be strengthened.

The beginnings of such a process are already visible in the textile and clothing industry. The implantation of the clothing industry in the dominated countries provides international finance capital with scandalously high profits, thanks to the derisory wages paid by the monopolies in those countries, while the clothes made at this derisory cost are sold in Europe at prices equivalent to those which would be charged were they made within a high wage economy. The imperialist who whines that it is 'Third World competition which is ruining the textile industry in Europe' is indulging in a revolting falsehood, a racist attempt to fan conflict between the workers in Europe and the dominated countries, while the capitalists amass huge fortunes.

None of this means that Africa should not be industrialized for fear that we shall be robbed even more than before. But it does mean that, without an effort to break the mechanisms of domination at every level, the industrialization of Africa cannot resolve the problem.

African Industrialization Not Autocentric

A second important characteristic of the present process of industrialization in Africa is that it is not 'autocentred'. The various manufacturing facilities do not form a coherent and integrated whole.[97] Because the big industries are geared to exports, they do not and cannot fit into an integrated national or, *a fortiori*, Pan-African economic system. This leads to a whole range of contradictions, both in terms of the prospects for integrating the various African economies and in terms of the economy of any single country. We will return to the point later and draw the relevant political conclusions. For the moment, let us simply note that it follows from the above that:

> In this sense, one ought not speak of 'underdeveloped national economies' but to reserve the adjective 'national' for the autocentric developed economies which alone constitute a true, structured national economic space, within which progress is diffused from industries that deserve to be regarded as poles of development. The underdeveloped economy is made up of sectors, of firms, which are juxtaposed and not highly integrated among themselves, but which are, each on its own, strongly integrated into entities whose centre of gravity lies in the centres of the capitalist world. What we have here is not a nation in the economic sense of the word.[98]

Naturally, simple class instinct is enough to drive the African bourgeoisie to seek some solution to this dilemma. But even if it does try, it will be out of pure self-interest rather than out of some concern for the 'interests of the people', 'of the nation' or any other such notions, all of which leave the African neo-colonial bourgeoisie quite unmoved.

However, it is clear that the African bourgeoisie is trying to do something about the situation. The programme for an integrated Pan-African infrastructure envisaged under the auspices of the O.A.U. includes projects such as the creation of a Road Development Fund (which has already been set in motion) geared to finance inter-African road links; the setting up of a Union of African Railways; the creation of an African Shipping Consortium; studies examining the reorganization and eventual fusion of African airline companies; a projected African Telecommunications Union, etc.

At the O.A.U. Ministerial Conference held in Accra from 19-23 February 1973, an expert report presented to the Ministers stressed the advantages of such a common African policy and effectively declared that:

> The sovereignty which the African states will be able to exercise over their own resources will be a key element in the pursuit of the aims set out for the Second Decade of Development. They will have to take concrete steps concerning methodical prospecting and evaluation of their resources, so as to draw up a common African policy for the exploitation of mineral and energy resources on a regional scale. Given the importance of electrical energy for large-scale industry, the African states will need to reach agreements concerning common exploitation of these resources.[99]

In the context of industrialization policy, the aim should be not just the extraction of minerals but also their refining and processing, to the greatest possible extent, prior to exportation. Similarly, the implantation of industries using these minerals should be a priority. African national and multinational firms will have a specific role to play here.

On paper, the programme looks attractive. But, since we have now come to the end of this much vaunted Second (?!) Decade of Development, it seems legitimate to examine what has actually been achieved. Let us take the example of bauxite in Cameroon, for instance, where it is mined in Adamoua, near N'gaoundere. Instead of promoting 'concerted inter-African policies' right from the prospecting stage, Ahidjo's Government has opted for a deal with the monopolies:

> The project, proposed by the *Societe des Bauxites du Cameroun* (a subsidiary of S.N.I.) holding 40% of shares, in association with a French company, B.R.G.M., Pechiney Ugine-Kuhlman, holding 50%, and the Bonn-based *Vereignigte Aluminium Werke*, holding 10%, will figure as part of the Third Plan (1971-76) and production will not begin until the Fourth Plan is under way.[100]

The S.N.I. (*Societe Nationale d'Investissements*) is, therefore, the only Cameroonian participant in a venture which is clearly dominated by the monopolies. As for the infrastructure associated with the bauxite mines, it is clear that the Trans-Cameroonian Railway, which could have been extended towards Bangui to further greater economic integration throughout the Lake Chad — Gulf of Guinea basin is still only a means of getting bauxite to Edea-Douala and thence to Europe.[101] This policy is all the more incomprehensible in that, even before independence, the Pechiney Group had already managed to co-ordinate Guinean bauxite and the Edea aluminium industry. When one thinks that Guinea has committed itself to a vast programme geared to develop the aluminium industry, a programme which has caused the country to drift steadily to the right in order to secure the necessary foreign finance (as will be shown in the Epilogue to this volume), one cannot but ask oneself what are the real reasons preventing some co-ordination of Guinean and Cameroonian aluminium policies. The matter is particularly worrying since, as we shall show later, in 1970 Sekou Toure Ahmed was already proclaiming to all and sundry that Ahidjo Birawandu Ahmed was nothing less than his companion in arms in the world anti-imperialist struggle, a veritable 'Giant of African Unity'. Comedy apart, the facts are that two African countries which are rich in bauxite and could easily co-ordinate their production of aluminium prefer to deliver themselves into the hands of the monopolies, despite the recommendations of O.A.U. experts and notwithstanding the proclaimed 'anti-imperialist' orientation of the two presidents. Perhaps these two 'companions in arms' find it easier to co-operate over such issues as the liquidation of the Union of Cameroonian Peoples — the real subject-matter of the communique jointly signed by Sekou and Ahidjo, not only in 1971 but more recently in February 1981 during Sekou's official visit to Yaounde.

There is, however, no reason to think that the servility of the Cameroonian buffoon or the absurdity of the pseudo-revolutionary jargon used in the country of the one-party state are in any way exceptional. For instance, look at Niger. Its uranium resources, which provide over half the country's exports, are evaluated at about 40,000 metric tons of concentrated uranium ore. They are, therefore, larger than France's, if one excludes what France unashamedly steals from the African countries. The Atomic Energy Commission (the French organization C.E.A.) discovered Niger's uranium as far back as 1959. Then:

> On 1 February 1968, following a series of agreements on Franco-Niger co-operation signed by ex-President Diori Hamani in Paris on 7 July 1967, the SOMAIR [*Societe des Mines de l'Air*], a mining company backed by private and public capital, was launched. In February 1970, two companies, one German and the other Italian, bought holdings in SOMAIR. Today, 35% of stock is held by the C.E.A., 18.24% by the *Societe Miniere Pechiney-Mokta*, 16.75% by the Republic of Niger, 14.66% by the *Compagnie Francaise des Minerais d'Uranium*, 8.152%

by *Urangesellschaft* (West Germany) and 8.125% by *Aig Nucleare* (Italy).[102]

Following the *coup d'etat* which overthrew yet another of French imperialism's puppets, Diori Hamani, many observers wondered whether Niger would take steps to protect its national interests on the question of uranium. It was not long before Lieutenant-Colonel Seyni Kountche, the leader of the Niger military who overthrew Diori, was at pains to calm any fears that might have troubled Niger's 'partners':

> Our movement is not a revolutionary movement, whatever people may have been led to believe, both here and abroad . . . Negotiations have already been initiated. We only ask that, when these negotiations are reopened, our partners will try to understand our position. But there is no question of us turning our backs on our partners and jeopardizing the whole policy. We have no intention of changing or modifying the participation arrangements.[103]

Domination by monopolies is almost standard practice in Africa. We shall return to the point later, but it should already be clear that, despite its occasional desperate efforts, the African bourgeoisie on its own is incapable of emulating the European bourgeoisie of a century ago and creating a modern industry. This is mainly due to the historical conditions under which this African bourgeoisie is emerging and developing. It lacks the necessary financial and technical means, especially as it has shown itself quite unsuited to make any judicious use of the relevant technical and scientific cadres. Even in 'purely economic' terms, the neo-colonial bourgeoisie cannot industrialize Africa without accepting the imperialist diktat. In other words, *unless Africa is politically united by socialism, under the leadership of a worker-peasant alliance, there can be no genuine liberation of the continent*. The African bourgeoisie has no choice but to make do with a few crumbs of secondary industry and submit to the requirements of international finance capital.

The Absence of Forward and Backward Linkages
A third aspect of the present industrialization process in Africa is the industrial sterility of the factories which have been implanted in most countries on the continent over the last few years. This industrial sterility characterizes any industry which has no 'offspring', which does not lead to the emergence of further industries; in other words, it is a characteristic of an industry which is essentially oriented either to direct consumption or to markets abroad.

Using the examples of Fria in Guinea and Alucam in Cameroon, Gerard de Bernis, a French economist, has shown very simply that some industries intrinsically advance industrialization while others do not. For instance, the Pechiney complex at Edea in Cameroon has made a disappointingly small contribution to the industrialization of the country, especially when compared to, say, Renault in France, which has given a big boost to other sectors of industry such as machine tools. The Pechiney complex at Edea is surrounded by an industrial desert. The Edea factory was truly 'a Cameroonian solution to a Pechiney problem, not a Pechiney solution to a Cameroonian problem'. From his concrete analysis, de Bernis draws out the idea of 'industrializing industry', a happy phrase which pinpoints the only kind of industry which can genuinely lead to accelerated and coherent industrialization in Third World countries.[104]

Are the industries which are presently being developed in Africa industrializing industries? Do they provide grounds for hoping that the industrial sector will grow increasingly autocentric and coherent? Are they leading to a serious restructuring of the pattern of industrial activity in Africa? Do they make it possible for new industrial plant to be set up, with a view to increasing the productivity of labour in the various sectors of industrial activity? Do they increase people's control over the process of production?

One does not need to be an economist to see that the answer to all these questions is a resounding *No*. The example of Pechiney in Cameroon is striking. Apart from a timid effort by Alucam-Pechiney's SOCATRAL subsidiary to manufacture saucepans and corrugated metal sheets, there has been no significant initiative from the big French monopoly, and no real effect on the industrial structure of Cameroon.[105]

The supply of new machinery to industry as a whole has been completely neglected in the present process of industrialization in Africa. Instead of producing capital goods such as machine tools, this process has been essentially concerned with the supply of consumer goods to satisfy the debauched requirements of the ruling neo-colonial African bourgeoisie.

Apart from in the extractive industries (mines and oil), which we shall deal with below, it is clearly difficult to increase productivity substantially without machines. Yet the fallacious theses of the bourgeois economists of the imperialist countries are accepted wholesale by the African neo-colonial bourgeoisie, who are willing to believe, amongst other things, that the development of agriculture is *the* priority in the solution of Africa's problems. For example, the model of growth proposed in the Second Five-Year Plan for Cameroon, as drawn up by the Ahidjo Government in late 1964 following the grotesque failure of their first plan, was worked out by a French 'expert' from the French National Institute of Statistics and Economic Studies. One of this model's basic hypotheses is that 'growth in productivity is slow, which means that technical progress can be left out as a parameter of the model'.[106] Yet this same model was re-adopted for the Third Plan, covering the period 1971-76. As we have seen previously, the difference in the productivity of labour between the developed and the dominated countries is one of the main aspects of the inequality of international exchange, along with all the ways imperialism dominates African countries, blocks the development of their productive forces and further accentuates inequalities in development. In the light of all this, the choice made by Ahidjo's Government in Cameroon is a clear example of the hypocrisy of the African bourgeoisies' complaints about 'deteriorating terms of trade'.

In the extractive industries, productivity is high, on a par with that of the same sectors in the imperialist countries. But these industries have little or no industrializing effect on the rest of the economy of the countries in which they exist. The main reason is that they are geared towards the export market rather than towards the domestic economy. Hence the idea that 'oil may be in the Middle East geographically speaking, but, in economic terms, it is in the West'.[107] The same applies to the oil reserves of Gabon, Nigeria and Cameroon. Ahidjo has already decided to give the French neo-colonialists a free hand in the matter, for all his demagogic declarations.

As for the worker's level of control over his product, it is obvious that, if there is one area in which it is strictly nil, that area is the mining and petroleum sector.

The industries which could genuinely promote Africa's industrialization include the manufacture of steel, machine tools and transport equipment, the energy industry and the chemical industry, especially the production of fertilizers. These industries would have a direct effect upon agriculture, through modernization and raised productivity.

It has often been argued that the steel industry could not be implanted and developed in Africa, due to the lack of iron, coal, energy, and so on. The argument was far more current at the time of direct colonialism than it is today, since by 1957 Africa was already supplying Britain with 29%, France with 36% and West Germany with 10% of their respective iron ore requirements. In 1963, Nkrumah, in his book on neo-colonialism, pointed out that:

> [Africa's] iron reserves are put at twice the size of America's and two-thirds those of the Soviet Union's, on the basis of an estimated two billion metric tons. Africa's calculated coal reserves are considered to be enough to last for three hundred years.[108]

Furthermore, in 1974 it was announced that Eastern Senegal's iron reserves were of the order of a thousand million tons, all 'high grade ore'.[109] In other words, Africa's total iron reserves are at least equivalent to the Soviet Union's and two and a half times larger than America's. All of which, of course, just goes to show how appallingly poor in natural resources the continent of Africa really is . . . .

Monopoly capital is now doing everything in its power to accelerate the extraction of these important minerals. Soon, there may be little left of them. Mauritania's reserves are estimated at 115 million tons of 63% iron ore. The Anglo-French consortium, which extracts 5 million tons of this ore annually, will have gone through the lot in 23 years, Mauritania's nationalization of its reserves notwithstanding. In Senegal, where very rich phosphate deposits have been handed over to a Franco-Belgian finance and mining combine by Senghor's crew, the country's 40 million tons of raw phosphates will be exhausted within 20 years if the present rate of pillage continues.

If we now consider the possibility of Africa manufacturing its own fertilizers, it is worth noting that, by 1957, all of France's phosphates and 71% of West Germany's phosphorites came from Africa.[110] The existence of substantial oil reserves further confirms that an African fertilizer industry is eminently possible. For example, in 1974 (before the liberation of the country by Frelimo), it was announced that:

> Soekor, a South African company which aims to develop the exploitation of Mozambique's Pande natural gas fields (estimated reserves of two billion cubic feet), will be able to transport the product to South Africa by means of a 900-km. pipeline linking Pande and Johannesburg. Should this prove impracticable, major petro-chemical complexes would be set up at Pande itself, with a view to the manufacture of chemical fertilizers and oil.
>
> During the last three years, the Petrangol Group has discovered oil reserves larger than all those the Group had previously discovered in 18 years of prospecting in Angola. Since 1972, new fields have been discovered at N'zombo in the north and at Bento, near Luanda, bringing the number of fields discovered in one short year up to four.[111]

Since more than 40% of the world's hydro-electric potential is also in Africa, it is quite absurd to claim that our continent lacks the natural resources required for industrialization. Few Cameroonians, for instance, are aware that: 'Engineers have calculated that the Sanaga River, which has its source at an altitude of 1,400 metres and a throughflow three times that of the Rhone at Genissiat, can provide more energy than all the Alpine rivers put together.'[112] There is no question. The materials for setting up the industries mentioned earlier are amply available in Africa.

Another argument is that, as the population of the African countries is 90% rural, the development of agriculture and agricultural production in one form or another should be given maximum priority. Occasionally a rider is added, stressing that agricultural exports are Africa's main source of the foreign currency needed to pay for factory plant and other industrial equipment. According to this line of reasoning, a country like France should never have industrialized in competition with Britain. On the contrary, it should have done everything to develop agricultural production, so as to buy British machinery throughout the 18th and 19th Centuries.

Let us turn to more serious matters. Given the steady fall in the prices of agricultural products exported by African countries, it is quite useless to wear oneself out trying to increase the volume of agricultural exports. To take only one example amongst many, Ghana's production of cocoa in 1954-55 reached 210,000 tons, which brought in £85.5 million when sold. In 1964-65, some 590,000 tons of cocoa were harvested, almost three times as much, yet it fetched only £77 million. In 1954-55, Nigeria harvested 89,000 tons of cocoa which was sold for £39.25 million. The 1965 harvest in Nigeria was an estimated 310,000 tons, almost four times the 1954 harvest. And what did this bumper crop earn the country? £40 million. Nkrumah's book on neo-colonialism is full of such revealing details.

The truth is that it would be extremely difficult for anybody to prove that African countries stand to gain any advantage whatsoever by specializing in a particular product, especially an agricultural product. Despite the efforts of mercantilists and confusionists to hide it, the fact remains that:

> Whatever product or industry a dependent economy specializes in, it will still suffer the effects of unequal exchange when it integrates into the world economy. In other words, the countries with dependent economies are invariably exploited by the countries of the centre. The international division of labour is based on capitalist relations of production, favours the central or developed economies, and blocks the development of the productive forces in the periphery.[113]

Nonetheless, it is true that since 80-90% of the African population is still rural, any major economic progress in Africa will necessarily involve an increase in agricultural productivity. But this progress is only possible on the basis of an industrialization of the continent, an industrialization which is emphatically oriented towards the production of capital goods rather than consumer goods, yet does not neglect the basic needs of the masses for certain consumer items.

This kind of industrialization cannot be carried out unless there is at least a measure of integrated regional planning. The scale of industry required is far beyond the potential of the present African micro-countries.[114] Consequently, it seems indubitable that real industrialization of Africa, which is a necessary precondition to the continent's economic liberation and hence to its liberation in every other sense, is intimately linked to African unity. The scale of the industrial projects described earlier makes a common policy based on the application of a coherent overall plan absolutely essential.

Inequalities in Economic Potential and Degree of Underdevelopment: Effects on Economic Integration

If one considers Zaire, Congo Brazzaville, Nigeria, Benin, Cameroon, Gabon and Togo, for instance, it is immediately apparent that the human and material resources of these countries are not all of the same order of magnitude. On top of these inequalities in economic potential, there are inequalities of development — or, more accurately, of underdevelopment — in that this or that African country may be more industrialized than its neighbours. The consequences of these two features can easily be observed in the daily practice of the African bourgeoisies' efforts to industrialize the continent.

On 20 April 1973, when Nixon announced the elimination of U.S. import quotas for both crude and refined oil, on the understanding that taxes would be imposed on these products to promote refining within the U.S. itself, it was obvious that the price of oil was going to rise in keeping with the expected increase in U.S. for imported oil. Shortly afterwards, the price of oil did indeed rise, dramatically. A host of reasons were advanced to explain the phenomenon, but it is the increase itself which concerns us here.

One result was an apparent divergence of interest between various African countries. The oil-producing countries, such as Algeria, Nigeria, Libya and Gabon, benefited, but the majority of African countries who were not exporters of energy in the form of oil and its derivatives saw the cost of their imports shoot up and their foreign currency reserves fall correspondingly. The interests of the various African bourgeoisies were objectively contradictory and this contradiction stemmed purely and simply from inequalities in economic potential.[115]

If — to take another case — we examine a question such as the association of African countries with the E.E.C. (capitalist Europe's Common Market), the first divergence that emerges is that between 'Francophone' and 'Anglophone' nations. But even between 'Anglophone' countries, there were divisions, in that: 'The smaller countries were in agreement. The more powerful ones, however, were essentially concerned about whether wider access to the European market would compensate for the loss of the advantages they enjoyed under the Commonwealth.'[116]

The 'more powerful' nations in Africa were thus primarily concerned to trade under the most favourable conditions, with guaranteed markets for their products. In fact, the more powerful countries referred to in the text were not all 'Anglophone'. True, they did include Nigeria, which originally declared its aversion for the E.E.C., before bowing to imperialist pressures and the interests of Nigeria's business bourgeoisie.[117] But the term also referred to Zaire. These two countries' economic potential, relatively high level of 'development' (especially Nigeria) and consequent need for markets initially led them to affect hostility towards any association with the E.E.C. They announced that they preferred the development of 'inter-African co-operation' in economic matters to any such association. Zaire's position, for instance, was expressed by Bo-Boliko Lokonga, then President of Mobutu's rump Parliament. With all the presumptuous arrogance characteristic of those who are not even aware of the extent to which their countries are under the neo-colonialist thumb, this gentleman proclaimed:

> It is our profound belief that co-operation, as we conceive it, cannot be simply limited to relations between a part of Europe and a part of Africa. This is why Zaire defends and will continue to defend its open door policy. In the context of this openness to the outside world, we have only one concern: to choose our commercial partners freely and to increase their number, for the good of our economy.[118]

Boliko is simply expressing the class position of Zaire's bourgeoisie. A form of co-operation limited to exchange between Europe and various African countries leaves even fewer crumbs for the African bourgeoisie. Their class interests demand something more, notably the growth of 'inter-African' exchanges, as Kamanda wa Kamanda puts it. The bourgeoisies of Nigeria and Zaire have much to gain from such 'inter-African' exchanges.

Kamanda's repeated attacks on the association between the African countries
and the E.E.C. when he was Deputy Secretary-General of the O.A.U., were
straightforward expressions of Zaire's position. At that time, Kawanda wa
Kawanda, who seems to have lost his tongue since Zaire's signing of the Lome
Convention in February 1973, could be heard to say: 'Africa must not allow
those who are organizing themselves on the basis of regional economic and
monetary integration to divide our continent up into zones of influence, to
block inter-African co-operation or to hinder our socio-economic
integration.'[119]

Experts from the countries most inclined to re-associate with the
metropoles (mainly the French neo-colonies) and from the imperialist
capitalist countries agreed in 1973 that 'the Associated African and Malagasy
States do not all have the same problems in terms of marketing their products'.
Unsurprisingly, these experts suggested the creation of National Foreign
Trade Promotion Centres, in three associated states — namely, Ivory Coast,
Cameroon and Zaire! Of all the associated states (with the possible exception
of Madagascar), these three are potentially the strongest, in that their level
of development (or — to be more precise — underdevelopment) is the highest;
they are thus the three countries which would be likely to experience the most
problems in marketing their products.

The present system produces, it is clear, undeniable contradictions
between African countries, contradictions which are due both to inequalities
in economic potential and to differing levels of development. *These economic
contradictions make it extremely unlikely that 'concerted action' by African
states, as promised by the African bourgeoisies and their imperialist
accomplices, will ever produce much in the way of tangible results.*

It is important to realize to what extent monopoly capital is the root
cause of these contradictions. The inequalities in potential may have a 'natural'
origin, but the inequalities in level of development/underdevelopment
certainly do not. Generally speaking, the latter are the expression of neo-
colonialist intentions, in that industries are installed in Africa according to
the strategic or economic needs of imperialist capital, not in accordance with
the needs and aspirations of the African countries concerned. In many cases,
an African country may have real potential in a particular area, but until
the neo-colonialists are convinced that the operation will be profitable in
their terms, nothing can be done. To take just one example:

> In its meeting of 20 March (1974), Upper Volta's Council of Ministers,
> led by the President, General Lamizana, adopted a motion to set up a
> General Projects Office at Tambao. The Tambao site, 300 km. north-
> west of Ouagadougou, is particularly rich in manganese. Reserves are
> estimated at over 15 million tons. No investor has yet expressed any
> practical interest in these deposits, partly because moving of the mineral
> to the port of Abidjan would involve building 300 km. of railway from
> Ouagadougou to Tambao.[120]

Compare this with the fact that international finance capital built up an 'economic miracle' from scratch in Ivory Coast, in order to provide a counterweight to Kwame Nkrumah's anti-imperialist Ghana. Compare it to the ease with which the Trans-Gabonese railway was got underway, despite the complications which the corruption of Bongo and his clique were likely to cause. Compare it to the fact that the project of a Trans-Cameroonian railway was shelved for 20 years and only re-emerged when it became apparent that the Amadoua bauxite deposits were extremely 'interesting'.

Regional Association: African Bourgeoisies' View of Their Significance for African Unity

A few years ago, when Barbatoura El Hadj Ahmadou Ahidjo, President of the 'United Republic of the Cameroons', announced that he was pulling out of OCAM (the puppet organization originally known as *l'Organisation Commune Africaine et Malgache*, then as *l'Organisation Commune Africaine et Mauricienne*, so as not to change the acronym), he implied that Africa had lapsed into micro-nationalism. Therefore, apart from the O.A.U., only regional organizations on the lines of UDEAC could claim any usefulness or significance. The reader may care to refer back to pp. 53, and particularly to the quote from Ahidjo's Biravandu's apologia for micro-nationalism, as delivered in Addis Ababa in May 1963, some ten years before Cameroon's withdrawal from OCAM in 1973. Micro-nationalism is not quite such a new phenomenon as Ahidjo would have us think. He can hardly expect us to believe that he has suddenly been converted to some form of genuine African unity, even a regional one, in accordance with the interests and aspirations of the patriotic workers and youth of Africa!

So why do Ahidjo and friends proclaim that UDEAC — and, of course, the O.A.U. — are the only possible interesting organizations in Africa?

It is well known that Cameroon occupies a privileged position within UDEAC, to say the least. For instance, the UDEAC General Secretary is automatically a Cameroonian. This position rests on the inequalities in economic potential between the member countries (inequalities in capitalist terms, where might is right) and also on disparities in their respective level of underdevelopment/development. Cameroon and Gabon are seen as the two 'richest' countries in UDEAC, but Cameroon has the advantage of a larger population and, at the moment, a greater pool of skilled manpower. Above all, UDEAC constitutes a crucial market for the Cameroonian economy, an outlet it could not do without under present circumstances. Recent figures show just how important this market is for Cameroon. In 1972, Cameroon's exports to UDEAC-Chad increased by 25.2% and amounted to some 3,590 million CFA francs in value, a remarkable figure. In chemicals, plastics and cement, the increase represented 75.3% of the total trade figure. Also in 1973, Cameroon's exports of light engineering manufactures increased by 43.7%, compared to the previous year. In the same year, out of total industrial exports worth 16,884 million CFA francs, trade with UDEAC-Chad represented almost 27%, amounting to 4,531 million. During the first nine months of 1974, exports to UDEAC-Chad were again up by 25%, compared to the same period in 1973. The steady rise in exports to UDEAC-Chad corresponds to a definite increase in Cameroon's industrial production and has enabled the country to reduce its enormous trade deficit with France, relatively speaking of course.[121]

Given all this, it is easy to see why business circles in Cameroon are enthusiastic about UDEAC, and why Ahidjo is constantly praising and toasting this beneficial Union.

Turning to another case of sudden enthusiasm for regional economic groupings in Africa, the Ivory Coast, we saw in the first chapter that Houphouet-Boigny did more than anybody to disrupt the old colonial A.O.F. and A.E.F. federations. That was in 1958 and 1961, when he believed that a federal executive should only be set up in Paris, certainly not in Dakar. But now that the gentleman in question feels the need to defend the interests of the new African bourgeoisie in the Ivory Coast, he is more inclined to make declarations like this one, delivered at the Tenth Summit of the O.A.U. in May 1973 at Addis Ababa: 'Now is the time for large African economic groupings, articulated on the basis of existing regional or sub-regional economic communities. From now on, these groupings should be our main concern.'[122]

It is well known that the Ivory Coast bourgeoisie, notably the plantation owners, are keenly interested in the *Conseil de l'Entente*, whose members are Ivory Coast, Benin, Niger and Upper Volta. This interest centres on the essential role played by the members of the poor peasantry, especially those from Upper Volta, who have been transformed into an agricultural proletariat for the Ivory Coast plantations. It is, therefore, not at all surprising to hear Houphouet-Boigny (who is himself probably the biggest Ivory Coast land-owner, despite his supposed 'gift' of his estates to the state in 1977) praising 'existing regional and sub-regional economic communities' — provided they are on the lines of the *Conseil de l'Entente*.

The countries whose industrial production is growing are constantly searching for markets. Given the unequal competition they face from the imperialist monopolies in finding stable and penetrable markets outside Africa, these African countries increasingly concentrate their efforts on Africa itself. The recent trend towards expanding economic and trading relations between African countries is, above all, a necessity imposed by capitalist economics. Thus it is also apparent that those African countries who can hope to find specific African markets for their products have no interest in promoting the involvement of their major African competitors. Houphouet's insistence on the value of *existing* regional and sub-regional economic communities is one way of saying that, from the point of view of the Ivory Coast bourgeoisie, the future West African Economic Community must not in any way threaten the positions and interests *already acquired* by the Ivory Coast in the region, namely the interests of the Ivory Coast bourgeoisie. To take another example, Zaire's sudden withdrawal from the pseudo-Community of Central African States, which Mobutu himself had set up, came hard on the realization that the project would boil down to a head-on clash with Chad and therefore had no economic or commercial interest for Mobutu's bourgeois clique.

Another case which attracted a great deal of attention, especially from 1972-73 onwards, was the Nigerian bourgeoisie's efforts to gain access to the important West African market. These efforts took the form of a full-scale offensive aiming to set up a 15-member West African Economic Community stretching all the way from Senegal to Cameroon. Another association, the *Communaute Economique de l'Afrique de l'Ouest* (C.E.A.O.), had already been set up, under the aegis of French neo-colonialism and its two main agents, Houphouet and Senghor; it had only six members, all French neo-colonies. Senegal, whose President seems to delight in quixotic attitudes, threw itself presumptuously and unthinkingly into the battle against the Nigerian project. Official declarations were issued in quantity, notably this one:

> Senegal is not in favour of participating in the present project for a 15-member West African Community, in which a single state (Nigeria) would clearly dominate the other 14. This was the gist of the statement issued by Mr. Daouda Sow, the Senegalese Minister of Information, at a press conference on 2 January [1974].[123]

It is indeed true, on the surface at least, that the Nigerian project represented a threat to the C.E.A.O. But an African cannot fail to notice the remarkable intellectual and political consistency of men like Senghor and Houphouet who are prepared to let their countries remain under the very pronounced domination of European imperialists, but become extremely 'vigilant' the moment there is any question that they might come under the more or less real 'domination' of another African country. This kind of ploy has a long history. Ever since the colonial era, the imperialists have used it very adeptly to block any real move towards African unification.

The Nigerian bourgeoisie's attempt to draw Cameroon into its projected 15-member community also threatened to break up the membership of UDEAC, namely Cameroon, Gabon, the Congo and the Central African Republic. Senghor and Ahidjo immediately recognized their common interest and soon afterwards, in January 1974, during an official visit to Cameroon by Abdou Diouf, then Prime Minister of Senegal, the two governments issued a joint communique, part of which read: 'As for African problems, the two parties expressed their conviction that the advance towards African unity should be based on existing sub-regional bodies such as the C.E.A.O. and UDEAC.'[124]

Less than two months later, in February, Senghor himself was in Bangui on an official visit. The joint declaration he signed with Bokassa — then Field Marshal for Life and later Emperor — stated: 'The two heads of state laid particular stress on the need to develop regional groupings in Africa, such as the C.E.A.O. and UDEAC, which are the very foundations of political organizations such as the O.A.U.'[125]

In the end, however, the Nigerian project was carried through: the Economic Community of West African States (ECWAS or CEDEAO) now co-exists with the C.E.A.O. Although this outcome may seem contradictory, one need only remember the enormous influence exercised by the Western European imperialists over nearly all the 16-member states of ECWAS to see that, once the African bourgeoisies had bowed down to the E.E.C. at Lome in 1975, Senghor's campaign was doomed, in that his masters and allies were no longer interested in his little battles.

Clearly, if 'reason has become foolishness and good deeds a curse' (Engels) — in other words, if the great, wise and glorious U.A.M./OCAM as a huge umbrella organization has become useless, while the economically based regional organizations like UDEAC and C.E.A.O. are increasingly of great interest and other similar regional or sub-regional economic communities are all the rage — there must be some very powerful factors at work. The fact is that certain countries are impelled by an 'economic force' which dwarfs them, a sort of capitalist economic determinism: they have to find outlets for their goods. They are thus compelled to do everything in their power to set up a regional division of labour, an unequal regional sub-specialization. This is the real and fundamental ecnomic content of all the supposedly new theories, and the withdrawal of countries such as Cameroon from organizations like OCAM.

Some progressive forces treat these withdrawals from OCAM as 'progressive acts', while recognizing that the motives involved have very little to do with the real interests of the African people. But this way of looking at things is both analytically and factually incorrect. On 25 November 1973, before a National Council of cadres from his fascist U.N.C. Party assembled at Yaounde, Ahidjo had this to say concerning OCAM: 'In the present context of Africa's search for unity, its aims are not only anachronistic but in contradiction to our own national aims.'[126] This from the man who fought so fiercely against our U.P.C. when we denounced the newly founded OCAM as a neo-colonialist body whose aims were fundamentally opposed to the interests and aspirations of the African people as a whole and of Cameroonians in particular.

The tendency for capitalism at the centre to marginalize trade with the periphery, as already noted, makes the African bourgeoisie's new policy both necessary and feasible. Necessary, in that if the developed capitalist countries do not import sufficient quantities of the goods African economies have for sale, then those goods have to be sold somewhere. Feasible, because the tendency for the capitalist centres to trade increasingly only amongst themselves means that markets on the periphery become more easily accessible. But this accessibility is only relative since, while it is true that the developed countries' trade with Africa is marginal, it is only marginal compared to the volume of world trade as a whole. These developed countries' exports to Africa remain very substantial when compared to the level of inter-African trade, both in terms of quantity and in terms of the competition they impose on African products within Africa itself. The new strategy has a clearly limited scope.

In order to overcome these difficulties, the African bourgeoisies have also begun to modify their fiercely anti-Communist stance and to establish trading relations with Eastern Europe and the progressive countries of Asia. Although the alacrity with which they have embraced this new policy has surprised some observers, it is clear that they have done so with the full approval of their neo-colonialist masters and allies. The whole point of this move is to find new markets. It has nothing whatsoever to do with progressive ideas or non-alignment, as has been suggested, even in some anti-imperialist circles. On the contrary, the African bourgeoisies hope thereby to isolate the revolutionary African forces who are struggling against neo-colonialism.

Once these withdrawals from OCAM and other puppet bodies are put in their correct perspective, it becomes obvious that they are by no means necessarily a manifestation of some anti-imperialist change of heart, as those opportunists who seek the slightest pretext to claim that Ahidjo's regime is evolving towards a progressive stance would have us believe. The demagogues of Pan-Africanism are always eager to find some way of justifying their association with the assassins of Um Nyobe, Moumie, Lumumba, Ben Barka, Ouandie, etc., whether it be by a cynical appeal to some hypothetical *raison d'etat* or by claiming that they themselves are in fact the 'Great Strategists of the African Democratic Revolution', etc. The tragedy is that the more naive and ill-informed of our compatriots may believe them.

Imperialist Domination and Inter-Imperialist Conflicts' Impact on Pan-African Integration

Imperialist domination is the decisive element which, in the context of international integration and specialization, is blocking any genuine Pan-African integration. It has long been apparent that the economic structure of Africa has been shaped to suit the interests of the imperialists. Twenty years after the achievement of formal independence, the situation is fundamentally unchanged. The imperialists do everything in their power to reinforce their position and adapt the form their domination takes to the new conditions under which it is exercised.

If one wishes to know how the French imperialists, for instance, hoped the situation would evolve five years ago — and still hope it will today — one only has to listen to Senghor:

> Europe? — a fascinating adventure. Eurafrica is the great opportunity facing the two continents. An association of all the states of the continent with the E.E.C. would be ideal[!]. That is why it is so important that economic communities should evolve which embrace both Anglophones and Francophones, in order that we should all have the same position *vis-a-vis* the E.E.C.[127]

In other words, Senghor's ideal was achieved at Lome in February 1975, when nearly all the African states signed the Convention of Association with the E.E.C.

The journal from which the above quote is drawn goes on to say that President Senghor has adopted a very clear line on the association of Anglophone Africa with 'the biggest market in the world'. According to the journal, in 1973, before Lome I, Senghor was apparently to be heard deploring the fact that the Anglophones 'do not see the trap into which some Americans and some Asians seek to push us'. The poet of Dakar goes on triumphantly: 'As for the Americans, they oppose our privileged relations with Europe. I have this to say to them: you have your arrangements with South America; well, then, we are Europe's South America.'[128] Senghor has rarely revealed himself to quite this extent as a servile agent of the imperialist bourgeoisie and true mouthpiece of the privileged classes of Senegal, who are quite content with the crumbs left them by the West European neo-colonialists.[129]

In this particular show, there was, of course, a U.S. puppet as well as a French puppet.[130] Mobutu's Kamanda wa Kamanda declared:

> Africa is not Europe's private hunting ground. Africa's unity does not and shall not depend upon Europe. Africa is not an extension of Europe or of Europe's problems . . . .
>
> The Africans themselves are the best architects of African development. When it comes to working out our development strategy, we Africans should remain amongst ourselves, just as the Europeans do when defining their own strategy.[131]

Kamanda may be contradicting Senghor and presenting himself as a true anti-imperialist African patriot. But what does he really mean when he speaks of Africans remaining 'amongst themselves'? Perhaps he had in mind something on the lines of the 1973 Kinshasa International Fair, which took place a few months later:

> With its 8,000 square metres and exhibitors from 30 countries, the fair is certainly impressive. One may be tempted to ask, however, whether these remarkable efforts have not been too heavy a drain on Zaire's public purse. 'Not at all', replies the project supervisor, Mr. Kiwana, 'it is far from being a mere prestige operation. Obviously, we had to put a great deal of money into it, but the fees for the stands, the number of exhibitors and the dialogue which has been established between local and foreign businessmen are ample compensation for our investment.' The figures certainly back up these assertions: since 1969, when a very liberal investment climate was instituted, about 5,000 million French francs have poured into what used to be the sole empire of the *Union Miniere du Haut Katanga* (now known as *Gecamines*), notably from Belgium, the U.S., Japan and most of the European countries.[132]

If that was the situation in 1973, the reader may well imagine what it must be like now that the I.M.F. experts have been granted full control over the Zaire economy, in response to the imperialists' realization that Mobutu and friends had brought this amazingly well-endowed country to the brink of total ruin.

£500 million in five years! Such generosity! This massive new influx of international finance capital, coming on top of an already remarkable level of foreign investment, shows Kamanda's speeches for what they really are: verbiage! Imperialist capital never ceases in its efforts to set up new structures through which to dominate Africa. For instance:

> After two days of particularly animated and fruitful discussions, the delegations of the African, Malagasy and French Consular Companies decided to set up a research and co-ordination office, the Permanent Conference of African, Malagasy and French Consular Companies. The purpose of this body is to encourage and organize multilateral co-operation in such matters as professional and technical training, information, economic linkages and the promotion of trade generally, amongst all French-speaking countries.[133]

Faced with French initiatives of this kind, and given that the Lome Agreement, which brought nearly all the African countries under a single banner, had not yet been signed, it is hardly surprising that the 'Anglophone' countries should

> think there was some connection between the preferential terms granted to the E.E.C. by the ex-French colonies and the continued monopoly over those countries' imports exercised by French companies. From such a conclusion, it is only a short step to the idea that the Yaounde Convention [which preceded Lome I, E.M.] is merely an instrument of French 'neo-colonialist' interests in Africa, a step which some people have taken all too eagerly.[134]

The various forms of domination exercised by this or that imperialism over this or that group of African countries and the unequal levels of development/underdevelopment create cleavages amongst the countries of Africa, dividing them up into 'more advanced' and 'less advanced', with 'the latter ready to make any concessions demanded of them, provided that FED support is guaranteed, and the former more concerned with their future economic independence', as the neo-colonial journal quoted above puts it so frankly. Does this mean that, even in the future, the 'less advanced' countries will have no economic independence in view? If so, Cameroon will certainly be one of them, given the present policy of Ahidjo's U.N.C. To put it more bluntly, the weaker African bourgeoisies are only after one thing: regular annual payment of a few million dollars from the coffers of the FED or U.S.A.I.D. However, the stronger local bourgeoisies on the continent already have other ambitions, which are unfortunately cramped by the power of imperialist capital.

It seems obvious that simple economic interest ought to bring the African bourgeoisies together in a single bloc which could stand up to imperialist capital, if only because:

> Competition among the products of the underdeveloped countries in the markets of the rich countries always seems stronger than that among manufactured goods in the markets of the underdeveloped countries . . . . This competition is even less when political domination is superimposed on relations of economic domination.[135]

In practice, nearly all the African bourgeoisies are too weak even to realize what their true interests are.

The domination exercised by the various imperialisms over Africa and the internal struggles these imperialisms wage against one another have a decisive influence on the course of events in the continent. They continue to have a very negative effect on the possibilities for genuine African integration, precisely to the extent that this domination continues to keep each African country tied to a particular neo-colonial metropole)or to the imperialist camp as a whole). This is, of course, precisely what is at stake in the inter-imperialist struggles, as each imperialism tries to gain the upper hand over its fellow competitors.

Faced with this situation, the African bourgeoisies can, at best, merely rail against those imperialisms which do not dominate them directly, while remaining tactfully silent about their own masters. The petty-bourgeoisie especially has a tendency to indulge in pseudo-revolutionary phraseology, denouncing 'all imperialisms in general' so as not to have to tackle the concrete imperialism which dominates their country 'in particular'. This is often the case when the masses in a particular country are fairly aware politically, following specific socio-historical developments. For instance, everybody knows that, despite the revolutionary phraseology which is *de rigueur* in Conakry, large sectors of the Guinean economy are still dominated by American trusts and the French giant Pechiney-Ugine-Kuhlmann, some 20 years after independence. As we shall show later, this domination will probably increase in the coming years and may involve various other multinationals. In the meantime, of course, the country has ostensibly become a 'Democratic Revolutionary Republic', led by 'The(!) Great Strategist of the Democratic and Popular African Revolution', etc. Similarly, the 'People's Republic of the Congo' has been ruled by a 'Marxist-Leninist' party, the Congolese Labour Party, for many years now, yet in 1973 the following (typical) report appeared:

> President Marien Ngouabi has yet again denounced international capitalism 'especially French capitalism which controls everything in the Congo' during a speech to trade unionists in Brazzaville. The

President stressed that: 'We do not have to buy everything in France. [Each year] 10,000 million of ours flows into France and only 2,000 million of theirs comes here. All your money goes to France. You must grasp this point. All the money goes to France.' 'What really matters,' the President added, 'is the health of our nationalized industries.'[136]

So we can conclude that, although French capitalism controls everything in this 'Marxist-Leninist' Congo, the most important thing is for the Congolese workers to ensure the smooth operation of the state enterprises! There can, of course, be no question of touching anything controlled by French capitalism — which controls everything. What Marien Ngouabi is really saying, either consciously or unconsciously, is that the Congolese bureaucratic bourgeoisie is fully aware that imperialism, especially French imperialism, dominates everything in the Congo; at the same time, this bourgeoisie dares not wage any effective radical struggle against this domination, since the Congolese working class and poor peasants might eventually take over such a struggle and overthrow both imperialist capital and the Congolese bureaucratic bourgeoisie. Consequently, the bureaucratic bourgeoisie's own interest dictates that it is 'after all' better to maintain the present situation under which 10,000 million francs produced by Congolese workers is stolen by the French neo-colonialists, who then send back 2,000 million to the Congolese bureaucratic bourgeoisie through the state enterprise system. Thus, it is hardly surprising that the President lays such stress on the smooth operation of these state enterprises.

Any serious analysis of the overall policies adopted by many African regimes who claim to be revolutionary will reveal contradictions so substantial that one can only conclude that the greatest caution is required before any of these regimes is deemed entitled to call itself 'anti-imperialist', 'revolutionary' and 'socialist', as they apparently wish to do.

Nationalizations: Implications for Socialism

Up to the present time, in nearly all the known cases of nationalization in Africa, the nationalized wealth has been transferred to the neo-colonial state, promoting the development of a form of state capitalism. The regimes which have carried out such nationalizations are then categorized as 'anti-imperialist', as opposed to the 'out-and-out puppets' who have not. Indeed, these 'anti-imperialist' regimes are often even characterized as 'socialist', albeit a rather peculiar kind of socialist. Some examination of the objective basis for this nationalization policy (or policies, since there are several varieties) and of the exact content of 'socialism' in certain African countries, therefore, seems called for so that we may assess its true scope and importance.

We have already shown how imperialist domination leads to a marked inequality in any eventual struggle between the monopolies and local capital. Inequalities in the level of underdevelopment of various African countries have also been pinpointed as a factor affecting choice of policy. If we now consider a country which is relatively developed in its underdevelopment, a country where local capital has reached the stage when it can no longer develop within the confines imposed upon it by imperialist capital, it is quite clear that the neo-colonial bourgeoisie of such a country has no other choice but to challenge the positions secured by foreign capital. When, on the contrary, local capital can still develop within the confines imposed by imperialism, the local bourgeoisie will allow foreign capital a free hand and concentrate unprotestingly on its own little affairs. Can one really say that the eventual differences in choice of policy in two such countries are necessarily differences in the degree of their orientation towards socialism? Obviously not. What differences do emerge will simply be the expression of the banal fact that bourgeoisies use different methods to solve the different problems arising out of different material conditions, as part of their overall effort to ensure their own capitalist development. Socialism has nothing to do with it. The interest of the African workers is the last thing the African bourgeoisies in question are concerned with. When it carried no obvious disadvantages, the African bourgeoisies have not been in the least reluctant to carry out the kind of nationalization we are talking about here. These nationalizations have indeed — in certain cases — been anti-imperialist in that imperialist interests have, to varying extents, suffered thereby, but this does not imply that 'socialism' was a factor. There are many examples: Egypt under Nasser; in the Maghreb, settler lands and even industries were nationalized; in Zaire, the *Union Miniere du Haut Katanga* was forcibly transformed into *Gecamines* and in 1971-73 there was a wave of nationalizations known as Zairianization, most of which, as it happens, were later rescinded when the World Bank and the I.M.F. started putting pressure on Mobutu and his mafia in 1976-77; in part of East Africa, trade was nationalized, etc. In each case the neo-colonial bourgeoisie confiscated the nationalized wealth and appropriated it for themselves.

Usually this process of nationalization involves 'buying back' assets which imperialist capital had originally appropriated for itself by force and theft during the colonial period. But a problem arises in that local capital rarely possesses the means required by capitalist norms to make these purchases. Only the state has the financial capacity to do so. *In other words, state control is a solution imposed on the African bourgeoisies by their own weaknesses, not by any desire for a socialist party.*

The nationalization strategy of the neo-colonial African bourgeoisie is based on a variety of tactics, two of which have been particularly fashionable in recent years: namely, the Africanization of management staff and the demand that African individuals or institutions should hold shares in the foreign companies operating in Africa.

The African bourgeoisie's call for the Africanization of company management functions is a direct response to the fact that fewer and fewer places are available in the already over-expanded state bureaucracy. Twenty years ago, nearly all the imperialist puppets, notably in the French neo-colonies, vehemently rejected the idea put forward by anti-imperialist militants that 'cadres at all levels should be Africanized'. The state bureaucracy had not yet developed to the point where it was causing bottle-necks in the neo-colonial machine. Now that their previous course is no longer tenable, the puppets affect a new militancy. Even Albert Omar Bongo, the French lackey in Gabon, recently called on private firms in the country to employ more and more Gabonese managers. School-leavers, including those who are not particularly careerist, need jobs. In a country like Cameroon, the state hierarchy displays a remarkable propensity to subdivide itself endlessly, from the Governors, Prefects, Sub-Prefects, District Officers, etc., down to their assistants, secretaries and the great host of 'technical advisers' who never advise anybody. The administrative units which official propaganda used to praise as the epitome of efficiency are increasingly broken down to allow for bureaucratic expansion. All this temporarily solves the problem of absorbing the mass of people who have set their sights on a place within the bureaucracy. An ultra-selective education policy in the schools, from the primary level up to university, also helps cut down the overflow in the short term. In Nigeria, too, the Federal Military Government deemed it necessary to launch an Africanization policy affecting private industry. Not long ago, Dr. Adetoro, the Federal Commissioner for Industry, reproached Pioneer Metal Products Ltd., a company for whom he was inaugurating an extension at Ikeja, for a 'lack of interest in the Africanization programme' and for neglecting to employ Nigerians in key posts. The problem manifests itself in almost identical form in practically every African country today.

Naturally, no African revolutionary would dream of opposing the complete Africanization of all management positions. The U.P.C., for instance, stated as early as 1960 that Africanization was an absolutely essential element of any Minimum Programme aiming to achieve true national independence, in marked contrast to the traitors of the present U.N.C. who vainly sought to prove the opposite.[137] Nonetheless, a distinction must be made between, on the one hand, an Africanization which genuinely advances the liberation of Africa, in keeping with the interests and aspirations of the working masses, and, on the other, a technocratic Africanization geared to the interests of the various strata of the bourgeoisie. Under the present conditions, the latter course cannot amount to more than a form of co-option of the intellectual petty bourgeoisie, either by the bureaucratic bourgeoisie who control the state apparatus or by private capital, which offers opportunist African intellectuals the illusion of penetrating the antechambers of international finance.

Laws stipulating that there should be a significant national shareholding in all foreign companies are also entirely in keeping with the interests of the neo-colonial bourgeoisie. As Samir Amin points out, wholesale nationalization has its problems, notably the 'compensation' owed to foreign capital. In Africa, even the state has fairly limited financial resources. National share-holdings not only reduce this kind of difficulty but also increase the flow of royalties directly into the pockets of the neo-colonial bourgeoisie. For instance:

117

Although the Nigerian Government's 35% stake in Shell-B.P. will bring considerable advantages to Nigeria in the long term, it poses an immediate financial problem. Shell-B.P. estimates that, over the last 35 years, they have invested about 1,000 million naira (about £800 million) in Nigeria. The Government's shareholding will therefore involve Nigeria in payment of compensation amounting to several hundred million naira. Lagos estimates that this compensation can be paid off out of oil resources within two years, after which the Government will begin to register a substantial profit in taxes and dividends as a result of the new agreement.[138]

Shell-B.P. may well have invested £800 million in Nigeria over 35 years. What is left out of the equation, however, is the sum that Shell-B.P. has taken out of Nigeria over the same period. It is worth remembering that imperialist firms generally reinvest part of the profits provided by their original investment. It would be quite wrong to assume that this £800 million all came in to Nigeria from abroad. But, clearly, the Nigerian bourgeoisie has no time for such quibbles. They will pay – or more exactly, they will get the working people of Nigeria to pay – the compensation demanded by Shell-B.P., for which they will be rewarded with an increased flow of dividends, the better to live their *dolce vita*.[139]

The various African political leaders who claim that they exercise real control over their country's oil resources are thus clearly exaggerating, to put it kindly. Nor does it make much sense to describe Nigeria as 'anti-imperialist', whatever various Cameroonian opportunists may say on the subject.

The real point of these observations is that they present the African revolution with two major problems. First, we must ask whether anti-imperialism in the last quarter of the 20th Century can really be reduced to developing the embryo of a more or less stunted form of state capitalism. Although under certain conditions the appropriation of assets 'belonging' to an imperialist company can effectively figure as an anti-imperialist action on the part of an African state, the fact remains that, inasmuch as such actions remain on the juridical level, they do practically nothing to eliminate the exploitation exercised by international finance capital (sometimes the changes amount to no more than a change in which is the dominant imperialism). Their anti-imperialist content is thus extremely limited. The unequal exchange relations which characterize the world market imply that, as long as a country remains integrated into the world capitalist market, the development of state capitalism in that country is by no means a *sufficient* criterion of an anti-imperialist policy. It would thus be bizarre to consider such countries as socialist, unless, of course, one was referring to some kind of 'underdevelopment socialism' which imposes less demanding criteria than the 'other' variety.

The second problem the African revolution faces is this: Is socialism really reducible to the appropriation of the means of production (*in toto* or, *a fortiori*, in part) by a state bourgeoisie in the context of the class societies which prevail in Africa today? African revolutionaries must ask themselves this question as clearly as possible, and work out an equally clear answer. Since forces outside Africa constantly do their best to convince Africans that any regime which goes in for nationalization must necessarily be 'engaged in the construction of socialism', it is crucial that we should consider the question in some detail.

We are, of course, not the first to face this question. False and inconsistent theories aiming to characterize various forms of statist nationalization had already emerged by the 19th Century. Friedrich Engels showed very simply in his *Anti-Duhring* that state take-overs could easily represent no more than ordinary economic necessities:

> In one way or another, with trusts or without, the state, the official representative of capitalist society, is finally constrained to take over the direction of production.
>
> I say *is constrained to*, for it is only when the means of production and communication have actually outgrown direction by joint-stock companies and therefore their nationalization has become *economically* inevitable — it is only then that this nationalization, even when carried out by the state of today, represents an economic advance, the attainment of another preliminary step towards the seizure of all the productive forces by society itself. But since Bismarck became keen on nationalizing, a certain spurious socialism has recently made its appearance — here and there even degenerating into a kind of flunkeyism — which, without more ado, declares *all* nationalization, even the Bismarckian kind, to be socialistic. To be sure, if the nationalization of the tobacco trade were socialistic, Napoleon and Metternich would rank among the founders of socialism. If the Belgian state, for quite ordinary financial and political reasons, constructed its own main railway lines; if Bismarck, without any economic compulsion, nationalized the main Prussian railway lines simply in order to be better able to organize them and use them in face of war, in order to train the railway officials as the government's voting cattle, and especially in order to secure a new source of revenue independent of parliamentary votes, such actions were in no sense socialistic measures, whether direct or indirect, conscious or unconscious. Otherwise the Royal Maritime Company, the Royal Porcelain Manufacture and even the regimental tailors in the army would be socialist institutions (or even, as was seriously proposed by a sly dog in the 1830s during the reign of Frederick William III, the nationalization of the brothels).[140]

In certain West European capitalist states, entire branches of industry have been nationalized, notably the railways, posts and telecommunications, steelmaking and air travel. Nobody has sought to say that this means that those countries are socialist or 'in the process of building socialism'. One can then only be surprised at the ease with which various regimes in Africa have been labelled as socialist simply because they have nationalized an industry here and there.

The appropriation by society as a whole of the means of production and exchange – in other words, the abolition of private ownership of those means of production – is a *necessary* condition of socialism but not a *sufficient* one. If even this condition is not realized, the society is certainly not socialist, whatever else it may be. Socialism is not a matter of proclamations, however sincere.

The embryonic state capitalism which has cropped up here and there in the majority of African countries today is in no way a challenge to private ownership of the means of production or to capitalism, which is based on that ownership.[141] From this point of view, African state capitalism does not differ fundamentally from the state monopoly capitalism which prevails in certain industrially developed European capitalist countries. Apart from Angola and Mozambique, there is nowhere in Africa where the principle of eliminating private ownership of the means of production is upheld or put into practice as such. The embryonic state capitalism in certain African countries (including nearly all those who loudly proclaim themselves socialist or are dubbed so with alarming facility by many friends of Africa) amounts to little more than statist rather than social appropriation. Nationalization serves as a means for the ruling neo-colonial bourgeoisie to confiscate certain assets 'belonging' to the imperialists. The strictly limited character of such actions illustrates that, under the present international circumstances, it is quite illusory to expect any attack on the capitalist imperialist system to succeed unless it is based on a radical political revolution, a complete overthrow of the existing political and social superstructure and a complete political break with imperialism.

Consequently, all the fine economistic phrases about economic liberation and so-called economic independence (yet to be obtained) are simply empty words. What is this 'socialism' which does nothing to secure the necessary basis for socialism, namely the abolition of bourgeois private property? Perhaps one could describe it as 'social-verbalism' and leave it at that.

Of course, some people will claim that in this or that country the abolition of private property is well under way, and that the socialization of the means of production and exchange necessarily involves statism as a first stage, the implication being that, wherever statism is at its most advanced in Africa, socialism is, in practice, being built. Unfortunately, even statism is not particularly 'advanced' in Africa, as is generally known by everybody who follows African affairs closely rather than simply taking an interest whenever there is another of the usual 'surprise *coups* amongst warring tribes' (*sic*).

But even if statism were a more real force, it would be necessary to remember that, while state ownership of the means of production and exchange – in other words, expropriation of the 'private' as opposed to 'state' bourgeoisie – is a necessary condition for socialism, it is far from being sufficient. Capitalism is not reducible to private ownership of the means of production and exchange. One also needs to know which social forces and which classes control the nationalized assets and hold power.

As Engels puts it:

> But neither conversion into joint-stock companies (and trusts), nor conversion into state property deprives the productive forces of their character as capital. This is obvious in the case of joint-stock companies (and trusts). But the modern state, too, is only the organization with which bourgeois society provides itself in order to maintain the general external conditions of the capitalist mode of production against encroachments either by the workers or by individual capitalists. The modern state, whatever its form, is an essentially capitalist machine, the state of the capitalists, the ideal aggregate capitalist. [This qualification shows that by 'modern state' Engels means the 19th Century capitalist state, not the worker's state during the transition to socialism he goes on to describe a few pages later. E.M.] The more productive forces it takes into its possession, the more it becomes a real aggregate capital, the more citizens it exploits. The workers remain wage workers, proletarians. The capitalist relation is not abolished, rather it is pushed to the limit. But at this limit, it changes into its opposite. State ownership of the productive forces is not the solution of the conflict, but it contains within itself the formal means, the handle to the solution.[142]

The experience of African 'Socialism' is a clear case in point. In African societies dominated by bourgeois state capitalism, state ownership of the means of production and exchange allows the ruling neo-colonial bourgeoisie to create and dominate a whole political, ideological, philosophical, legal and religious apparatus. This superstructure enables a thoroughly rotten neo-colonial bourgeoisie to trick the working masses into accepting as universally valid various purely bourgeois ideas. Because of its need to dominate politically, this neo-colonial bourgeoisie

> is compelled, merely in order to carry through its aim, to represent its interest as the common interest of all the membrs of society, that is, expressed in ideal form: it has to give its ideas the form of universality and represent them as the only rational universally valid one.[143]

Nationalizations are a typical example, as is the notion of the importance of economically healthy state enterprises, when in fact these enterprises benefit only the ruling African state bourgeoisie. The 'need' for a 'national', 'united', 'one-party' state is also a typical manifestation. The one-party state is merely a tool with which to domesticate the working classes and impoverished peasantry according to the requirements of the ruling neo-colonial bureaucratic bourgeoisie. With a few rare exceptions, the one-party state, which is the rule throughout Africa, is an instrument of this bourgeois class dictatorship. This does not prevent this one-party state being presented as a necessary instrument of development, as Ahidjo Birawandu had the gall to describe it during the second Congress of his fascist U.N.C. party in February 1975.

It has long been clear that:

> The ruling ideas are nothing more than the ideal expression of the dominant material relationships, the dominant material relationships grasped as ideas; hence of the relationships which make the one class the ruling one, therefore, the ideas of its dominance.[144]

Throughout Africa, the ideas spread by the one-party state are the ideas of the class which controls that party, the ideas which help that class rule and make it the dominant class — in short 'the ideas of its dominance'. In nearly all African countries, that class is the corrupt neo-colonial bourgeoisie. There are practically no countries in Africa where the ideas of the working class are really in command.

If state control has merely transferred economic power (and hence political power) from the hands of the imperialist to the hands of a bureaucratic state bourgeoisie — as is the case in nearly all the 'anti-imperialist, revolutionary and socialist' countries of Africa — then it has done nothing to resolve the problem of the transition to socialism.

But we must further realize that even when the working class, under its own organization, has led a socialist revolution and abolished the economic basis of capitalism through a properly conducted systematic expropriation of the bourgeoisie, the question is still far from settled. As Vladimir Lenin says:

> Expropriation alone, as a legal or political act, does not settle the matter by a long chalk. There can be no equality between the exploiters — who for many generations have been better off because of their education, conditions of wealthy life and habits — and the exploited, the majority of whom, even in the most advanced and most democratic bourgeois republics, are downtrodden, backward, ignorant, intimidated and disunited.[145]

This is, of course, even more relevant when we are talking of the so-called 'socialist countries' of Africa, where even expropriation has not been fully effected and no real state capitalism has developed, in the sense of major state intervention in the economic life of the country. In Africa, the nationalization of a few businesses for the benefit of the ruling bureaucratic bourgeoisie has had little effect on the economy of the countries concerned. According to these criteria, even Ahidjo might qualify as a socialist, since his system of so-called 'planned liberalism' is characterized by the fact that: 'The state participates increasingly in the important companies which are being created in partnership with investors, and reserves the right to buy back any shares and allocate them to private citizens who lack sufficient capital at the moment.'[146]

Here we have a typical case of quasi-state capitalism, in which the nationalizations effected, thanks to the resources of the Cameroonian workers (state shareholding), will later be used to finance private business — and this is openly proclaimed!

The journal *Marches Tropicaux et Mediterraneens* (the old *Marches Coloniaux*), which specializes in colonial and neo-colonial affairs and lucidly expresses the opinions of the imperialists, especially the French imperialists, published an article in early 1974 under the title 'Congo: un bilan economique de l'annee 1973'.

> Finally, and above all, 1973 was the year in which the new Franco-Congolese Agreements were negotiated. They were eventually signed on 1 January 1974: the Congo remained in the Franc Zone and agreed to recognize the 'fundamental rights' pertaining to French nationals and their property.
>
> The private sector was not really thrown into question, despite the country's socialist orientation; instead, 'honest collaboration' was demanded. Nonetheless, the private sector was held responsible for the general rise in prices, which was especially manifest in October when the price of bread doubled, rising from 10 to 20 SFA francs for 130 grammes.[147]

The journal, to which our readers must by now be getting quite used, can at least be trusted as an accurate judge of whether the interests and 'fundamental rights' of French imperialism are being respected or not. Commander Ngouabi, then head of state in Congo Brazzaville, confirmed the journal's report in the speech we have previously mentioned, when he publicly recognized that 'French imperialism controls everything in the Congo', despite the 'socialist orientation' of the country, naturally.

It is thus sadly amusing to read that:

> After a four-day official visit to Gabon, President Senghor arrived in the Congo, where his host, President Ngouabi, showed him round various achievements of the socialist regime, notably the Kinsoundi textile complex. The Senegalese head of state expressed a keen interest in the Congolese experiments and in return was complimented by his host who told him: 'We have learnt a great deal from you and, once again, you have convinced the militants of the *Parti Congolais du Travail* that you are fully familiar with the principles of Marxism-Leninism.[148]

The situation is not without its humorous side: the most senior officials of the 'Marxist-Leninist' Congolese Workers' Party and French neo-colonialist high finance are in complete agreement on two points. They both recognize that French imperialism controls everything in the Congo and that the Congolese Government of Marien Ngouabi does not really challenge this domination exercised by an implanted private sector which is under no threat whatsoever, 'despite the country's socialist orientation'. The result is that, through Senghor, the ex-slave trading imperialist French bourgeoisie can treat itself to the luxury of giving Marxist-Leninist militants lessons in socialism and Marxism-Leninism! The conclusion seems inescapable: socialism in Africa is in danger of collapsing into demagogic putrefaction.

The plain fact is that the socialism in question in most states in Africa is merely vociferous verbiage. The neo-colonial African bourgeoisie uses it as a slogan to mystify the working and peasant masses, in a deceitful effort to convince them that their problems are being solved. Nationalization in Africa has very little to do with socialism. It should now be clear that current fashionable thought amongst certain progressive circles in Europe, according to whom one should 'not be too demanding concerning the socialist regimes in Africa' as this would be ultra-leftist, is essentially paternalistic and does nothing to promote healthy relations between African and European revolutionaries.

Conclusions

Ever since formal independence was achieved in the 1960s, the African economy has undergone an evolution, the main lines of which have remained fundamentally determined by the economies of the centres of world capitalism. These central economies have shaped the evolution of the African economy as follows.

First, the quest for the highest possible profit and the scientific and technical revolution in industry have thrown developed capitalism into a headlong race. In the industrially developed countries, certain industries have proved insufficiently profitable for the imperialists who insist on high productivity in the West. It is, therefore, becoming possible to transfer some of these less profitable industries to Africa (and, of course, elsewhere in the periphery). At the same time, imperialism ensures that this transfer does not trigger off a process which might evade its control. For instance, the imperialists are very careful as to where and how they set up industries which might have a 'knock-on' effect, promote autarchic development and break with the present pattern of disparate, uncoordinated economic activity geared to European and American needs. Not surprisingly, the present industrialization of Africa is far less oriented towards the production of capital goods than towards the production of consumer goods, an orientation which suits the frivolous and wasteful African bourgeoisies perfectly.

Second, a variety of factors are resulting in real contradictions between the various African countries. These include the tendency towards a relative diminution of the overall importance of inter-African trade and trade with Africa; the need for imperialism to maintain its domination over Africa as a reservoir of raw materials; the extensive use of classical 'divide and rule' tactics; inter-imperialist contradictions reflecting the increasingly internationalized character of capital as opposed to the still prevalently national character of the centres of decision; and inequalities in economic potential between African countries leading to unequal levels of underdevelopment. All this severely limits the scope of the various economistic attempts at Pan-African integration and push African countries to seek out markets by any means available.

Third, the relations of unequal exchange which constitute the very essence of world trade, based as they are both on inequalities in the development of the productive forces and the productivity of labour and on relations of economic and political domination between the imperialist countries and African countries, provide the ground for a deterioration in the terms of trade. These relations are also the root economic cause of the steady and inexorable impoverishment of the African workers. The outcome is inevitably an ever-increasing awareness on the part of the African workers and poorer peasantry that irreducible contradictions put their interests in opposition to those of both imperialism and the African neo-colonial bourgeoisie. The latter may be equally dominated by the foreign imperialist bourgeoisie, but they can always take their troubles out on the African workers. Within the limits imposed by imperialism, the neo-colonial African bourgeoisies strive to organize an African market, notably a labour market structured so as to enable them to move labour from point to point as they see fit. This, of course, suits imperialism as well.

Fourth, the inherent tendency of the capitalist system to broaden the market and the demagogic use of nationalization as a means for the neo-colonial African bourgeoisies to present themselves as 'nationalist' constitute two tendencies which enable these bourgeoisies to mystify the public. An inherent feature of developing capitalism, namely the possibility of developing inter-African trade, is used by the African bourgeoisies as proof that they are in the process of bringing about a measure of genuine Pan-African integration. In reality, nothing could be further from the truth.

At the moment, the relations of domination between imperialist monopoly capital and African countries remain the most important feature determining the evolution of the African economy, despite all the fine phrases to the contrary. Even if certain advances have indeed taken place, the main issues in the whole question of the liberation of Africa have remained fundamentally unchanged, despite the formal independence achieved in 1960. In other words:

> The change in the economic relationship between the new sovereign states and the erstwhile masters is only one of form. Colonialism has achieved a new guise. It has become neo-colonialism, the last stage of imperialism; its final bid for existence, as monopoly capitalism or imperialism is the last stage of capitalism. And neo-colonialism is fast entrenching itself within the body of Africa today through the consortia

and monopoly combinations that are the carpet-baggers of the African revolt against conditions and the urge for continental unity.[149]

In the medium term there is every reason to believe that these general tendencies will continue to dominate the evolution of Africa, as they have done for the last 20 years.

Notes

1. Useful works on this and other concepts sketched in this chapter include: N. Bukharin, *The Imperialism and World Economy*, (1915; republished New York, Fertig, 1966), Preface by Lenin; V. I. Lenin *Imperialism: the Highest Stage of Capitalism* (various editions); Kwame Nkrumah, *Neo-colonialism: The Last Stage of Imperialism*, (London, Nelson, 1965); Samir Amin, *Accumulation on a World Scale*, (New York, Monthly Review, 1974); Christian Palloix, *L'Economie Mondiale Capitaliste* and *Problemes de la Croissance en Economie Ouverte*, (Paris, Maspero); Pierre Salama, *Le Proces du Sous-Developpement*, (Paris, Maspero).

2. 'Thus, when we study the working of a particular national economy in which a certain mode of production seems to be dominant — for example, the economy of some country in Latin America in which large-scale private land ownership is dominant — we ought not, if we want to arrive at meaningful conclusions, consider this economy otherwise than in *its mode of relations with the modes of production which are dominant on a world scale*; because we cannot understand this national economy if we do not grasp that it is a part of world production relations. It is thus as an integrated structure, for example as a structure dominated by the [North] American economy, that the specificity of development of this economy can be understood.

   'Similarly, the transformations of structure and different stages of transition that a national economy can undergo cannot be analysed in a valid way except by putting these transformations back into the world structural totality.' C. Bettelheim, *The Transition to Socialist Economy*, (Hassocks, Harvester, 1975).

3. 'Hence, the process of the formation of a market for capitalism has two aspects, namely the development of capitalism in depth, i.e. the further growth of capitalist industry and agriculture in a given, definite and enclosed territory; and the development of capitalism in breadth, i.e. the extension of the sphere of capitalist domination to new territories. In accordance with the plan of the present work, we have confined ourselves almost exclusively to the first aspect of the process, and for this reason we consider it particularly necessary to stress that its other aspect is of exceptionally great importance.' V. I. Lenin, *The Development of Captialism in Russia*.

4. See O. C. Cox, *Capitalism as a System*, (New York, Monthly Review, 1964), quoted in S. Amin, *Unequal Development*, (New York, Monthly Review, 1976), p.174.

5.   K. Marx, *Grundrisse*, (London, Penguin, 1973), p.872. Marx goes on
      to add that: 'One of the nations may continually appropriate for itself
      a part of the surplus labour of the other, giving back nothing for it in
      the exchange.'
6.   This was already true in antiquity, when 'the towns of Asia Minor thus
      paid a yearly money tribute to Ancient Rome. With this money Rome
      purchased from them commodities and purchased them too dear. The
      provincials cheated the Romans, and thus got back from their
      conquerors, in the course of trade, a portion of the tribute.' K. Marx,
      Capital, (London, Lawrence and Wishart, 1954), Vol.I, p.160.
      Nowadays, not only do Africans pay tribute in a thousand and one
      different ways, but the imperialist conquerors proffer 'aid' which
      enables them to keep Africans (and dominated peoples generally) in
      perpetual debt. The dominated countries are then forced to pay very
      dearly for goods from the imperialist countries, and are thus rooked
      twice over; the imperialists extort via trade far more than the value of
      the loans and aid they extend. Yet the neo-colonial bourgeoisies are
      still full of praise for these aid programmes.
7.   Adam Smith expressed his law of comparative advantage as follows:
      'If a foreign country can supply us with a commodity cheaper than we
      ourselves can make it, better buy it off them with some part of the
      produce of our own industry, employed in a way in which we have
      some advantage. The general industry of the country, being always in
      proportion to the capital which employs it, will not thereby be
      diminished, no more than that of the above mentioned artificers;
      but only left to find out the way in which it can be employed with the
      greatest advantage. It is certainly not employed to the greatest
      advantage when it is thus directed towards an object which it can buy
      cheaper than it can make.' Adam Smith, *The Wealth of Nations*, Vol.IV,
      (various editions). According to this theory, the presently dominated
      countries should not bother to develop any industries at all, since they
      could buy just about anything that can be bought 'cheaper than we
      ourselves can make it'.
8.   Cf. Karl Marx, *Capital*, Vol.III, Book 1, Chapters 13 and 14. The law
      can be summarized as follows: The total capital 'advanced' by a
      capitalist in any industrial enterprise is, according to Marx, of two kinds.
      On the one hand, there is *constant capital*, that portion of the capital
      which exists in material form as means of production such as machinery,
      raw materials, etc. This capital is constant in the sense that it does not
      directly produce any extra value. On the other hand, there is *variable
      capital*, that portion of the capital which is 'advanced' to the workers
      and which does produce extra value, as we shall see.
          The working day can be broken down into two parts. During the
      first part, the worker merely 'pays back' the capitalist for the wages
      the latter has paid him. But there is also always a second part to the day,
      during which the value produced by the worker's labour goes straight
      into the capitalist's pocket, for free. The work done by the worker
      during this second part is thus quite simply *stolen* from him by the
      capitalist, since the worker is not paid for it. Marx calls the value
      produced by this unpaid labour *surplus value*, and the extra and unpaid

labour of the workers is known as *surplus labour*. The accumulation of values created by the surplus labour of the workers is, in fact, the basis of the capitalist mode of production.

For example, in an eight-hour working day, the salary paid to the worker will be the equivalent of, say, five hours, in which case the remaining three hours supplied by the worker will be surplus labour, and the value produced during those three hours will be the surplus value pocketed by the bourgeois. The relationship between necessary labour (which reproduces the worker's salary) and surplus labour is, naturally, not fixed. It varies according to the balance of forces in the permanent class struggle waged between the capitalist class (the bourgeoisie) and the workers.

Let S stand for surplus value, V for variable capital and C for constant capital. Marx defines the rate of surplus value R, as the ratio of S over V, in the formula $R=S/V$. Marx goes on to define the rate of profit as the ratio of surplus value over the whole capital. This can be expressed as the rate of profit, $P=S/C+V$. Naturally, $C+V$ represents the total sum of capital involved. The rate of surplus value is the amount of surplus value divided by the sum of the variable capital, whereas the rate of profit is the amount of surplus value divided by the sum total of all the capital. The rate of surplus value is thus always greater than the rate of profit. But it is the rate of surplus value which expresses the exact degree of exploitation suffered by the worker, since it expresses the ratio between what has been stolen from the worker (surplus value, S) and what the capitalist has given him, his salary, V.

Given the definition of R, the rate of surplus value, it follows that S, the surplus value, equals R, the rate of surplus value, multiplied by V, the variable capital paid to the worker.
$P=S/C+V : R=S/V : S=R.V$. If we replace S by $R.V$ in the formula which defines P, the rate of profit, we get the relation $P=(RxV)/C+V$ which can also be expressed as $P=RxV/C+V$, or $P=R. (1/1+(C/V))$.

Assuming a constant rate of surplus value, R; if C increases compared to V, then the ratio C over V increases. The denominator in the expression P above increases and the fraction diminishes, since its numerator, 1, remains constant. Since we have assumed that R, the rate of surplus value, is constant, then P as a whole also diminishes. However, this fall is only tendential. Marx has pinpointed many countervailing tendencies to this falling rate of profit. Indeed, we can express his observations in the following law: for a given level of exploitation of constant labour (that is to say with a fixed rate of surplus value), the rate of profit has a tendency to fall as constant capital, C, increases relative to variable capital, V. Marx has also shown that, as the capitalist mode of production develops, constant capital increases relative to variable capital (as Marx puts it, the organic composition of capital increases). The law of the tendency of the rate of profit to fall is thus an inherent feature of the capitalist mode of production.

What does it mean to say that constant capital increases relative to variable capital? Quite simply that the portion of capital which takes the material form of machinery, etc., increases relative to the portion which is set aside for the worker's wages. It is a way of saying that the productivity of labour increases. Marx concluded that the tendency for the rate of profit to fall was simply the way progress in the social productivity of labour was expressed under the capitalist mode of production. It is, therefore, not at all surprising that this tendency for the rate of profit to fall should be so much more marked in the more industrialized capitalist countries, and that the imperialists should try to find a way around it by exporting capital to countries where, because of the shortage of machinery, the productivity of labour is still low and increases more slowly than in the economically developed capitalist countries.

9. A simple example: from 1957 to 1964 the U.S. invested about $14,000 million abroad. Over the same period, they withdrew about $27,000 million, in *net profits*, from the countries which they invested in. They therefore took back *twice* what they had put in. The average rate of profit was thus about 200%! But let us suppose that, instead of considering all the foreign countries in which the U.S. invested, we consider only the underdeveloped countries. We then see that, in 1966, the U.S. invested some $500 million in the countries concerned. During that same year, the U.S. withdrew $2,500 million in profits, *five* times what they invested. The average rate of profit was thus 500%. See Ahmed Akkache, *Capitaux Etrangers et Liberation Economique*, (Paris, Maspero, 1971), pp.22-3.

10. K. Marx, *Capital*, Vol.III (London, Lawrence and Wishart, 1974), p.237.
11. K. Marx, *Capital*, Vol.III, op.cit., p.256. 'If capital is sent abroad, this is not done because it absolutely could not be applied at home, but because it can be applied at a higher rate of profit in a foreign country.'
12. The rate of surplus value is in fact very high in these parts of the world. Salaries are very low. In a country like Gabon, to which the misleading estimates of U.S. exports attribute a yearly *per capita* income of $3,000 (a sum which no Gabonese worker or peasant ever sees), the minimum guaranteed industrial wage is $120, and this in one of the French industrialists' supposedly wealthy 'oil provinces'.
13. Karl Marx, *Capital*, Vol.III, op.cit., p.238.
14. See the Algerian paper, *El Moudjahid*, No. 723, 16 October 1967.
15. The figures are from Nkrumah's *Neo-colonialism: the Last Stage of Imperialism*, op.cit., p.58, quoting V. Perlo, *American Imperialism*, p.28.
16. Lenin's masterful work, *Imperialism: the Highest Stage of Capitalism*, published in 1916, explains the contradictions which led to the 1914-18 War.
17. Kwame Nkrumah, op.cit., p.61.
18. See *Marches Tropicaux et Mediterraneens*, 23 November 1973, p.3,408.
19. Karl Marx, *Capital*, Vol.III, op.cit., p.484.
20. Paul A. Baran, *The Political Economy of Growth*, (New York, Monthly Review, 1957). See also P. A. Baran and P. M. Sweezy, *Monopoly Capital*, (New York, Monthly Review), and Charles Bettelheim, *Planification et Croissance Acceleree*, (Paris, Maspero, 1973), Chapter 5.
21. 'The old imperialism levied tribute: the new imperialism lends money at interest', as H. N. Braisford put it in his *The War of Steel and Gold*,

published over 60 years ago.

22. N. Bukharin, *Imperialism and World Economy*, op.cit., p.138.
23. Having originally actively supported Angolan puppets such as UNITA, the FNLA and FLEC, the French bourgeoisie suddenly decided to recognize the People's Republic of Angola, against the advice of their E.E.C. allies. A little while later, this same bourgeoisie co-operated with the U.S. to save Mobutu.
24. S. Amin, *Unequal Development*, op.cit., p.160.
25. Ibid., p.159.
26. See Christian Palloix, *L'Economie Mondiale Capitaliste,* op.cit., Vol.II, pp.193-4.
27. In *Capital*, Marx quotes F. J. Dunning to point out that capital may fear disorder but will venture into criminal discord if the profits to be won are high enough.
28. Yet, in April 1974, Senghor was promising that 'conditions will be laid down to regulate polluting industries', *Marches Tropicaux et Mediterraneens*, 19 April 1974, p.1,069.
29. See Gerard Destannes de Bernis, 'Industries Industrialisantes et contenu d'une politique d'Integration Regionale' in *Economie Appliquee*, Vol.XIX, 1966, p.415-73.
30. See Arghiri Emmanuel, *Unequal Exchange*, (New York, Monthly Review, 1972).
31. Samir Amin, *Neo-colonialism in West Africa*, (Harmondsworth, Penguin, 1973).
32. See Note 8 above.
33. Otto Bauer, *Die Nationalitatenfrage und die Sozialdemokratie*, (Vienna, 1924). Bauer's subsequent opportunism does not invalidate this point.
34. Christian Palloix, *Problemes de la Croissance en Economie Ouverte*, op.cit., p.84.
35. Karl Marx, *Capital*, Vol.III, op.cit., p.215.
36. See P. Florian, 'Emmanuel chez les philistins', *Critique de l'Economie Politique* (a Trotskyist journal published in Paris), No.3, 1971.
37. Samir Amin, *Unequal Exchange*, op.cit.
38. A. Emmanuel, *Unequal Exchange*, (London, New Left Books, 1972), p.264.
39. The minimum industrial wage in Holland was £340 a month in 1977. In West Germany, a road sweeper earns more than £500 a month.
40. Only Japan lags behind in this respect.
41. See Christian Palloix, *L'Economie Mondiale Capitaliste*, op.cit., Vol.I, p.131.
42. The fact that the bourgeoisie of the imperialist countries appropriates for its exclusive use the bulk of the values stolen in this way does not really come into it. Naturally, internationalist militants in the dominated countries are fully aware that pillage by unequal exchange benefits mainly and primarily the bourgeoisie in the imperialist countries. Were we to forget this truth, we would end up with an absurd strategy based on a clash of interests between the workers of the dominated countries and the workers of the imperialist countries, to the delight of our common enemies.
But it is also worth remembering that: 'The receipt of high

monopoly profits by the capitalists in one of the numerous branches
of industry, in one of the numerous countries, etc., makes it economically possible for them to bribe certain sections of the workers and,
for a time, a fairly considerable minority of them, and win them to
the side of the bourgeoisie of a given industry or given nation against
all the others . . . . And so there is created that bond between imperialism
and opportunism, which revealed itself first and most clearly in Great
Britain, owing to the fact that certain features of imperialist development were observable there much earlier than in other countries.' V. I.
Lenin, *Imperialism: the Highest Stage of Capitalism*, Selected Works,
(Moscow, Progress, 1963), p.765.

Although we should never confuse the imperialist bourgeoisie
with the workers of the dominant countries, no one can prevent us
observing that the following is still as relevant today as when Engels
wrote it, in a letter to Marx on 7 October 1878: 'The English proletariat
is actually becoming more and more bourgeois, so that this most
bourgeois of all nations is apparently aiming ultimately at the possession
of a bourgeois aristocracy and a bourgeois proletariat *alongside* the
bourgeoisie. For a nation which exploits the whole world this is, of
course, to a certain extent justifiable.'

On 12 September 1882, Engels wrote to Karl Kautsky, who had
asked 'what the English workers think about colonial policy', 'The
workers gaily share the feast of England's monopoly of the world
market and the colonies.'

43. Karl Marx, *Histoire des Doctrines Economiques* (Costes), Vol.7,.
p.93. The reader will thus not be surprised to learn that: 'The profits
realized abroad by American multinationals rose from $500 million in
1950 to $3,700 million in 1973 and to an estimated $10,000 million
in 1974.' See A. Faire in Y. Fitt, A. Faire, and J. P. Vigier, *The World
Economic Crisis*, (London, Zed Press, 1980).
44. For instance, the Trotskyist journal mentioned in Note 36.
45. Samir Amin, *Accumulation on a World Scale*, op.cit., p.72.
46. See A. Akkache, op.cit., p.44.
47. *Marches Tropicaux . . .*, 10 May 1974, p.1,237.
48. Senghor also helped France set up its notorious Inter-African Strike
Force.
49. Christian Palloix, *L'Economie Mondiale Capitaliste*, op.cit., Vol.I,
p.41.
50. MIFERGUI-NIMBA is made up of various European and Japanese
companies, in association with Guinea-Conakry, Liberia, Nigeria and
Algeria. Its purpose is to mine the iron ore deposits in Guinea's Nimba
Mountains. Expected production, starting in 1977, is expected to reach
15 million tons of high grade ore a year. More recently, Guinea has
been actively inviting capital from the most reactionary Arab countries.
51. Cameroon, for instance, has only just managed to create a National
Maritime Transport Company after 15 years of independence. And
even now, most of the senior staff is still German. Cameroon withdrew
from the neo-colonial airline, *Air Afrique*, controlled by France's U.T.A.,
only to put itself into the hands of *Air France*. Although CAMAIR is to
some extent Cameroonized, it is mainly used for the frivolous pleasures

of the bourgeoisie.
52. *Marches Tropicaux* . . ., 23 March 1973, p.856.
53. Ibid., p.885.
54. Ibid., 15 March 1974, p.656.
55. Karl Marx, *Capital*, op.cit., Vol.I, chapters 26 to 31. The chapters of *Capital* dealing with primitive accumulation are a brilliant expose of the mechanisms of theft and pillage instituted by the bourgeoisie.
56. Cf. Samir Amin, *Unequal Development*, op.cit.
57. Cf. Andre Gunder-Frank, *The Development of Underdevelopment*, (New York, Monthly Review).
58. Mobutu sided with nazi South Africa and supported the puppet FNLA and UNITA movements.
59. V. I. Lenin, *The Development of Capitalism in Russia*, op.cit., Vol.3, p.67.
60. V. I. Lenin, *A Characterization of Economic Romanticism*, Collected Works, Vol.2, Moscow, Progress, 1963, p.209.
61. *Marches Tropicaux* . . ., 15 March 1974, p.666.
62. Karl Marx, *Capital*, Vol.III, op.cit., p.637.
63. V. I. Lenin, *The Development of Capitalism in Russia*, op.cit., p.40.
64. The history of German expropriation of the people of Cameroon culminated in the murder of Chief Duala Manga in August 1914. Chief Duala Manga led the struggle of the Duala people against expropriation. In Germany only Rosa Luxemburg and her group condemned the silence of the German socialists over this affair. See also V. I. Lenin's article *On the Junius Pamphlet*.
65. See B. Etahoben, 'Cameroon: "Green Revolution" fails to develop farming', *New African Development*, September 1977, p.915.
66. See *Marches Tropicaux* . . ., 5 October 1973, p.2,952.
67. See *l'Effort Camerounais*, No. 879, September 1973 and No. 880, October 1973, for extracts from Tonye Mbog's press conference. The latter was at the time Ahidjo's Minister of Youth.
68. While the young people of Cameroon rot in unemployment, Ahidjo's CONAJEPCA (National Youth and Popular Education Committee), set up by presidential decree in 1967, contents itself with singing the praises of its creator, 'His Excellency, El Hadj'. Perhaps the regime needs to give itself the illusion that it is not backed only by a handful of self-seeking opportunists.
69. Mbog had the face to announce that in the face of this chronic unemployment 'the Government has bravely decided to do something for these young people, so that their unemployed capacities should be put to use to promote their own material well-being.
70. Even Amnesty International's report on political prisoners in Cameroon was reported only in *Le Monde*.
71. The C.F.A. franc is linked to the French franc by a fixed parity. 1 French franc = 50 CFA francs. The parity has not changed since 1959. A pseudo revolt launched by some neo-colonial African regimes against this situation fizzled out back in 1974-75.
72. A striking contrast with the nonsense put out by *Wife*, the journal of Ahidjo's puppet women's organization, OFUNC. See *Wife*, June 1973, p.12.

Africa's Economy and World Capitalism Since 1960

73. The joke gains in the telling: In April 1974, a colloquium on education, attended by 73 representatives of the Protestant Churches, in Cameroon, concluded that: 'The cost of keeping one pupil in secondary education in Cameroon is at present eight times the average income of a farm worker.' The peasantry represents some 80% of the total population. Yet the Baptist pastors of Douala present Ahidjo as God's gift to Cameroon. For details of this alliance between the Protestant and Catholic clergy (notably the reactionary Archbishop of Yaounde) with the regime, see *Resistance*, No. 16-17, U.P.C., January 1975.

74. See 'A travers le Kamerun', *Cahiers Upecistes*, April 1974, and *Resistance*, Nos. 14 and 15, 1974.

75. Declaration made by Ayissi Mvodo to the assembled Administrative Council of the Social Welfare Fund, of which he was President, February 1974.

76. El Hadj Birawandu Ahmadou Ahidjo, *Pour la Revolution Verte*, (Imprimerie Nationale, 1973).

77. Figures based on *Marches Tropicaux . . .*, August 1973, pp.2,519-20.

78. Ibid., February 1974, p.443.

79. While Houphouet forces Ivory Coast diamond miners to work solid eight-hour shifts in the Korogho mines for £40 a month, the *European volunteers* he invites are paid £600 a month. And Houphouet has no qualms about building himself palaces of imported European marble.

80. *Marches Tropicaux . . .*, 12 April 1974, p.1,011.

81. Ibid., 5 April 1974, p.951.

82. Ibid., pp.954-5.

83. Ibid.

84. Ahidjo, on the other hand, believes in 'planned liberalism' in which the use of productive resources for profit is seen as a progressive element. See Third Plan, 1971-76, Planning Ministry, (Yaounde, 1973), p.40.

85. *Marches Tropicaux . . .*, 5 April 1974, p.954.

86. Ibid., 10 November 1978, p.2,977. Corruption in Kenya is legendary.

87. Samir Amin, *Unequal Development*, op.cit., p.352.

88. *Marches Tropicaux . . .*, 17 January 1975, p.352

89. B. Ryelandt, *L'inflation en Pays Sous-developpe*.

90. Samir Amin, *Accumulation on a World Scale*, op.cit., Vol.II, p.464. There can be no doubt that, in a country such as Cameroon, the real buying power of the population has steadily declined since 1960. In real terms the price paid to a peasant for a kilo of 'Robusta superieur' coffee has fallen by about 50% in five years. See *Marches Tropicaux . . .*, 29 October 1976, p.2,900.

91. The Zairean bourgeoisie was not being particularly innovative: 'The traditional policy of ruthless direct exactions from the peasants was supplemented by a number of other devices calculated to maximize the aggregate economic surplus. Wages of workers employed in non-agricultural activities were rigorously held down to rock bottom — a principle that was easy to enforce in a labour market glutted with agricultural surplus population. Even more important was the systematic inflationary policy initiated by the Meiji administration, which resulted not merely in further redistribution of income in favour

of capital accumulation but also in expansion of the economic surplus
through the utilization of previously unemployed resources.' Paul A.
Baran, *The Political Economy of Growth*, op.cit., p.155. All this took
place in Japan around 1870-90, when the Emperor initiated the changes
which were to lead to the development of capitalism in Japan. Same
aim, same methods.

92. In Mauritius, which is a full member of OCAM, 'The number of
unemployed is increasing by 10,000 each year (total employed 200,000,
total population 800,000, of whom 54% are under 18). Salaries are very
low. An unskilled worker gets a 100 francs (£10) a month, a semi-
skilled worker receives 300 francs (£30). Employers have no social
security contributions to pay.' See *Usine Nouvelle*, the journal of the
French bosses, No. 39, 24 September 1970, 'L'ile Maurice sera-t-elle
un nouveau Hong Kong?' Under Sir Sewoosagur Ramgoolam, Mauritius
sold the island of Diego Garcia to the U.K. which in turn rents it to the
U.S. as a military base. Mauritius has also become a playground for
white South African tourists.

93. See Friedrich Engels, *The Condition of the Working Class in England*,
and Karl Marx, *Capital*, Vol.I, Chapters 10, 15, 25 to 31 for striking
descriptions of the appalling poverty which prevailed in Europe at the
time.

94. Karl Marx, *Capital*, Vol.I.

95. V. I. Lenin, *On the So-Called Market Question*, Collected Works, Vol.I,
op.cit., p.102.

96. See *Marches Tropicaux . . .*, 23 February 1979, p.512.

97. Ahidjo and his ilk may call for 'auto-centric development', but in their
mouths the slogan becomes meaningless verbiage. See his 'Report' to
the 2nd U.N.C. Congress, February 1975.

98. Samir Amin, *Accumulation on a World Scale*, op.cit., p.289.

99. *Marches Tropicaux . . .*, 4 May 1973, p.1,241.

100. *Afrique Industries Informations*, No. 43, November 1973, p.46.

101. At the end of a no doubt most enjoyable safari in the forests of the
Central Africa 'Empire', the French President once promised Bokassa
a railway. The people are still waiting.

102. *Marches Tropicaux . . .*, 26 April 1974, p.1,135.

103. Ibid., p.1,136.

104. Gerard Destannes de Bernis, 'Industries Industrialisantes et contenu
d'une politique d'integration regionale', *Economie Appliquee*, Paris,
Vol.XIX, pp.415-73, 1966. De Bernis says: 'I refer to these industries
or groups of industries whose fundamental economic function is to
transform the inter-industrial matrix around them, transforming the
functions of production by making new machines available to industry
as a whole and thereby increasing productivity and man's mastery
over his production and his products. These transformations in turn
lead to a social and economic restructuring, to a transformation of what
can be done in the given context and to a renewal of social structures;
they thereby constitute both a pre-condition and a consequence of the
industrialization process.'

105. Anybody who goes to Edea cannot but be struck by the isolation of
the Pechiney complex. The staff live in a sort of encampment and

management strives to limit all contact between officials (including the Cameroonian ones) and workers. After 20 years, the Cameroonian state still has a disgracefully small stake in Alucam-Pechiney's capital.

106. The authors of the second and third plan are Mlle Etienne and M. G. Winter, respectively: Ahidjo obviously has more confidence in French 'experts' than his French masters do.

107. E. Teilhac, 'Le petrole dans l'Economie du Moyen Orient', *Economie Appliquee*, No. 4, 1954, pp.399-489. Appearances to the contrary notwithstanding, this observation still holds good today.

108. Nkrumah, *Neo-Colonialism: The Last Stage of Imperialism*, op.cit., p.1.

109. *Marches Tropicaux . . .*, 15 March 1974, p.657.

110. Nkrumah, op.cit., p.2.

111. *Marches Tropicaux . . .*, 8 March 1974, p.618.

112. Cheikh Anta Diop, *Les Fondements Economiques et Culturels d'un Etat Federal d'Afrique Noire*, (Paris, Presence Africaine, 1974), p.57.

113. Jagdish C. Saigal, 'Reflexions sur la theorie de l'echange inegal', in S. Amin, *Unequal Development*, op.cit., N.B. Saigal refers to 'capitalist relations of production *and trade*'.

114. See Cheikh Anta Diop, op.cit.

115. At first, the imperialists shed gallons of crocodile tears over the millions of pounds African countries would thus have to pay the Arabs. It was only later that they realized that perhaps setting Arabs and Africans against one another was not such a good idea, since Arab reaction was fully prepared to ally itself with neo-colonialism against Black Africa.

116. *Marches Tropicaux . . .*, 30 March 1973, p.915.

117. In the end, the Lagos authorities preferred to drop their initial position in exchange for the flattering role of sole spokesman for the African nations at the Second Yaounde Convention. The West European neo-colonialists thus managed to enroll nearly all the countries of Africa, the Caribbean and the Pacific, now conveniently known as the A.C.P. countries.

118. *Marches Tropicaux . . .*, 6 April 1973, p.977.

119. Ibid., 2 March 1973, p.661.

120. Ibid., 5 April 1974, p.955.

121. Ibid., 17 January 1975, p.159.

122. Ibid., 1 June 1973, p.1,485. What marvellous demagogy!

123. Ibid., 11 January 1974, p.84.

124. See *Unite*, the official journal of Ahidjo's fascist U.N.C., 2 February 1974, p.4.

125. *Marches Tropicaux . . .*, 8 March 1974, p.598.

126. OCAM has in fact never been anything more than a head of state's trade union, camouflaging the exploitation of African workers by African bourgeoisies and French neo-colonialism. One of its main roles has always been to sink any moves towards genuine African unity, a role now played to the full by the O.A.U. OCAM is now useless to its masters, precisely because the O.A.U. has taken over its functions as an active brake on African unification, notably by neutralizing those who struggle against established regimes.

127. *Marches Tropicaux . . .*, 11 May 1973, p.1,295.

128. Ibid.
129. In 1958-59, he and Houphouet even defended the French position on Algeria at the U.N., right in the middle of the Algerian people's war of liberation. These things get forgotten too easily.
130. It has long been common knowledge that Mobutu is a C.I.A. agent. His vaunted 'anti-hegemonism' and 'non-alignment' are simply examples of just how far cynicism and hypocrisy can be pushed today in the international arena.
131. *Marches Tropicaux* . . .,2 March 1973, pp.661-2.
132. See *Le Monde*, 22-23 July 1973, p.20.
133. *Marches Tropicaux* . . ., 25 May 1973, p.1,436.
134. Ibid., 9 March 1973, p.737.
135. Samir Amin, *Accumulation* . . ., op.cit., p.128.
136. *Marches Tropicaux* . . ., 23 March 1973, p.884.
137. See the Minimum Programme for a United Front in *Proclamation Commune*, 16 December 1960. Quoted in *Le Courant du Manidem*, I, U.P.C., (1974), p.11.
138. *Marches Tropicaux* . . ., 20 July 1973, p.2,282. A new agreement later gave Nigeria a 55% stake (Cf. Ibid., 26 April 1974, p.1,137).
139. Thus, in Nigeria, there has been 'extensive liberalization affecting a wide range of articles, notably foodstuffs, meat, fresh fruit, beer, whisky, rum and other alcoholic drinks which had been tightly controlled if not banned outright'. (*Marches Tropicaux* . . ., 19 April 1974, p.1,076). Any comparison between the list of freely imported products and the prevailing average salaries in the country makes it clear who this measure was intended to serve.
140. Friedrich Engels, *Anti-Duhring*, (Peking, Foreign Languages Press, 1976), pp.358-59.
141. 'Socialist' Algeria's Agrarian Reform Charter states that: 'Although the agrarian revolution does not abolish private ownership of the means of production, it does abolish man's exploitation of his fellow man.'
142. Engels, *Anti-Duhring*, op.cit., pp.358-9.
143. Karl Marx and Friedrich Engels, *The German Ideology*, (New York, International Publishers, 1970), p.66.
144. Ibid., p.65.
145. V. I. Lenin, *The Proletarian Revolution and the Renegade Kautsky*, op.cit., Vol.28, p.252.
146. See the *Third 5-year Economic and Social Development Plan*, Ministry of Planning, (Yaounde), p.40.
147. *Marches Tropicaux* . . ., 15 February 1974, p.373.
148. Ibid., 8 March 1974, p.518.
149. Kwame Nkrumah, *Neo-Colonialism: the Last Stage of Imperialism*, op.cit., p.31.

3. The Politics of Pan African Demagogy in Practice

Emerging Contradictions Between Neo-Colonial Bourgeoisies and Imperialism

Around 1972-73, a bizarre fever took hold of many observers of the African political scene. The sickness developed to near malignant proportions. Everybody fell prey to the illusion that important changes were taking place in the policies of several neo-colonial African regimes. First, it was Ould Daddah's Mauritania, which withdrew from OCAM and then from the Franc Zone. Next, Ahidjo the drunkard established diplomatic relations with the People's Republic of China and the Royal Government of National Union in Cambodia.[1] Some time later, he also announced his country's withdrawal from OCAM since, as he put it, he had discovered that its aims were contrary to the interests of Cameroon (such clarity of thought!). Finally, Leopold Germanicus Senghor, not wishing to be left out, noisily announced that he was going to recognize the Provisional Revolutionary Government of South Vietnam. Shortly afterwards, vying with each other in this belated 'nationalism', nearly all the puppets of French neo-colonialism called for a revision of the unequal treaties they had signed ten years before with their masters and which had, until then, been presented as expressions of 'African wisdom and of France's eternal friendship with Africa'. What was really going on?

Conditions were increasingly ripe for the emergence of contradictions between the African neo-colonial bourgeoisies and their imperialist masters and allies.

The transition from classical colonialism to neo-colonialism implied the need for imperialism to promote the ascendancy of a local bourgeoisie which could be entrusted with the running of the state apparatus and the exercise of a direct class dictatorship over the African workers. Within limits defined by the overall interests of international finance capital, imperialism was forced to allow this African bourgeoisie to play the role of a pseudo national bourgeoisie. The contradictions inherent in imperialism's own strategy meant that this African bourgeoisie had to be given a little bit of room for manoeuvre within the neo-colonial economic system.

This introduction of local capital, even on a very limited scale, could not but lead to some sort of accumulation, given that concentration of capital is inevitable in a 'competitive' African economy, especially with the prevailing rates of profit. Local capital was thus bound to find itself up against imperialist capital — in a very weak position, of course, but nonetheless a factor to be reckoned with. The African bourgeoisies eventually wanted a larger slice of the cake produced by the African workers. In other words, when we see African bourgeoisies standing up to the monopolies, it is essentially because it is in their own interests to limit, but even then not eliminate, the exploitation of the country as a 'national community'; this, of course, is very different from being opposed to the exploitation of the workers — which the African bourgeoisie is not.

This is the real meaning behind what has been called the contradiction between imperialism and its allies, the neo-colonial African bourgeoisies. The African bourgeoisies are convinced that 'nothing can be done against monopoly capital, it is too strong, too well organized'. Consequently, they are only seeking a better position on the chessboard of world capitalism. Their struggle for a 'second independence' is thus little more than a second piece of trickery. They are trying to draw the African workers into a *fool's crusade* which would use the strength of the African masses to obtain concessions from the imperialists which would benefit only the African bourgeoisies, and would, in fact, lead to even fiercer exploitation of the African workers, both by imperialist capital and by this bourgeoisie.

This 'Formal' Dispute Between Bourgeoisies: The Example of Chad

During 1973-74, there was a striking example of this type of 'formal' dispute between bourgeoisies which are fundamentally in agreement. For several months, especially in 1973, Francois Tombalbaye and his followers in Chad were constantly denouncing imperialism. He even launched the famous formula stating that co-operation = colonialism = hypocrisy. Some people were led to believe that Tombalbaye was 'going red'. Yet on 28 January 1974, 'an important French delegation, led by Mr. Robert Puissant, technical adviser to the French Secretary of State for Foreign Affairs, arrived in Ndjamena, Chad. Then, on 31 January, shortly before midnight, the French Secretary of State, Francois Deniau, arrived in Ndjamena for three days of talks with his Chadian opposite number on the 'implementation of the 1960 co-operation agreements and several other economic and social matters'. Deniau actually stayed for five days rather than three, and only left on 4 February, after having been received twice by Tombalbaye. On 8 February, a joint communique informed African and world public opinion that, in fact, there had never been more than 'certain misunderstandings' between the two countries. Indeed, the Franco-Chadian Commission, convened for the occasion

> sought particularly to dissipate certain misunderstandings which were making any effective implementation of the co-operation agreements difficult. . . . Franco-Chadian co-operation will now be got underway by a strict implementation of these agreements.

The French delegation 'was pleased with the atmosphere of open collaboration [*sic*!] which prevailed during the Commission's activities.' The Chadian delegation expressed 'its satisfaction at seeing the co-operation [i.e. colonialism and hypocrisy. E.M.] between the two countries thus reinforced, and thanked the French authorities for the spirit of understanding which had characterized the Commission's meetings.[2]

All of which becomes perfectly understandable when one realizes that French civil and military technical assistance was on offer:

The desired staff levels for 1974 were worked out and outlined in an agreement between the two parties. The Chadian delegation presented a variety of projects as suitable for funding by the Aid and Co-operation Fund. The French delegation agreed in principle to some of these, while others were referred for further study.[3]

The objective necessity for the African bourgeoisies to make common cause manifests itself on two levels. First, they have to cope with the various imperialisms and contradictions inherent in that relationship, as outlined above. This tendency for the African bourgeoisies to 'struggle' against their masters is itself full of contradictions and conditioned by contingencies, given the level of imperialist domination over Africa. The example of the bourgeois ruling clique in Chad and all the other puppets of French neo-colonialism is particularly revealing, especially when it comes to currency questions. Second, the bourgeois bureaucrats who rule nearly all the African countries are forced to develop a class solidarity amongst themselves which comes into full play against the working class and poorer peasantry of Africa.

The conditions which prevailed during the first two decades of formal independence have led the neo-colonial African bourgeoisie to concentrate on breaking the working class and its revolutionary organizations. This development is, in fact, linked to the conditions under which these bourgeoisies came to power, often under the direct protection of colonialist troops deployed against African patriots. By now, most African workers have been dragooned into bourgeois and often plainly fascist trade unions. The African bourgeoisies could not conduct their affairs as they chose if the workers were free to hound them through constant struggle. Furthermore, there could be no joint demands made on imperialism if each state supported workers' struggles in neighbouring countries.

Impact on the O.A.U.
In short, the regrouping of the various semi-continental organizations of 1958-62 (the Casablanca and Monrovia-Lagos-Brazzaville blocs) into a single body, the O.A.U., is primarily the result of an awareness amongst all the African neo-colonial bourgeoisies of their need for a reactionary class alliance. The so-called 'advanced', 'non-aligned', 'anti-imperialist' political and

diplomatic positions of the O.A.U. which are so lauded by sundry opportunists searching for a market and prepared to tell the African people any lie required to secure that market, are thus only expressions of the African bourgeoisies' class consciousness. Such positions merely express the African bourgeoisies' awareness that they should perhaps try to free themselves a little from the claws of their imperialist masters and creators. But, of course, there is still a vast difference between knowing and doing.

One of the more amusing aspects of this contradiction was clearly illustrated during the 1974 O.A.U. crisis concerning the initiatives of the Secretary-General of the organization. Mr. Nzo Ekha Ngaky, who was soon replaced by his colleague and compatriot Eteki Mboumoua, had actually managed to sign an agreement with·Lonrho (London and Rhodesian Mining and Land Company) which authorized Lonrho to act as consultant to the O.A.U. member states affected by the oil embargo launched a few months previously. Lonrho was to advise and assist these states in consultation with their governments. Ekha Ngaky decided that the nature of Lonrho as an organization was irrelevant. It did not matter that Lonrho was a sizeable economic group of companies with important interests in Africa, where it operates in about 15 independent countries. At the time, Lonrho held stakes in the Ashanti Gold Mines in Ghana, various mines in Rhodesia, direct and indirect holdings in West Africa and South Africa, a majority holding in the biggest platinum mine in the Transvaal, the Western Platinum Mine, holdings in Mozambique, which was still under Portuguese colonial domination, etc. Lonrho has maintained its presence in a wide variety of African countries to this day. In short, Lonrho is one of the octopus-like organizations which organize the survival of racist and colonial domination over the peoples of Southern Africa. It is precisely the sort of body the O.A.U. and the African heads of state claim to detest and fight against constantly, as Ahidjo Birawandu reiterated at the May 1974 Yaounde session of the O.A.U. Liberation Committee. Ahidjo's progressive qualities are so well appreciated by his O.A.U. colleagues, and his regime is deemed by them to be so committed to a merciless struggle against 'the colonialists, the zionists, the racists, the Lonrhos of this world' that they twice appointed Ahidjo's candidate as Secretary-General of the O.A.U. After all, perhaps it was just an accident that in 1973 Ahidjo's Government set up a *Societe Nationale Industrielle et Commerciale du Cameroun*, in which Lonrho was one of the substantial shareholders.

In his masterly analysis of the economic foundations of neo-colonialism in Africa — a work which Amilcar Cabral described as 'a profound materialist analysis of the terrible reality of neo-colonialism in Africa'[4] — President Kwame Nkrumah illustrated the nature of companies like Lonrho as follows (the quotation is long but extremely instructive):

> Mr. Kiek is chairman of Chicago-Gaika Development Co. Ltd., a company existing since 1897 and having 17 gold claims in the Sebakwe district of Matabeleland, Rhodesia, which was at one time within the jurisdiction of the British South Africa Company. Mr. Kiek's other

associations are with the London & Rhodesian Mining and Land Co. Ltd., owning directly 384 gold-mining claims, base-metal claims and lands covering 757,000 acres in Rhodesia. Some of the properties are leased on a royalty basis, and ranching operations are also carried on.

Subsidiary companies of London & Rhodesian include Mazoe Consolidated Mines Ltd., Lonrho Exploration Co. Ltd. and African Investment Trust Ltd., which took over all the company's investments in 1958, except shares in subsidiaries and trade investments. Its associates include Arcturus Mines Ltd., Homestake Gold Mining Co. Ltd., Coronation Syndicate Ltd. and North Charterland Exploration Co. (1937) Ltd. Among further interests acquired by London & Rhodesian in 1961 were 90% of Consolidated Holdings (Pvt) Ltd., 100% of Mashaba Gold Mines (Pvt) Ltd., which operates the Empress Gold Mine at Mashaba, near Fort Victoria, Rhodesia, 36 2/3 % of Kanyemba Gold Mines and 51% of Associated Overland Pipelines of Rhodesia (Pvt) Ltd., in exchange for 1,500,000 shares in London & Rhodesian and an option on another 2 million.

That London & Rhodesian Mining comes within the Oppenheimer Group interests there can be no doubt, despite the separate front that is kept up.[5]

The reader may wonder what is this Oppenheimer Group with which Ahidjo and the neo-colonial bourgeoisie have allied themselves through Lonrho's participation in the *Societe Nationale Industrielle et Commerciale du Cameroun*. Kwame Nkrumah explains:

The king of mining in South Africa, indeed in Africa, is Harry Frederick Oppenheimer. One might even call him the king of South Africa, even the emperor, with an ever-extending empire. There is hardly a corner of Southern Africa's industrial and financial structure in which he has not got a very extended finger of his own or the hook of some affiliate or associate . . . .

Mr. Harry Frederick Oppenheimer is Director, Chairman or President of some 70 companies. Dominating this complex of companies are the Anglo-American Corporation of South Africa Ltd. and Consolidated Gold Fields of South Africa Ltd. (p.110)

Dominant in South Africa's economy is the Anglo-American/De Beers Group, part of the empire of Harry Oppenheimer which extends into South West Africa and Zambia, and is linked with mining companies in many other African states. (p.120)

Biggest octopus in the Oppenheimer sea of operations is probably the Anglo-American Corporation Ltd . . . . Gold, uranium, iron, asbestos and coal mines are among the corporation's most notable undertakings in South Africa, forming the solid foundation on which the Oppenheimer empire stands. Copper mining is the principal occupation in the Rhodesias, though it exploits also lead, zinc and cadmium, and has the distinction of being the only producer of coal in Rhodesia, where it controls the Wankie Colliery. Through associated companies, its interests spread out into Tanganyika, Uganda, the Congo, Angola, Mozambique, West Africa and even into the Sahara and North Africa, as can be seen from this list of direct investments. (p.127) [The list covers the next four pages of the book, and includes 124 companies, E.M.]

Diamonds are a major concern of Mr. Harry Oppenheimer, and it is through De Beers and the Diamond Corporation, with their associated companies and alliances that the operations of his Anglo-American Corporation stretch out from South Africa into South West Africa, Angola, the Congo, East and West Africa, to control until recently the production and sale of pretty well 85% of the world's diamonds. Even the distribution of the Soviet Union's quite important production has been added, by the arrangement to dispose of 'Red' diamonds through De Beers' selling organization. (p.137)[6]

So this is who Ahidjo and his gang are associated with through their links with Lonrho — not that this stops them signing endless communiques condemning apartheid in Southern Africa, or being applauded by opportunists for their 'progressive Pan-Africanism'.

Pan-African Demagogy and Close Relations with Pretoria

It should now be clear why Mr. Nzo Ekah Ngaky was so sensitive about his ties with Lonrho and in such a hurry to explain that his initiative had been approved by several African governments. The existence of relations between the nazis in Pretoria and many of the most reactionary bourgeois cliques in Africa have since become almost common knowledge. Even as early as 1973, the people of Africa did not have to look far to find revelations like this:

West Africa (especially Ivory Coast, Zaire and Gabon) remains an 'open' market for South African trade, despite the suspension over a year ago of the official policy aimed at maintaining a dialogue between the country and the rest of Africa north of the 10th parallel. The point was stressed by M. G. Le Pan de Ligny, a French economist, during a conference on exporting held recently in Johannesburg. M. Le Pan de Ligny told the conference that countries like Ivory Coast, Zaire and Gabon 'have at their disposal the means whereby to sustain a very active trading policy and have already established commercial links with South Africa, including direct air and sea trade routes'.

South Africa continues to maintain regular contacts with certain West African states, notably in terms of investments and technological assistance.

For instance, in Gabon, South Africa, along with France and the Netherlands [those great slave-trading nations of yesterday. E.M.], has a considerable stake in an international consortium which has successfully tendered for the construction of the Trans-Gabonese railway, a project launched by President Albert (Omar) Bongo with an eye to the future development of the economic resources of the Gabonese interior.

Furthermore, an important South African civil engineering company, Roberts Construction, is negotiating with the Gabonese authorities concerning several major infrastructure projects.

During a recent press conference, B. J. Vorster, the South African Prime Minister, insisted that South Africa was maintaining unofficial links with several African countries despite the temporary suspension of the 'dialogue' between them, as defined by Mr. Vorster and President Houphouet-Boigny of Ivory Coast in 1971.[7]

Since that date, there have been several meetings between Houphouet and the South Africans. Until 1974-75, these were kept secret, but now they have become insolently public occasions, held in Switzerland or in Ivory Coast itself. Senghor, Bongo, Tolbert, Bokassa and others of that ilk have also not been loath to entertain such contacts. South Africa has offered substantial export credits to several independent countries such as Ivory Coast, Gabon, the Central African Republic and Zaire, and has participated in various economic projects in many of these countries, for instance in Mauritius. The South Africans also provide countries like Mobutu's Zaire with political-military support. None of this prevents the various heads of state from indulging in wildly demagogic anti-South African diatribes. In 1963, when the O.A.U. was being set up in Addis Ababa, Houphouet proclaimed:

> Faced with the unspeakable behaviour of the Portuguese leaders, their systematic blind refusal to respond to the demands of history, the inhuman suffering inflicted by that country upon our brothers who struggle for the life-breath of freedom, the heroic resistance of the Angolans who fight without arms or backing, the martyrdom of so many others whose grief is an insult to our own liberty and a denial of our own independence, we solemnly declare that our country has overruled our desire for negotiation and has called upon us to seek out, in concert with all of you, the most practical means to put an end to Portugal's criminal stubbornness and to the apartheid which rules in South Africa and which stains the honour of our entire continent.[8]

This combination of demagogy and collaboration with the African people's worst enemies goes hand in hand with an increasingly systematic reactionary struggle against all African revolutionaries who resist the neo-colonial bourgeois regimes. It is highly significant that most African regimes, and especially the most reactionary ones, strive to appear progressive to the outside world while becoming ever more fascist domestically. As we have seen, the problem for these regimes is to find new markets and customers. It is notable that, on the whole, the countries whose underdeveloped economies are the most dynamic — in other words, those whose trade is most likely to

143

develop — are also the most 'dynamic' when it comes to putting on a display of 'progressiveness' to the outside world.

Roots of the Contradiction

The Neo-Colonialist Bourgeoisie's Need for Markets

This need for new markets emerges very clearly when one considers the trade imbalance between a country like France and the whole of Africa from 1970 to 1972, shortly before the neo-colonialist bourgeoisie launched its new broader-based international trading policy.

> France's exports to Africa increased in value terms by 10% from 1970 to 1972. Compared to 1970, France's imports from Africa fell by 8.5% in 1971 and by 1.5% in 1972; French imports as a whole rose by 28% over the same period.
> French imports from African countries outside the Franc Zone have remained almost stable since 1970. On the other hand, French exports to those countries rose by 26.5%.
> Africa accounts for 9.3% of France's imports and is last but one in the list of continents supplying France with goods. By contrast, Africa is France's second largest client (10.4%), slightly above America.[9]

One should remember that oil and minerals account for a decisive share of these African exports to France. This is clear when one considers that France's major African suppliers (in value terms) are Algeria, Libya, Nigeria (oil), Zambia, South Africa, Zaire (minerals) and Gabon (oil and minerals) rather than Senegal or Cameroon.

Thus, it is not surprising that these 'dynamic' African countries should turn to the socialist states of Europe and certain Asian countries in their quest for new markets to conquer. An outward display of 'progressiveness' is essential to the success of this effort. Furthermore, the imperialist countries have a real interest of their own in seeing this tendency develop. The wealth which such trade may provide will inevitably eventually be accumulated in those imperialist countries themselves, given the domination they exercise over their African neo-colonies.[10]

It is worth noting that this whole evolution is favoured by the increasingly prevalent mercantilist trend in world affairs. Those who are committed to the socialist revolution can only conclude that we are witnessing a terrible recrudescence of *economism*, on a scale never seen before.

Economism Criticized

Economism can be defined as an ideological current which claims that the socialist revolution (throughout the world or in a single country) can be accomplished solely, or even essentially, by economic means. In countries with a backward level of capitalist development, such as the African countries today, one variant of this theory goes like this: The socialist revolution can be achieved only by the working class, which is itself a product of capitalism. Therefore, since capitalism leads historically to socialism, it is both necessary and sufficient to develop capitalism in Africa, to industrialize these countries and thereby create a working class which will eventually make a revolution. In this way, socialism is sure to triumph, sooner or later.

This is yet another variant of the theory of historical inevitability, without struggles or efforts. The advocates of economism may, of course, put their case less crudely. They may even condescend to recognize the struggles of the 'young and inexperienced' African proletariat, providing these struggles are for higher wages — in other words, only those struggles pertaining to the domain of economics.

On the world scale, economism consists in asserting that, from now on, the struggle between socialism and capitalism will be fought out only (or mainly) in terms of *economic competition*. The conclusion which flows from this 'theory' is that, in order to develop the economic capacity of the socialist system, there must be a systematic quest for further 'state to state economic relations, with every country in the world, irrespective of social system or any other consideration'. Meanwhile, the capitalist system, be it the imperialists themselves or the neo-colonial dictatorships, are all too insistent that political concessions should accompany trading links.

Nonetheless, despite all the efforts made by African reaction to disguise its real policies, two decisive elements will, in the final analysis, determine the course of the present process, namely, the domination exercised by imperialist capital, on the one hand, and the ever-increasing proletarianization of the African masses, on the other.

The African Bourgeoisie's Weakness in the Face of Imperial Capital

It is now clear that the more and more unitary, integrationist and 'Pan-African' tendencies of the O.A.U. merely express the African bourgeoisies' growing awareness of their weakness in the face of imperialist capital which more or less brought them into being in the first place. Houphouet-Boigny voiced precisely this concern in May 1973 at Addis Ababa, although his choice of words may have misled some people with little grasp of the real motives of the African bourgeoisie at the present time. Why should Houphouet now clamour for Pan-African integration when ten years ago he fought so vehemently against similar projects put forward by Kwame Nkrumah? The French puppet of Abidjan can now be heard declaiming that:

It has become essential for us to concentrate all our attention and efforts towards breaking our ties of economic dependence. . . . We must strive to develop a far more efficacious response to the pressing need for ever more structured and mutually complementary common economic fronts than we have managed in the past. It is high time there were broad-based African groupings capable of making their voices heard at the table of the money giants. We must never forget that our

international negotiating strength is directly proportional to our ability
to define common and hence firm positions concerning the key
commercial and monetary problems.[11]

Houphouet-Boigny, one of the most influential spokesmen for the neo-colonial
bourgeoisies, is naturally also an incurable demagogue. To cut through the
mystifications he generates is not just a matter of exposing him personally;
he stands at the head of his class, and if he can be unmasked, so can the ruling
neo-colonial African bourgeoisie.

According to Houphouet-Boigny, it would seem that it only became
essential to break our ties of dependency in 1973. It would follow that, in
1958 for example, either we were already independent and thus had no need
to struggle to break the ties of our dependency, or we were dependent but
simply did not need independence. The former is historically absurd, the
latter is heresy since 1960, although, as we saw in the first chapter, Houphouet
and his friends were arguing that independence made no sense at all right up to
the moment when it was forced upon them. Another possibility is that
Houphouet is implying that independence was necessary even then, but that
unity and strength were not. Such ignorance of the realities of history would
not be beyond him. For instance, in 1958 this Yamoussoukro demagogue
was arguing that:

> Independence pure and simple runs against the tide of history. The
> paramount issue in the contemporary world is the requirement on the
> part of wealthy countries to provide for the underdeveloped countries
> in a way which does not imply subordination of the latter.[12]

Of course, Houphouet has never offered a single example of a formula
which did not 'imply subordination'. The sort of formulae his boundless
demagogy actually comes up with are invariably along lines similar to the
following example.

> Several mining and steelmaking companies, including the American
> company, Pickands Mather and Co. (a subsidiary of Moor McCormack
> Resources Inc.) and the *Societe pour le Development Minier de la Cote
> d'Ivoire* (Sodemi) have launched a joint project to study the commercial
> potential of the Klahoyo iron deposits near Man (Ivory Coast). The
> investment required is of the order of U.S. $450 million . . . .
>
> If the results of these investigations prove positive, the group
> will then undertake the extraction and treatment of the very large
> iron ore deposits of Mount Klahoyo. The mineral content of the
> deposit is estimated at around *385 million tons of high grade magnetite*.
>
> The mineral will be mined and processed by a company in which
> Mitsubishi Corp. (Japan) would have a 27% stake, British Steel (U.K.)
> a 20% stake, Sumitomo Shoji Kaisha (Japan) a 14% stake, *Union
> Siderurgique du Nord et de l'Est* (France) and Hoogovens Ijmuiden a

10% stake each and, finally, Pickands a 15% stake. The *Societe pour le Development Minier de la Cote d'Ivoire* would hold 5% of the shares.

A spokesman for Pickands recently announced that, if the operation went ahead, the company would be set up in early 1975 and production would begin in 1979 or 1980.[13]

So much for 'broad-based African groupings capable of making their voices heard at the table of the money giants'.

It is all too obvious that it is Houphouet and his friends (Ahidjo, Senghor, etc.) who have consistently 'run against the tide of history'. The same Houphouet who called for 'firm positions' in 1973, once told a French journalist, Andre Blanchet, that such language was simply a reflection of 'that spirit of vengeance against the old colonizing nations which was expressed so clearly at Bandung'.

Fear of Popular Struggles

Meanwhile, the workers' struggles are developing, albeit slowly and in spite of savage and indiscriminate repression. As time goes by, these struggles cannot but become increasingly radical, as is shown by numerous examples. Strike movement and political struggles are developing in Chad, Mauritania, Cameroon (for instance, the major strikes in January 1976 led by U.P.C. militants and MANIDEM activists in the factories of Douala and Yaounde, involving several thousand workers and effectively paralysing Douala for several days), Nigeria, Tunisia, Ivory Coast, etc.[14]

In Nigeria, with a population of around 80 million, according to conservative estimates, and a relatively large working class, strikes have been illegal almost since the Civil War in the late 1960s. The ban was again extended for a renewable six months in 1975, 'to avoid disorders'.[15]

As well as these popular struggles in the neo-colonies – the most notable in 1977-78 being the risings in Zaire – there is the valiant struggle, in the face of intense repression, of the peoples of Southern Africa against an odious system of imperialist oppression. The situation is not evolving favourably for the racist settlers; their furious spite against the courageous neighbouring regimes is more a sign of a profound disarray than a proof of real strength. It is evident that the peoples of Southern Africa are developing their struggle at every level. To take only one example amongst many:

> The Confederation of Building and Metal-working Trade Unions (C.M.B.U.), with a membership of over 80,000 White, Coloured and Indian South African workers, has decided to set up trade unions for African workers. The creation of African trade unions has been called for by both the employers and the Trade Union Congress of South Africa (TUCSA).
>
> Mr. McCann, the C.M.B.U. President, has explained that the movement of Black workers into jobs once reserved for Whites, Coloureds and Indians was threatening the job security and wage levels

of his members. 'Furthermore,' Mr. McCann added, 'we believe that African trade unions are inevitable and that South Africa's economic progress and future industrial peace will be best served by setting up those unions as of now.' Mr. McCann concluded by inviting the Government to co-operate with the trade unions in setting up the new African unions. 'Tomorrow may be too late,' he said, 'the White, Coloured and Indian workers may no longer be on top of the situation.'[16]

African regimes' tendencies towards autocracy, cynical dictatorship and the most appalling counter-revolutionary repression are mainly a response to the fact that the struggles of the oppressed working masses could easily become uncontrollable, given the slightest opportunity.

The increasingly apparent systematic co-operation between all the neo-colonial African bourgeois regimes, notably as seen in the initiatives by the O.A.U. to ensure that counter-revolutionary repression prevails throughout the continent, expresses the class solidarity of these bourgeoisies. It also expresses their common fear of the 'threat of revolution', as Tunisian President Bourguiba put it to the Pan-African Youth Congress assembled in Tunis in July 1973. The following agreement between Libya and Niger is just one example amongst many of this new fraternal spirit.

> According to the Libyan Information Agency, a joint declaration was simultaneously released in Tripoli and Niamey on 22 March, announcing the signature of a Defence and Security Treaty between the two countries.
> The Treaty stipulates that the 'two countries undertake to provide each other with whatever assistance proves necessary should the internal security of either one of them come under threat from within or from outside.'[17]

The usefulness of such treaties became clear in 1979 in Uganda, for instance, when the Arab People's Socialist Jamahahiriya of Libya sent troops to try and save the reigning buffoon, Idi Amin Dada, from a popular uprising. This action, firmly in keeping with the orientations of Arab-Islamic reaction in Black Africa, exposed Libya's 'progressivism' in foreign affairs for what it really was, as well as bringing her Sub-Saharan expansionist ambitions to the attention of African and world public opinion.

Independent African Capitalism Nevertheless Impossible

Despite all these manoeuvres, the prevailing conditions in Africa, given the dominance of neo-colonialism, condemn the African bourgeoisies' attempts at developing an independent African capitalism to inevitable failure. In other words, the much vaunted African unity of the ruling neo-colonial bourgeoisies can of its very nature only be a sham. In the context of the world capitalist market, there can be no major accumulation of capital such as would enable the African bourgeoisies to become genuinely independent of the imperialist monopolies. In other words, the major investments will continue to be foreign or foreign-controlled. As the facts show all too clearly, this means that the eventual flow of profits back to the imperialist countries will remain far in excess of the original investments. For example:

> For Chad and the UDEAC countries as a whole (Cameroon, Central African Republic, Congo-Brazzaville and Gabon) the average yearly flow of profits back to the metropole between 1960 and 1968 amounted to 44,200 million CFA francs. Public spending and the inflow of foreign investment remained below 34,400 million CFA francs. Gross profits exported represented 13% of the Gross Domestic Product in both Ivory Coast and the UDEAC/Chad countries.[18]

As Ahmed Akkache rightly points out:

> Practically all investments are completely recouped, and in many cases transferred back home, within two or three years at the most. From then on, the company's activities are fuelled entirely by the 'beneficiary' country's resources and amount to a cost-free accumulation of profits. Once the first short period when capital inflow is greater than capital outflow is over – in other words, once exploitation has been got underway – the flow of capital is reversed and the excess of capital exported over capital imported begins to grow faster and faster.[19]

One thing is clear. Getting out of the world capitalist market is an essential precondition to winning the battle against underdevelopment.

But it is precisely because they are neo-colonial bourgeoisies that the classes now in power in Africa cannot take the required fundamental decisions and commit themselves to this kind of policy. Yet as long as our countries remain yoked to the world capitalist market, it is quite illusory to expect any real economic development, just as it is quite illusory to expect any genuine Pan-African integration which would serve the interests and aspirations of the workers and poor peasants who make up more than 90% of the population in Africa. The world capitalist market is ruled over by imperialism and monopoly capital. The present evolution is inseparable from that fact and it is in this sense that imperialist domination over Africa continues to be a determining element.

The other element is the proletarianization of the popular masses and Pan-Africanization of the proletariat, semi-proletariat and poor peasantry. This can only lead to an exacerbation of the class contradictions between the working class, poor peasantry and their allies, on the one hand, and the neo-colonial bourgeoisie and their allies, on the other. The result can only be an increasing awareness amongst all the working classes that their enemies are the bureaucratic bourgeoisies who now exploit and oppress them. The inevitable outcome is a growth in the struggles of the proletariat and poor peasants to free themselves from the yoke of capital, be it imperialist or African. *It is this liberation of workers and the poor peasantry of Africa which will liberate Africa from foreign domination.*

Pan-African Demagogy

It should by now be firmly established that for all the noise and vociferations, the so-called policy of African unity launched by the ruling African bourgeois classes is no more than *Pan-African demagogy*.

Pan-African demagogy consists in claiming to build African unity while knowing that one is incapable of following such a course or even that one is *hostile* to its ends. The watchword of African unity is then used purely and simply for the sake of misguiding the African workers and people.

How can the people of Africa be expected to put the slightest faith in a man who has successively announced that: 1) African unity will never be achieved; 2) African unity, political unity, with a single federal government and a central parliament, is what we all desire? Houphouet-Boigny made the first of these declarations in November 1959 during his trip to the United States. The second was issued during a press conference on 8 June 1961 at the Palais d'Orsay, during his state visit to France. Previously, on 7 September 1958, during a speech at the Abidjan Geo-Andre stadium, he had proclaimed his 'refusal to believe in the possibility of achieving a kind of unity that no other people has ever achieved on a continental scale'.[20]

Why such inconsistency from this representative of the African bourgeoisies? Why did the most reactionary regimes in Africa accept the O.A.U. in 1963 in Addis Ababa, even though these regimes, then members of OCAM's predecessor, U.A.M. (African and Malagasy Union), had constantly attacked the Casablanca Group countries as 'Reds who do nothing but spout threats and slogans'? For the simple reason that, from their point of view, Africa has developed an urgent need for what Houphouet calls 'complete tolerance' between states, meaning in practice active co-operation in the struggle against revolutionary organizations and the workers of Africa.

Consciously or by class instinct, the masses of Africa know that African unity *can* get them out of the misery and exploitation in which they, and Africa, have been plunged for centuries. And they are right. Real African unity, geared to the interests and aspirations of the workers and poor peasants, is a practical and concrete means of liberation, a possible and necessary step towards the real liberation of the African masses themselves.

Deliberate Deception of the Masses
In the meantime, the African neo-colonial bourgeoisies use the apparently and sometimes even objectively Pan-African character of certain elements in their present policies in order to deceive the African people. They deceive them by pretending that the African unity desired by the workers is precisely what is now being built, under the 'revolutionary' leadership of the heads of

state, regrouped under the auspices of the O.A.U. The Conakry regime recently published a brochure, entitled *The Road to Unity*, which contains a fine example of the neo-colonial bourgeoisies' approach to the task of mystification. Some extracts will illustrate the point.

In keeping with the traditions of hospitality characteristic of authentic Africa, in keeping with the demands of our revolution and its commitment to the restoration of the African peoples' freedom and dignity, in keeping with the aspirations of a whole emerging continent, the people of Guinea enthusiastically welcomed the visits, on 25-29 May 1972 and 31 May to 4 June 1972, of two great sons of Africa in struggle, President El Hadj Ahmadou Ahidjo of the United Republic of Cameroon and President Houari Boumedienne of the Popular Democratic Republic of Algeria. These two visits take on their full significance when one realizes how urgently Africa needs soft-hearted leaders with strong hands and the determination to fight a common struggle against indignity, especially today, when imperialism seeks to divide us in so many ways.

The respected leaders of Algeria, Cameroon and Guinea have long led their people in this struggle. They have fought side by side, each under their specific historical conditions, through the whole process of disintegration of a shameful colonial system.[21] They have striven to build national unity in their countries, out of the chaotic plethora of micro-groupings which colonialism had built up for all too obvious reasons.[22]

Today, Africa has outgrown the tiny groups created and maintained to preserve an imperialism condemned by history. Africa is fully adult because it has launched itself on the road of unity and real independence for its working masses. [Anyone would think colonialism had been already vanquished and that all that was left to do was to sing the praises of the existing regime! E.M.] Africa is fully adult because it knows how to impose its wishes on its worthy sons, who are more than ever committed to the future of their continent.

It is in this context that we salute the visit of our brother, President Ahidjo, who has come with a mandate from the African people of Cameroon to meet the Great Strategist, Ahmed Sekou Toure, so that they may work jointly towards a broader based African democratic revolution. By broadening the bases of the African democratic revolution, they simultaneously undermine the neo-colonial organizations which remain on the continent.

As the two comrades in arms, Ahmed Sekou Toure and Ahmadou Ahidjo, have repeatedly pointed out, Africa, like freedom and dignity, is indivisible, is one.

The Guinean, Algerian and Cameroonian peoples will march arm in arm with the other peoples of Africa, to continue the work begun by Samory, Alpha Yaya, Behanzin, Abd-el-Kader, Nkrumah, etc. [It would of course not have been polite to mention Lumumba, Um

151

Nyobe, Moumie, Ouandie, etc. E.M.]
The Guinean, Algerian and Cameroonian peoples will march
behind their leaders, Ahmed Sekou Toure, Houari Boumedienne and
Ahmadou Ahidjo, three giants of African unity.[23]

So much for the official Conakry version of the African democratic
revolution. It is all too clear that the 'progressive, Pan-Africanist' tendencies
of the various African bourgeoisies express political necessities inherent in
the contemporary African economies and nothing more than that. The
organization of these economies runs completely contrary to the interests
and aspirations of the African workers, and, given the present context, could
not do otherwise. It can certainly not go very far in bringing about the genuine
African unification so devoutly wished for by 90% of the masses of our
continent.

Fate of the Former Revolutionary African States of 1958-62

What then, are the Pan-African revolutionaries of today, who fight alongside
and for the workers and poor peasants of Africa for the triumph of socialism,
to think of those regimes which were once part of the group known as the
Revolutionary States and who were effectively anti-imperialist under the
conditions prevailing from 1958-62?
*The fundamental point to notice is that these regimes were led by
political organizations controlled by the petty bourgeoisie.*[24] Now, under
neo-colonialism, a ruling petty bourgeoisie which is not controlled effectively
by the working class and poor peasantry will inevitably turn into a bureaucratic bourgeoisie which may or may not retain an inclination to follow
revolutionary phraseology. The first ten years of neo-colonialism in Africa
provide a conclusive demonstration of this tendency. The interest of the new
bureaucratic bourgeoisie soon centres on retaining its own power, which
usually implies remaining at peace with its neighbours, hence the 'complete
tolerance' called for by Houphouet-Boigny. As for those regimes which were
completely neo-colonial from the start (e.g. Ahidjo's Cameroon, Houphouet's
Ivory Coast), the very conditions which gave birth to them had forced them to
establish such 'tolerance' right from the beginning.

The Case of Guinea-Conakry
The nationalist petty bourgeoisie of one country, which was to a greater or
lesser extent oriented towards revolutionary Pan-Africanism from 1958-62,
itself described what happened in the ensuing years as follows:

Since the proclamation of independence on 2 October 1958, the
Government of the Republic of Guinea has constantly maintained
friendly and co-operative relations with fraternal African countries.
No fraternal country on the continent, neighbour or not, can reproach

Guinea with having offered asylum to individuals or groups of foreign nationals in order that they might prepare expeditions or armed coups aimed at the sovereignty, independence or territorial integrity of that country.

It is well known that, from the moment it acceded to independence, the Republic of Guinea did indeed welcome certain African brothers who were having difficulties in their own countries. This was notably the case with a small group of Cameroonians affiliated to the *Union des Populations du Cameroun* (U.P.C.), led by brother Felix Moumie. During the French period, hospitality was granted to these political refugees, but [since independence] no Cameroonian refugee has ever been authorized to set up, on Guinean soil, a military or paramilitary organization directed against Cameroon, the Cameroonian state or the national institutions of that fraternal country. Furthermore the Guinean Government has repeatedly sought to persuade the group in question to return to their country and participate in the electoral process, as organized in 1960 by the legitimate government under the then President of the Council, Mr. El Hadj Ahmadou Ahidjo.

These are undeniable and easily verifiable historical facts. The Government of the Republic of Guinea has always considered that to allow its territory to be used as a base for activities which might threaten the sovereignty, independence or territorial integrity of any other African state would run counter to elementary morality and to the fundamental principles which ought to guide all bilateral or multilateral relations between states in an international community.[25]

In other words, the petty bourgeoisie, as exemplified by Sekou Toure's regime, considers that the struggles of a 'group' like the U.P.C. against a reactionary neo-colonial regime are the same thing as activities which threaten the sovereignty, independence, etc. of an African country. This petty bourgeoisie has now come round, both theoretically and practically, to the political positions of the African neo-colonial bourgeoisie. Let us not forget that neo-colonial regimes such as Mobutu's now invariably castigate the slightest popular revolt against them as a Soviet-Cuban aggression.

Nonetheless, the Conakry regime did provide crucial assistance to the comrades from Guinea-Bissau in the national liberation struggle against the NATO-backed Portuguese colonialists. In that respect, no serious Pan-African revolutionary would deny that the regime has made an important contribution to the anti-colonialist struggle in Africa. However, this is by no means the whole picture.

To begin with, colonialism and neo-colonialism are two aspects of the same reality, two different forms of the same imperialist domination; in the last analysis, the two phenomena are to be accounted for in terms of the same international finance capital. Second, all existing African regimes are constantly proclaiming their willingness to fight for economic independence, 'against imperialism', etc. etc. In so doing, these regimes admit and recognize that Africa is still dominated, even if the form of that domination has changed somewhat.

The Case of Congo-Brazzaville

One conclusion should be immediately obvious to any serious African anti-imperialist militant today, namely that the struggle against classical colonialism must be indissociably linked to the struggle against neo-colonialism, in all its aspects and specific manifestations, if it is to be more than lies and hollow words. For instance, consider the line of the 'Marxist-Leninist' P.C.T. (Congolese Workers' Party). The President of its Central Committee, Marien Ngouabi, recently declared that 'we cannot align ourselves with any movement struggling against any one of the African regimes which have already achieved independence'.[26] In other words, he agrees with Sekou Toure's sentiments, quoted above.

Ngouabi's regimes which have already achieved independence' is not a selective definition. Ahidjo's Cameroon, Bokassa's Central African Republic, all the 'independent' neo-colonies are included. Furthermore, Ngouabi is talking about regimes, not countries. Presumably he means us to believe that these regimes are genuinely struggling against classical colonialism and the racist settler regimes in the southern parts of the continent. If so, we would ask him to consider the following details: 1) Ahidjo's contracts through Lonrho with that pillar of apartheid, the Oppenheimer Group; 2) Bokassa's repeated delegations to Pretoria; 3) Houphouet, Tolbert and Senghor's secret and, later, open meetings with the racist South African Government; 4) Mobutu's manoeuvres in Angola, with the connivance of imperialists the world over, etc. etc. Everybody knows that Ian Smith's racist regime in Zimbabwe was theoretically isolated completely by the O.A.U. countries. The U.N. itself voted for a total embargo on Rhodesian products. The African bourgeoisies would occasionally make some timid (and sickeningly hypocritical) protestation to the effect that the imperialist countries were not concretely enforcing the U.N. decision. The O.A.U. even sent a delegation, under President Kenneth Kaunda of Zambia, to convince the European countries of the need for sanctions that were really enforced. In the meantime, it was well known that:

> In the restaurants of Zaire's capital, the Europeans take a mischievous delight in asking the chef where all the abundantly available red meat comes from. The answer is to be found at the airport, where every night DC7s, registered in Gabon but piloted by Rhodesians, are to be seen unloading sides of meat flown in from Rhodesia. Should one decide to afford oneself the [costly] pleasure of finishing the meal with fruit, it is a pretty good bet that it will come from South Africa.[27]

This co-operation between Zaire and the South African nazis is not only restricted to commercial affairs. Indeed, when Mobutu found himself faced with a popular uprising in Shaba Province in 1977, he called South Africa, as well as the other imperialists, to his aid. The press reported the dictator's manoeuvrings:

> Kinshasa, 8 April — A top official of South Africa's Bureau of State Security (BOSS) has been in Kinshasa secretly, to negotiate emergency aid — mainly fuel and support funds — to help the Zaire military campaign to hold off Katangese rebels in southern Shaba Province, according to three well-placed sources here. The high-ranking official of BOSS was reportedly in the capital last week to talk with the authorities in the office of President Mobutu Sese Seko. The highly reliable sources said that the Zaire Government accepted the offer of an undisclosed amount of fuel — and support funds, perhaps credits, to buy South African goods.[28]

Two months later, Mobutu brazenly declared to *Le Monde*: 'As long as Pretoria continues to maintain any form of racial discrimination whatsoever, there can be no dialogue between the South African Government and Zaire.'[29]

And what do Sekou Toure and Marien Ngouabi have to say about the fact that the newly elected (1977) President of the O.A.U. is the same Bongo Omar Albert whose disgusting complicity with racist Rhodesia and South Africa was just recently fully exposed by the imperialist press?

The African petty bourgeois regime's retreat from Revolutionary Pan-Africanist positions and their present endorsement of regimes which have been frankly neo-colonial right from the start indicates that a profound concordance of interests has developed. Under the prevailing neo-colonialism, the objective social interests of the nationalist petty bourgeoisie of 1958-62 have become practically identical to those of the pro-imperialist African bourgeoisie of the 1950s. This is the objective social basis for what can only be called the present-day bankruptcy of petty bourgeois Pan-Africanism.

The regimes which could once have been considered as having a Revolutionary Pan-Africanist position may have sunk to the level of Pan-African demagogy. And the original out-and-out neo-colonial regimes (Ahidjo's Cameroon, Bongo's Gabon, Mobutu's Zaire, Senghor's Senegal, Houphouet's Ivory Coast etc.) have not missed a chance to export counter-revolution. Sekou Toure's periodic accusations, over the last 20 years, that Houphouet, Foccart and Senghor were plotting against his Guinean regime are an implicit recognition of this fact. Commander Marien Ngouabi has repeatedly acknowledged the problem, notably in his accusation that Mobutu was plotting with the C.I.A. to overthrow his Brazzaville regime.

Where today are the much vaunted 'socialist', 'revolutionary' or even 'anti-imperialist' countries of Africa? On close examination, it emerges that, with the possible exception of the newly independent ex-Portuguese colonies, none of the states which claim to be socialist has implemented policies which would qualify as effectively fighting imperialism and building socialism. After 20 years of independence, the contrast between words and deeds is the most eloquent possible indictment.

Of course, there are distinctions which should not be blurred. The empty verbiage which prevails in Conakry should not be confused with Algeria's genuine efforts to build an independent national economy, for example. Until 1975 or thereabouts, the whole debate concerning the evolution of progressive African regimes centred on three cases, Guinea-Conakry, Congo-Brazzaville and Algeria. Since then, other progressive regimes have emerged (Madagascar, Benin), as well as some who are engaged in the transition to real scientific socialism. However, the three original cases remain very representative of the type of progressive regimes in Africa and thus make useful examples.

The comments above concerning the Popular Republic of the Congo are almost all there is to say about the regime's achievements; very little positive change has taken place apart from the regime's proclamation of its enthusiasm for Marxism-Leninism. This does at least have the advantage that Marxist ideas are widely circulated amongst the Congolese workers, unlike what happens in a country such as Cameroon, where such circulation can only take place in secret, whatever the official demagogy proclaims to the contrary.[30]

As for the 'Revolutionary Democratic Republic of Guinea-Conakry', with its 'Party-State led by the Great Strategist of the African Democratic Revolution', etc., etc., (don't laugh) we have already pointed out a great deal, enough to indicate just how seriously one should take a strategist who fights reaction arm in arm with notable revolutionaries such as Ahidjo for comrades.

Algeria: A Special Case

Algeria remains one of the few African countries where a revolutionary process is genuinely underway. Even there, however, many contradictory factors have determined the changing political orientations of the country since 1962.

To begin with, the historical conditions under which independence was won, and especially the popular war of national liberation, seriously limited the manoeuvring space of the petty bourgeoisie which eventually seized effective power. Second, because of the relative weakness and lack of autonomous political organization of the proletariat, as elsewhere in Africa, it is clear that the way the problems of the Algerian peasantry will be resolved is the crucial determinant for the medium-term evolution of the country. Hence, the vital importance of the Land Reform Programme, launched by Ahmed Ben Bella in 1963-64. But despite the adoption in 1976 of the F.L.N. Charter, which proclaimed the country's socialist orientation and stressed the need for agrarian reform — some 13 years after that reform was originally launched! — the situation has not improved that much. Indeed, in 1975, it was still true that:

> 420,000 farmers, representing 72% of the landowning peasantry, still
> held less than ten hectares each, an area which is generally recognized

as too small to provide a guaranteed minimum for subsistence under the prevailing technical conditions in agriculture. This unequal distribution of land is, of course, the main cause of what is generally known as 'rural overpopulation'; at present, unemployment officially affects one peasant out of two and 100,000 people leave the land every year, to go abroad or to the towns.[31]

It is worth recalling that in November 1965 the Council of the Revolution (the leadership of the June 1965 coup which overthrew Ben Bella) had decided to 'set up a Commission to prepare for the implementation of the Agrarian Reform by 1966[!]. This Commission was to define the areas which would come within the scope of the reform programme, determine the most profitable forms of land use and develop methods of organization and relevant administrative structures.' It seems obvious that if the Agrarian Reform is still at an embryonic stage ten years later, there must be some serious obstacles in its path. The key issue is whether the big and medium landowners will allow themselves to be expropriated. The settlers' lands which were nationalized in 1963-64, while Ben Bella was still in power, still form the bulk of the self-managed sector. Since then, there has been little progress: 'The self-managed sector only covers 2.3 million hectares, some 5% of the cultivated land area. It employs only 370,000 workers. 70% of the Algerian population, some 7 million people, still depend on the private agricultural sector, which accounts for more than 40 million hectares.'[32] It is easy to understand why the Agrarian Reform Charter stipulated that, among other things:

> It is essential to do away with the complexities and diversities of legal status which prevail at present, so as to establish private land ownership on a modern legal basis. A full census of privately held land, conducted within the framework of the Agrarian Reform, should establish the facts and rights of each case and make it possible to determine a single type of private land ownership. These measures and the relevant administrative structures will help stabilize private farming and promote a higher level of productivity.
>
> The Agrarian Reform may not abolish private ownership of the means of production, but it does do away with man's exploitation of his fellow man.[33]

Provision, however, was made for paying compensation to the big landowners who were to be expropriated. It is quite obvious that, whatever the intentions of the people who thought up the project, it can, at best, only lead to the development of modern capitalism in industry or trade. Until recently, rents in kind were the normal pattern in Algeria, as in parts of Black Africa (Cameroon, for example). Under this system, the workers, who did all the work on somebody else's land, would receive only a fraction (one-third or one-fifth) of the product. Since the Algerian peasantry was clearly the fundamental force behind the war of national liberation, while the big landowners 'kept a low profile', when they did not overtly collaborate with the colonialists, it is not at all obvious that they deserve any compensation at all.

The money used to pay this compensation will, of course, be drawn from public funds, in other words, from the hard work of the Algerian workers. Delays of up to 15 years are envisaged before payment of the sums involved, some of which are very large, is complete. In the interim, interest at 2.5% will be paid. All this will provide these landowners with the capital they need to diversify into modern capitalism. This should prove all the easier given that the rural exodus will ensure an abundant labour supply. In many respects, the process is closely akin to that of primitive capital accumulation and seems likely to lead towards a capitalist form of development in Algerian agriculture.

Third, if one looks at the existing capitalist sector in Algeria, especially the more dynamic state capitalist branch, one cannot but have very strong reservations about the fact that, according to the Agrarian Reform Charter, 'there is no question of us seeking to build up an economy cut off from the world market'. This orientation will inevitably create the conditions most liable to cancel out the positive effects of any objectively anti-imperialist measures implemented in other domains. Such an orientation highlights the non-socialist character of overall policy.

One example of this refusal to break off from the world capitalist market is provided by the remarkable development of economic relations between Algeria and the U.S. In 1973, it was already observable that:

Relations between the U.S. and Algeria over the last four years have reached a contradictory phase: they are plainly bad on the political level — diplomatic relations have been suspended ever since the June '67 Arab-Israeli War — yet on the economic and commercial level, the links between Algiers and Washington are steadily becoming closer.

U.S. foreign policy, especially in South East Asia and the Middle East, is virulently attacked every day in the Algerian Press and has repeatedly been condemned by the Government. However, business contacts grow more and more fruitful day by day.

The Algerian leadership has chosen to keep business matters and politics quite separate in their dealings with the United States.

Hardly a month passes without the National Algerian Hydrocarbons Company (SONATRACH) announcing the signature of yet another contract for the sale of gas or oil to an American company.

The United States have purchased around 30,000 million cubic metres of Algerian natural gas, to be delivered over the next 25 years. Before the decade is out, Algeria will be the United States' largest supplier of liquified natural gas.

American and Algerian Government companies also collaborate closely. Many powerful Texan oil companies implanted themselves in

Algeria between 1966 and 1970.[34]

There follows a list of ten major U.S. companies. American firms (four are mentioned) are also involved in other crucial areas such as long-term planning. The journal from which the above extract is drawn goes on to claim that, because Algeria holds 51% of the stock in all Algerian subsidiaries of the U.S. companies concerned, the Algerian Government remains firmly in charge of the situation. This is by no means obvious. It is rarely the formal balance of forces (51% of the total shares against 49%) which really determines how decisions are taken. Furthermore:

> The envisaged massive Algerian oil and gas deliveries to the United States and the financial implications of the various contracts signed to this effect by SONATRACH and the U.S. companies have promoted increasingly close financial co-operation between the U.S. and Algeria over the last few years. Trade between the two countries is constantly on the increase and this trend seems likely to continue.
>
> However, the main characteristic of Algerian-American trade is the considerable deficit in the Algerian balance of trade. [Subsequent oil price increases may have enabled Algeria to make good this deficit, but the underlying trend remains. E.M.]
>
> Informed circles in both countries are optimistic about the future development of Algerian-American trade. The installation of major gas transport facilities in Algeria — installations which will make the massive deliveries to the U.S. possible and which have been partly financed by specially earmarked U.S. loans — will, at first, considerably increase the volume of American sales to Algeria. But it is widely expected that from 1976 onwards, when the first natural gas deliveries get underway, a balance will rapidly be re-established.[35]

It could be objected that this information comes from French business circles and inevitably reflects a certain bitterness on the part of French imperialism, which is seeing itself displaced by a rival imperialism. Right up to 1970, Franco-Algerian relations were held up as an 'exemplary' model by both partners. However, the information in question is publicly available; furthermore, French foreign policy in recent years (1974-80) has been so closely aligned with that of the United States that to talk of rivalries between them on Algeria requires some very fine distinctions. In any case, whatever this or that imperialism may think of the matter, the fact remains that U.S. capital is pouring into Algeria.

This integration of the Algerian economy into the world capitalist market is, to say the least, somewhat contradictory with the regime's proclaimed anti-imperialist position; especially as it has long been well known that — taking the dominated and exploited countries of the world as a whole:

Declared profits alone accounted for a flow of capital away from the developing countries which amounted to U.S. $23,000 million during the second half of the 1960-70 decade of development. This figure represents *two and a half times* the sum total of aid money provided by the countries in which the companies who made the profits in question are based.

The overall debt owed by the developing countries to the developed countries is of the order of U.S. $80,000 million. Servicing this debt costs around U.S. $9,000 million a year and this burden is one of the factors which force the developing countries to constantly borrow more, and thus sink further and further into a chronic balance of payments deficit.[36]

Under such conditions it is highly debatable whether the U.N. is the best framework in which to seek a solution to this problem. All the more so since the imperialists, as usual, saw fit to dictate their terms even before the U.N. General Assembly had finished its deliberations on raw materials and a 'New International Economic Order'. The desired effect had already been obtained: work had been found for a few technocrats and an enormous smokescreen had been put up to confuse the peoples of the dominated countries. The outcome? In early May 1974, world opinion learned that:

On the evening of 1 May, the U.N. extraordinary session on raw materials finally adopted, by general consensus, a declaration on the New International Economic Order and a programme of action geared to give this declaration practical effect. After these two texts had been adopted, there followed a series of speeches outlining the objections of a number of states, notably the U.S. and various E.E.C. countries, including France. These centred on the fact that the declaration proclaimed the permanent and integral sovereignty of each state over its natural resources and its economic activities, including the right to nationalize and regulate all national activities and to determine the sum of any eventual indemnities.[37]

Apart from these basic economic factors, which explain the current changes, there are also external factors whose role is not insignificant given the present context.

The economic orientation outlined above implies an increasingly frantic search for new markets on the part of those African countries with a more developed level of underdevelopment. One result is the need for dubious political compromises, especially in terms of Pan-Africanism. Many such compromises have been made with regimes which were quite rightly considered neo-colonial in Algiers up to 1964. This tendency towards compromise is generally reinforced by the situation in the Middle East and the overall strategy adopted by most Arab states on the subject. The fact that Algeria is, by definition, a member of both the Arab League and the

O.A.U. does not make it any easier for that country to define its position clearly. The September 1973 Conference of Non-Aligned Countries in Algiers, where genuinely anti-imperialist militants and heads of state rubbed shoulders with out-and-out lackeys of imperialism such as Houphouet, Mobutu, Ahidjo and Bongo, illustrated what non-alignment has come to mean today. For instance, the French daily, *Le Monde*, described Niger under 'non-aligned' Diori Hamani as follows: 'In all the key sectors — banking, public works, teaching, administration and even the army — the French hold over the country is so manifest that Niger is still considered to be France's private hunting ground in most foreign chancelleries.'[38] This did not stop Diori Hamani, then President of Niger, from attending the 'non-aligned' conference in Algiers just like anybody else.

Any attentive observer will have noted that, whenever Ahidjo visits Algiers, the Algerian press displays a remarkable selective memory concerning the history of Cameroon before 1960. This history is systematically presented as beginning in 1960-61, so as not to have to talk about what 'the great President Ahidjo' was doing before that date — he was at the time an active agent of the same French Government which was massacring the descendants of Abd-el-Kader and striving to destroy the U.P.C.'s struggle for national independence. Similarly, any attentive observer will have noted the number of militant Cameroonian revolutionaries who have been deported from Congo-Brazzaville to Algeria, with the encouragement of Ahidjo and the O.A.U., in order to 'keep these people as far as possible from Cameroon'.[39]

All this implies that the greatest caution is called for before one talks of 'revolutionary, socialist and anti-imperialist' countries in Africa. Great precision is required before one can justifiably describe countries which refuse in any way to break with the world capitalist market as 'revolutionary' or 'socialist'. The best results that such countries can hope for may be relatively substantial in certain domains, but they cannot really open up the way for a transition to scientific socialism, the only sort of socialism which has ever really proved itself.

Pan-Africanism Today: Basic Conclusions

We can now answer nearly all the questions raised at the beginning of this study. In the next chapters we will answer the next two questions: what does Revolutionary Pan-Africanism mean today? And what is to be done now? We have already established a number of points.

First, Pan-Africanism is the political theory which asserts that *Africa is a single entity with a common set of problems and which must unite to ensure its liberation from domination, exploitation and enslavement.* Throughout its history, there have always been two variants of this Pan-Africanism, a revolutionary form and a reactionary form. Revolutionary Pan-Africanism has, during each historical period, explicitly or implicitly represented the conscious and unconscious interests and aspirations of the

161

exploited African working people. Reactionary Pan-Africanism expresses the interests of those social strata in whose interests it is for Africa to remain enslaved. At each stage of the African people's struggle for liberation, Revolutionary Pan-Africanism has emerged as the ideology, political theory and programme of action which must inspire the Revolutionary Pan-African movement. This movement is itself the practical instrument which will enable the people of Africa to carry out the African revolution. At each important stage of the struggle, at each historical turning point, one of the fundamental tasks of African revolutionary militants is to define the African revolution correctly in terms of its explicit political contents and hence also in terms of the practical political content of Revolutionary Pan-Africanism. Today, in a period when neo-colonialism is triumphant, yet already undermined by countless insurmountable contradictions, one of the duties of African revolutionaries is to redefine and respecify the basis of Revolutionary Pan-Africanism.

Second, analysis of the situation in Africa at the moment shows that, although one cannot lump all the regimes together, no African government is implementing a consistent revolutionary Pan-African policy. This is particularly so given that even those few countries who are genuinely engaged in a transition to (scientific) socialism remain very cautious in their approach to the political unification of Africa. No doubt they are subject to pressures and influences of all kinds. If one considers the African regimes led by the nationalist petty bourgeoisie who, at the end of the 1950s and in the early 1960s, adopted a policy which, given the historical context at that time, was effectively revolutionary Pan-African, one will notice that, where those regimes have not been overthrown, they have sunk, without exception, into an opportunist policy based on systematic *Pan-African demagogy* (the second, and reactionary, current of Pan-Africanism). This policy consists in systematic collaboration with the regimes who had already become completely neo-colonized by the early 1960s, for the simple reason that they were themselves creations of colonialism. The political content of Pan-African demagogy is class collaboration on a continent-wide level. The African petty bourgeoisie, uncontrolled by the working class and poor peasantry, began by refusing to wage class struggle against the pro-imperialist colonial bourgeoisie and landed up eventually allying itself with those who had by then become the neo-colonial bourgeoisie. This nationalist petty bourgeoisie embraced Revolutionary Pan-Africanism up to about 1960 and then effectively turned its back on genuine African unity and sought refuge in a sort of trade union for heads of state, as embodied in the O.A.U. It thereby inflicted the worst defeat upon Pan-Africanism that it had ever suffered. In doing so, this class exposed its own bankruptcy.

Third, the bankruptcy of petty bourgeois Pan-Africanism is not a manifestation of the 'nastiness' or 'ingratitude' of that class. *The objective socio-economic conditions of neo-colonialism were the real basis for the African petty bourgeoisie's failure to accomplish the historic mission of leading the people of Africa towards independence, political unity and socialism.* The point is that neo-colonialism fulfilled all the objective conditions required to enable the petty bourgeoisie of the 1950s to get some advantage out of the prevailing system. The anti-imperialist struggle thus became superfluous as far as that class was concerned.

Fourth, the organizational manifestation of the bankruptcy of petty bourgeois Pan-Africanism is the Organization of African Unity. Indeed, the birth of the O.A.U. marked a historic turning point, at which the African nationalist petty bourgeoisie renounced genuine African unity, that unity which corresponds to the real interests and aspirations of the people of Africa. The political foundations of the O.A.U. — notably the blatantly hypocritical principle of 'non-interference in the internal affairs of each member state', the toleration extended to all regimes whatever their nature, the respect for the territorial integrity of existing countries, amounting as it does to absolute recognition of the colonial frontiers — are *all fundamental breaks with the quest for African unity*, as it was already defined by the Pan-African Congresses between 1919 and the Second World War. These basic principles of the O.A.U. establish beyond a shadow of doubt that there is a close link between Pan-African demagogy and micro-nationalism in Africa, since the principles insist on the maintenance of the existing *status quo*.

Finally, since the overall conditions of neo-colonialism are the basis for Pan-African demagogy, one can safely say that there is a close link between imperialism, in its neo-colonialist form, and the temporary victory of Pan-African demagogy over the Pan-African revolutionary movement.

It is the duty of all African revolutionaries today to change this situation radically.

Notes

1. A Kampuchean National United Front was set up in Cambodia following the U.S. aggression against the country in 1970.
2. *Marches Tropicaux et Mediterraneens*, 8 February 1974, p.333. Also *Le Monde*, 10-11 February 1974, p.22.
3. *Marches Tropicaux . . .*, 1 February 1974, p.256.
4. Amilcar Cabral, 'Speech for Kwame Nkrumah Day', *Presence Africaine*, No.85, (Paris, 1973), p.7.
5. Kwame Nkrumah, *Neo-colonialism: The Last Stage of Imperialism*, op. cit., p.184.
6. Kwame Nkrumah's book contains further details on the Oppenheimer Group from Chapter 7 onwards. The reader will discover that Oppenheimer is perhaps *the* central economic pillar of apartheid in Southern Africa, and can thus only be expected to do everything in his power, by any means available, to shore up that iniquitous system. For instance, in Chapter 10 the reader will learn that De Beers Consolidated Mines Ltd., the main De Beers Group mining company, owns 50% of African Explosives, a company which, as one would expect, manufactures explosives, and not just for the mining and quarrying industries. In fact,

African Explosives is associated with the biggest of the chemical and plastics companies, the Dupont Corporation. Hence its links with De Beers and Lonrho's connection 'with the modern military equipment industry that seems to issue inevitably from chemicals manufacture.' (Nkrumah, op.cit., p.139).

We cannot resist pointing out that the Dupont Corporation started its ascent by making *anti-black* explosives. 'Their first big order was to supply Napoleon, in his vain attempt to crush Toussaint de l'Ouverture and the people of Santo Domingo. See Victor Perlo, *The Empire of High Finance*, p.195.

Delivery of weapons of every kind, including nuclear reactors, to the Pretoria Nazis is a constant feature of French foreign policy. A notable example are the French Alouette 2 and Alouette 3 anti-guerrilla helicopters. The African people have a heavy score to settle with the French bourgeoisie.

7. *Marches Tropicaux . . .*, 31 August 1973, p.2,649.
8. *Addis Abeba, Mai 1963 . . .*, op.cit., p.74. By 1970, this passion for negotiation was quite overwhelming. Every kind of demagogy was grist to the mill when the O.A.U. was set up as a compromise to stymie the progressive states of the day.
9. *Marches Tropicaux . . .*, 20 July 1973, p.2,259.
10. It is well known that the gold and currency reserves of those African countries belonging to the Franc Zone are held in France, and that they can thus take no major action outside the Franc Zone without the prior consent of Paris. On 14 November 1973, a treaty signed in Paris with France's West African neo-colonies granted the Africans a few concessions, allowing them to hold up to 35% (and no more) of their assets in currencies other than the French franc. This 'benefit', which the French bourgeois press described with remarkable candour as 'giving the African states the feeling that they are masters of their own destiny', was nonetheless not extended to the states of Central Africa and Cameroon. The latter are affiliated to the by no means any less colonial *Banque Centrale des Etats de l'Afrique Centrale et du Cameroun*.
11. *Marches Tropicaux . . .*, 1 June 1973, p.1,485.
12. *Paris-Normandie*, 11 August 1958.
13. *Marches Tropicaux . . .*, 19 April 1974, p.1,073. Once again, it emerges that, when profits are at stake, the imperialists and their lackeys will make free even with the most elementary rules of arithmetic. $27 + 20 + 14 + 10 + 10 + 15 = 96$. If the imperialists hold 96% of the capital, how can Houphouet's Sodemi hold 5%? Has the company floated 101% of its capital?
14. In June 1973, the Abidjan bus drivers went on strike for better wages and working conditions. Houphouet immediately sent in the army and threatened to sack everybody. Naturally, the imperialist press, so punctilious about the defence of civil liberties elsewhere, never even mentioned the incident.
15. Yet, in 1975, a handful of Cameroonian opportunists in Conakry were still talking of Nigeria's 'anti-imperialist and revolutionary' position. He who pays the piper . . . .

16. *Marches Tropicaux . . .*, 31 August 1973, p.2,649.
17. Ibid., 5 April 1974, p.948. The treaty did not prevent one signatory, Diori Hamani, Niger's President, from being overthrown shortly afterwards.
18. Samir Amin, *Accumulation on a World Scale*, op.cit., p.331. In fact, U.D.E.A.C. contributed 10,000 million CFA francs per annum to the imperialists' coffers.
19. Ahmed Akkache, *Capitaux Etrangers et Liberation economique: l'Example de l'Algerie*, op.cit., p.28.
20. See *Europe-France-Outre-Mer*, No.389.
21. The reader will note the emptiness of these phrases. In fact, this is compounded by a feigned amnesia. Sekou Toure pretends to forget that, at the 1960 Addis Ababa Conference of Independent States, Ahidjo's puppet Minister of Foreign Affairs, Charles Okala, attacked the Guinean delegation for supporting the U.P.C. in its struggle for the independence of Cameroon and against French colonialism, which had just brought Ahidjo to power in Yaounde at the barrel of a gun. Sekou Toure and his friends seem intent on falsifying the historical record.
22. It would have been preferable if the Conakry authorities had been more explicit about the 'micro-groups' set up by colonialism, in Cameroon for instance. One typical example was the *Bloc des Democrates du Cameroun* (B.D.C.), founded by the settler Aujoulat and of which Ahidjo was a member. The latter then founded the *Union Camerounaise* (U.C.) to fight the U.P.C. which was struggling for the reunification and independence of the country. Once neo-colonial independence had been granted, this U.C. became the present U.N.C., through a forced incorporation of all the other parties (except, of course, the U.P.C., which could not accept so monstrous an imposture).
23. See *Bulletin de l'Ambassade de la Republique de Guinee en Europe Occidentale et Albanie*, No.8, 22 June 1972.
24. See Woungly Massaga, 'Sur quelques problemes de l'heure, lettre aux militants du Parti et aux patriotes kamerunais', *Resistance* (U.P.C., October 1972).
25. See *Revelations sur les Activites Criminelles de la Contre-Revolution*, (Conakry, August 1973), pp.231-2. The chapter contains a scathing attack on Senghor by Sekou Toure, condemning the poet of Dakar for his involvement in a reactionary alliance with the Portuguese colonialists against the PAIGC and Guinea in November 1970. (The O.A.U. Commission set up to investigate these accusations was made up of Senghor, Sekou Toure, Haile Selassie, Ould Daddah, Moussa Traore, Yakubu Gowon, Boumedienne, Tolbert and Ahidjo Birawandu.)
26. Ngouabi's 13 February 1974 declaration, reproaching the French publisher, Francois Maspero, for having published a book by our comrade, Woungly Massaga, entitled *La Revolution au Congo: Contribution a l'Etude des Problemes Politiques d'Afrique Centrale*. See *Marches Tropicaux . . .*, 22 February 1974, p.490. Marien Ngouabi was assassinated in March 1977. Despite our many differences with him, we cannot but pay homage to him for his contribution to the consolidation of a free Angola at a crucial juncture.

27. See 'La seconde independence du Zaire' in *Le Monde*, 22 February 1974.
28. *International Herald Tribune*, 9-10 April, 1977.
29. *Le Monde*, 12-13 June 1977, p.2.
30. In 1970, for the centenary of Lenin's birth, the Communist Party of the Soviet Union presented Ahidjo's fascist U.N.C. with the complete works of the Bolshevik leader.
31. Christian Leucate, 'Revolution Agraire en Algerie?', *Critiques de l'Economie Politique*, No.15, January-March 1974, pp.70-71 (Paris, Maspero).
32. Ibid., p.67.
33. Ibid., p.76.
34. *Marches Tropicaux . . .*, 20 July 1973, pp.2,267-8.
35. Ibid.
36. Houari Boumedienne, *Speech to the U.N. Extraordinary General Assembly on Raw Materials*. See *Le Monde*, 12 April 1974, p.7.
37. *Marches Tropicaux . . .*, 3 May 1974, p.1,175.
38. *Le Monde*, 18 April 1974, p.9.
39. See annex to Woungly Massaga, op.cit., Vol.I.

4. Revolutionary Pan Africanism Today

The Objective Basis of Revolutionary Pan-Africanism

What needs to be said about contemporary Revolutionary Pan-Africanism? The first thing is to show that a revolutionary Pan-Africanist policy has a contemporary objective basis and is not just a utopia.

> Leaving aside the question of 'race' — in Africa the people are neither more homogeneous nor less mixed, since prehistoric times, than are the other 'races' — a common, or kindred, cultural background and a social organization that still presents many similarities from one area to another make Black Africa a single entity. This living entity, vast and rich, did not wait for colonial conquest either to borrow from or to give of itself to the other great regions of the Old World. But these exchanges did not break up the unity of Africa's personality; on the contrary, they helped to assert and enrich it. And the colonial conquest strengthened this still further.[1]

This is just one objective basis for the unity of the peoples of Africa; it is far from being the only one.[2]

In previous chapters, we saw how the economic mechanisms operated by monopoly capital and the African bourgeoisies tend to promote a certain Pan-African integration, a certain 'unity'. As we saw, this tendency has definite limits. We have already stressed that these mechanisms could not, of themselves, lead to unity. One important consequence, that we also noted, of the existence of such mechanisms is the Pan-Africanization of the African proletariat, a tendency which once again confirms the famous thesis in *The Communist Manifesto* that 'workers have no country'.[3] However, these objectively integrationist tendencies cannot bring about a revolutionary African unity. Any such claim would amount to preaching economism — which we have already dismissed. Indeed, the African neo-colonial bourgeoisies, like their allies and masters in Western Europe, could use these inherent tendencies of the neo-colonial African economy in order to create an economically integrated Africa. If only international finance capital allowed them to, the African bourgeoisies would draw together Africa's capital, for their sole benefit. It is thus essential to use these objective conditions created by neo-colonialism to further a revolutionary perspective in keeping with the interests and aspirations of the African workers.

The Essential Requirement: A Break with the World Capitalist Market

All the fundamental features we have outlined previously point to one inescapable conclusion. *Since the mechanisms of the world capitalist market, operating through unequal exchange, are at the root of the pillage of Africa, the only way out, the only way to establish the necessary conditions for authentic economic liberation, is to break with the world capitalist market.* This does not necessarily imply economic autarchy. *It is simply the elimination of the mechanisms of domination through which international imperialism subordinates the economies of the dominated countries, including the African countries, to its own economic laws.* It is now generally recognized that:

> A break with the world market is the primary condition for develop-
> ment. Any development policy that accepts the framework of integra-
> tion into this market must fail, for it can only be a matter of pious
> wishes for 'much needed external aid' . . . . The failure of planning in
> the Third World[4] — which cannot be denied since the gap between it
> and the centre is widening — is essentially due to this refusal to break
> with the world market.[5]

We see the need for a break with the world capitalist market as one of the fundamental requirements of Revolutionary Pan-Africanism at the present stage of the struggle against neo-colonialism.

All the really progressive economists who are dealing with the contemporary economic development problems of the dominated countries are unanimous in saying that a break with the world market is a *sine qua non* of development.

> There can only be an equitable exchange of products between the more
> developed and less developed countries in one of two cases: when the
> less developed countries undertake a programme based on internal
> development, which is relatively isolated from the world market; or
> when the relations of production and exchange in the world economy
> are determined by the laws of a socialist mode of production rather
> than by those of a capitalist one.[6]

The Lesson of 19th Century France
Even an economist only as modestly progressive as Paul Bairoch has reached similar conclusions, notably from an analysis of the period of free trade

between France and Britain in the late 19th and early 20th Centuries, when France was relatively underdeveloped compared to Britain.

> The analysis we have just presented allows us to draw some very clear conclusions as to the effects of France's 1860 to 1892 liberal foreign trade policy. On the whole, these effects were very negative and the precise opposite of those predicted by liberal and neo-liberal theories.
> Economic growth was seriously slowed down, even once external factors have been discounted . . . . The rate of growth was slower than in the equivalent periods which preceded and followed the free trade interlude. Indeed, it was the slowest rate of growth France has ever known, if one excludes the troubled years of the Revolution and First Empire and the great crisis of 1930. From the available indices it would seem that innovation declined rather than prospered during the period.
> As trade increased, there was no sign of the theoretically predicted closing of the gap in the level of development between France and Britain. On the contrary, available indices show that economic growth was faster in Britain and that the gap therefore widened during the period. Far from producing the favourable effects promised by liberal and neo-liberal theories, free trade led to a slowing down of economic development and to all the consequences which that carries.[7]

When the bourgeois classes were still on the ascendant and progressive in the historical sense, they, too, had to deal with the question of the integration of an underdeveloped economy into the world market. Africa has precious lessons to learn from the experience of South America, which has evolved (or stagnated) under the domination of the developed capitalist states, especially the U.S., for almost 150 years.

The Lesson of Argentina
In Argentina, in the second quarter of the 19th Century, there was a great dispute as to whether integration into the world capitalist market would be good or bad for the development of the country. Even in those early days:

> Brigadier General Pedro Ferre argued as follows: 'I consider free trade to be a curse upon the nation. I think I will never understand how restrictions imposed on trade in this way could possibly harm industry . . . . Of course, a few wealthy men may have to endure some minor deprivations. The less wealthy will hardly notice the difference. But the condition of the great masses of the Argentinian people will begin to improve and we will cease to be haunted by the idea of the appalling poverty to which they are now condemned.[8]

The reader could be forgiven for thinking of those 'few wealthy men' in Africa who cannot go without their whisky, their champagne and their Christmas trees (in the middle of Africa), and who for this reason tie our countries to the world capitalist market.

The Lesson of the U.S.A.

The U.S. has now become the leader of the imperialist world and constantly sings the praises of the world capitalist market and of this or that liberal or neo-liberal trade theory. It sang a different tune when its own industry was still embryonic. Indeed, at the end of the Civil War, around 1865, the victorious General Grant announced quite clearly: 'When America has got all she can out of protection, she too will embrace free trade.'[9] This was Grant's answer to all those in the U.S. who supported a pro-British — or pro-imperialist — viewpoint; American lackeys of British imperialism at the time were clamouring for the doors of the country to be thrown wide open to British trade.

So some things at least are very straightforward: without a break with the world capitalist market, there can be no real development in Africa.

How to Achieve Such a Break

The next important question is whether such a break can be brought about. Just because a step is necessary does not mean it is immediately practicable as a viable alternative. It is particularly important to deal with this aspect of the question, since it leads us to an examination of the concrete conditions under which the break could be made.

The break is undoubtedly viable, possible and achievable. History gives many examples of units like Africa operating perfectly well outside the world market: notable cases are the early U.S., the U.S.S.R. and then China. From a strictly economic point of view, the necessary and sufficient condition is size of economic territory.

A Large Economic Territory via Revolutionary Political Unity

As soon as Africa achieves revolutionary political unity, the size of its economic territory will be sufficient to ensure that a break with the world market will be viable. Such an African economy would have access to an enormous domestic market, which does away with the need to seek outlets abroad, especially for an economy in transition towards socialism. The economy would be planned on a continental or quasi-continental level. Industry would base its expansion on the domestic peasant market and would no longer have to operate mainly in terms of foreign markets where conditions are so grossly unfavourable. This orientation towards an expansion of the domestic peasant market would make it essential to modernize agriculture (machinery, fertilizers, etc.) and to raise the peasant's level of consumption. The industrializing effects of such a strategy and the resulting tendency towards an increasingly autocentric industry are obvious.

In other words, the question comes down to showing that it is both possible and necessary to establish sizeable economic territories in contemporary Africa.

As we saw earlier in this study, the present-day African economies are all externally oriented and dependent. They do not constitute integrated wholes, even in a given micro-country. In many cases, it would be an abuse of language to describe the economy of these countries as a national economy. As Samir Amin puts it:

> Sectors are simply juxtaposed, with little integration between them; on the other hand, each sector is strongly integrated into distinct wholes whose centres of gravity lie in the capitalist metropoles . . . . There is no real nation, in the economic sense of the word.
>
> The weakness of national cohesion in the Third World is often a reflection of this fact, which is also the source of 'micro-nationalism': the area of interest to the export economy has no 'need' of the rest of the country, which may indeed seem a burden upon it, and so it may contemplate establishing a 'micro-independence'.[10]

So even from a purely economic point of view, Africa and the African workers would not be much inconvenienced by the dislocation of the little African states of today. Indeed, these states represent an obstacle to the real liberation of Africa, in that they prevent the development of the broad economic zones which are essential if Africa is to break with the world capitalist market and cease being so dependent on foreign markets. Given the prevailing neo-colonialism, renunciation of these foreign markets is indispensable if there is to be any real popular economic development.

The present Balkanization of Africa is one of the fundamental conditions (and consequences) of the domination of our continent by imperialism. This domination takes the form of a direct economic integration of each little African country with its imperialist 'metropole' or group of imperialist countries. It would even be fair to say that integration into the world capitalist market is *enough* to prevent any real unification of Africa. Consequently, a break with that market is *necessary* before any policy geared to promote the genuine unification and integration of Africa can succeed. This necessity has a second aspect. As soon as the African states break with the world capitalist market, they will be faced with the need to integrate economically and politically with each other, in order to survive as states within a wider whole. Conversely, the absence today of such an urgent necessity acts as a brake upon genuine unitary tendencies. *The break with the world capitalist market conditions the success of economic and political integration*; it is crucial to the realization of genuine unity in Africa.

The Existing Micro-States an Immovable Obstacle?

The existing frontiers resulted from the carve-up of the continent by the European imperialists at the end of the 19th Century. The African peoples themselves were not consulted, and some of them were split between two or even three of the newly created states.[11] However, one characteristic of developing capitalism is to ignore the national frontiers of bourgeois states. African small traders, for instance, pay no attention to formal frontiers. The neo-colonial bourgeoisies themselves make a mockery of the frontiers each time they involve themselves in contraband or whenever there is a need to transfer workers from Upper Volta to Gabon, from Cameroon to the Congo, from Nigeria to Equatorial Guinea, and so on. The tendency to disregard these absurd frontiers is, of course, particularly marked amongst peoples who have been artificially divided by them. Nonetheless, the majority of wars of secession in Africa over the last few years have taken place in areas where the development of local capital had already reached a certain level; imperialist manoeuvres played a role, but were not the sole factor. It would, therefore, seem that *developing capitalism creates objective conditions leading to the breakdown of these colonial frontiers.*[12] In the face of such socio-economic conditions, government propaganda and demagogy concerning a 'national unity' which has to be constantly reaffirmed, even though it has supposedly already been established thanks to the farsightedness of the head of state (*sic*), seems patently ridiculous.

Everybody is fully aware, in fact, that the national problem in most African countries manifests itself as 'tribalism' and 'regionalism'. Our Party has long argued that the solution to this problem is not the formation of single parties, which are supposed to unite the nation but in practice usually end up as strongholds of the worst kind of tribalists and regionalists. On the contrary, what is needed is a complete and systematic democratization of political life in the African countries.[13] Unfortunately, such a measure would be equivalent to a death warrant for the ruling African neo-colonial bourgeoisies, which is why no existing regime will ever put it into practice. The African workers, on the other hand, have nothing to gain from the preservation of the present system.

The natural conclusion from all this is that the *wholesale integration of Africa, on the widest possible geographical and political levels, is an absolute necessity for the political, economic and social liberation of the working people of Africa.* This, too, is a fundamental tenet of contemporary Revolutionary Pan-Africanism.

The African Bourgeois Class Cannot Lead the Struggle

Is the African bourgeoisie capable of carrying out this historic mission and freeing Africa for ever from domination by foreign imperialism?

Throughout this study, we have seen that the answer to this question is a resounding No. This is not only because, 'having been created within the setting of the small artificial states of today, the national bourgeoisie will rise only with difficulty above the limited horizons of these states'.[14] It is also because these bourgeoisies are essentially *bureaucratic bourgeoisies, state bourgeoisies*. They were created along with the neo-colonial state apparatus and their relationship with the latter is essentially parasitic; they are thus condemned to defend that apparatus against any form of genuine Pan-African integration. Furthermore, the African bourgeoisies, precisely because they are bourgeoisies, are themselves duped by the ideology which the world bourgeoisie uses to deceive the proletariat the world over, namely economism. As long as one remains content to fight on a purely economic battleground, there is no fundamental challenge to the world capitalist system or to imperialism. In our era:

> The basis of imperialism is the expanded reproduction of capitalist relations of production on a world scale. Whenever these relations of production are challenged, be it in Africa, Latin America or Asia, the imperialism of the capitalist nations manifests itself in political and military interventions supposedly aimed at defending 'liberty' or 'civilization'.
>
> Imperialism can provide itself with the material base it needs for domination and exploitation simply by ensuring that capitalist relations of production can reproduce themselves freely on a world scale, since the (automatic) corollary is the reproduction of existing inequalities in the development of the forces of production.[15]

In other words, imperialism is adaptable, and no longer demands outright support from its minions. It is enough if the expanded reproduction of capitalist relations of production is not interfered with. As long as this basic condition is met, imperialism has no objection to any pseudo-socialist solutions whatsoever.

This amounts to saying that the imperialist bourgeoisie will always win if economism is the name of the game. Just as 'in the purely economic struggle, capital is always stronger' than labour, so in a purely or even essentially economic struggle, monopoly capital will always be stronger than the African bourgeoisie.

The Example of the Oil Price Rises

Let us now turn to consider the efforts made over the last five years by certain countries in Africa and elsewhere to re-establish some equality in the terms of trade by increasing the prices for certain raw materials exported by those countries, notably oil and uranium. No serious progressive, let alone an African revolutionary, can do other than support such measures, especially if implemented by a government which is in the smallest degree anti-imperialist. On the other hand, serious militants cannot let the matter end there. They cannot endorse the mistaken belief that such measures will, in themselves, solve the problem of unequal international exchange or lead to some form of genuine independence.

At the risk of repeating ourselves, we must insist that the fundamental cause of inequality in international trade is not the price of this or that raw material. The fundamental causes are, first, differences in productivity due to unequal development of the forces in production in the various countries,

173

and second, the relations of domination through which imperialism imposes enormous differentials in the remuneration of labour (wages) and thereby steals a considerable portion of the surplus labour produced in the dominated countries. The ratio between the differences in productivity and the differences in wages is the essence of unequal exchange.

Although the struggle to raise the prices of various raw materials deserves to be supported — with the rider that it is the duty of revolutionaries to assess precisely who benefits from the resulting increase in revenues — it is more important to underline that this struggle is at best a palliative and cannot resolve the underlying problem.

The mechanisms which enable imperialism to perpetuate both its domination and unequal exchange are precisely those mechanisms which organize the world market and integrate the African and other underdeveloped economies into it as dominated and dependent economies. The key point is the need to break away from these mechanisms. Nothing else will serve.

Given the situation of the present world economy and the decisive importance of energy, and especially oil, it might seem that one could sidestep the problem by the simple expedient of specializing in oil production and increasing the price of the product as and when necessary. There would then be no need to withdraw from the world capitalist market. However, experience has shown that the advantages of such a strategy are more passing than permanent, and that unless one can raise prices at will — an ability yet to be demonstrated — such specialization does not resolve the fundamental problem, as most honest economists admit.[16]

Indeed, from a strictly economistic point of view, it would seem that a verdict can already be reached concerning the viability of such measures as a means of re-establishing equality in the terms of trade. 1973 and 1974 saw a very dramatic increase in the price of oil. Nonetheless:

> The Arabian American Oil Co., better known as Aramco, which exploits 90% of Saudi Arabia's oil fields, made a net profit of $3,200 million in 1973, as against $1,700 million in 1972. These figures, the first to be made public, were published by the [U.S.] Senate sub-committee on multi-national corporations.
>
> The four American shareholders in Aramco (Exxon, Texaco, Mobil and Socal) received $2,590 million in dividends, as against $1,560 million in 1972. Aramco did not welcome this publication of its accounts by the Senate sub-committee.[17]

If the American shareholders received $2,590 million of Aramco's $3,200 million profit for 1973, Saudi Arabian interests could not have been left with more than $610 million, a large part of which would have gone straight into the American bank accounts of the various kings, viziers, sheikhs, princes, El Hadj, etc. Meanwhile, in 1974, Exxon overtook General Motors as the world's largest company.[18]

For its part, the *Compagnie Francaise des Petroles* 'contented itself with very little' during the 1973 oil year:

> Mr. Rene Granier de Liliac does not approve of attacks on the oil
> companies; this is hardly surprising since he is the Chairman and
> Managing Director of the *Compagnie Francaise des Petroles*, the C.F.P.,
> which has just announced some rather embarrassing profits.
> The net profit figure, which has nothing to do with the real
> profits of the C.F.P., was 550 million French francs, representing an
> increase of 19.7% in one year.[19]

In 1979, the French neo-colonialists, who were themselves staggered at what
was happening, began to admit that they were literally bleeding African oil
countries controlled by the C.F.P., such as Gabon and Congo-Brazzaville:

> From 1971 to 1976, production had almost doubled, peaking at 11.5
> million tonnes (85% of which was through *Elf-Gabon* and the French
> *Societe Nationale Elf Aquitaine*). But in 1978 it fell back to 10.6
> million tonnes and will probably decline by a further 6% in 1979.
> *Elf-Gabon* (a company in which the government of Gabon took
> only a 25% stake, contrary to the recommendations of OPEC, of
> which Gabon is a member) enjoys a favourable tax climate (73% tax
> on profits, as opposed to 85% in the Gulf) and is allowed to set aside
> up to 10% of its turnover for diversified investments. The company
> has intensified its explorations over the last few years, in an attempt to
> counteract the decline in production.
> With the usual oilman's discretion, Mr. Cosse, the company's
> Managing Director, would only go so far as to say that 'Gabon is
> incontestably an oil-rich province'.
> Gabon is in fact *Elf Aquitaine*'s second largest source of revenue
> (after Lacq, in Southern France). In 1978, revenue from Gabon
> represented more than 20% of the French group's gross margin of self-
> generated finance (1,300 million French francs).[20]

We can thus fairly conclude that, unless the fundamental mechanisms
which determine international exchange are themselves challenged, increases
in the price of raw materials alone cannot solve the problem.[21]
It is still true that, although imperialist domination over Africa is rooted
in the economy, that domination will eventually be overthrown only by an
essentially political struggle. This argument is still as much at the centre of
Revolutionary Pan-Africanism today as it was when its main opponents were
Houphouet, Ahidjo and others who refused to struggle against colonialism
on the grounds that 'we could not even manufacture a pin'.
In the present neo-colonialist stage, the African bourgeoisie cannot
lead this political struggle. Even if it wished to, it could not do so on its own.
In any case, the duplicity and cowardice of the bourgeoisies in the semi-
colonial countries are well known. These classes could not fight without

the backing of other social strata. The African bourgeoisie may have been able to trick the African workers in the old days of colonialism, but under neo-colonialism a much truer picture has emerged. The contradictions between the African bourgeoisie and the working people of Africa now stand out starkly and will accentuate as time goes by. Only the working class and poor peasantry, allied with certain other strata, can carry out the necessary political revolution and bring about the unity of Africa. The so-called 'economic liberation' propounded by the ruling African bourgeoisies cannot lead to any real unity; all their speechifying on the subject is therefore mere Pan-African demagogy.

Appropriate Political Practice for Pan-African Revolutionaries

Let us now turn to questions of political practice. First, the objective socio-economic facts, as outlined in this study, indicate very clearly that Pan-African revolutionaries must resolutely break with any ideological or political tendency which preaches or inclines towards some form of micro-nationalism.

Obviously, this does not mean we should ignore present realities. The small countries do exist. To paraphrase Marx and Engels, what we can say is that, *although the revolutionary struggle of the African workers for their liberation through unity and socialism is not micro-national in essence, it takes on a micro-national form.* In other words, the various detachments of the African revolution in the various countries will proceed to 'settle accounts with their respective bourgeoisies'.

However, the African bourgeoisie has already taken the initiative in the continent-wide struggle. A systematic counter-revolutionary repression has been organized. Under such conditions, African revolutionaries would be mistaken to shut themselves into the present micro-countries. On the contrary, they must seize the weapon provided for them by an African bourgeoisie thrashing about in its own contradictions: that weapon is the Pan-Africanization of the revolutionary struggle. The multiplicity of isolated revolutions, now each cloistered in their own little state even though they share a common enemy — international finance capital — must combine to form a *single revolutionary Pan-African current*.

The Pan-Africanization of the revolutionary struggle of the African workers and poor peasants thus implies the rejection of the inherently counter-revolutionary principle of 'non-interference in the internal affairs of individual states'. The various African bourgeoisies use this principle solely to keep the working people of Africa quiet and docile. The principle is blatantly disregarded whenever counter-revolution can be exported, or whenever there are millions waiting to be stolen, as Houphouet-Boigny and Co. demonstrated over Biafra.

A further point is that the Pan-Africanization of the revolutionary struggle of the workers and poor peasants of Africa cannot remain simply a matter of declarations of principle. It must be translated into an actual organization. The only real limit upon this endeavour is the need to take into account the unequal development of the revolutionary struggle in various countries.

The principle must also be extended to the level of daily revolutionary practice. From this point of view, African revolutionaries should establish a firm basis of mutual aid. *The basic principle is simply that the revolutionary struggle in any part of the continent is the business of all African revolutionaries.*

A Revolutionary Pan-African Standing Organization is unlikely to emerge out of any assembly called and presided over by the 'Guiding Light Party' of this or that African micro-state. On the contrary, the required body will most likely develop through the revolutionary struggle. This struggle will be the ideological and practical cement which will hold together the various parties from the different little countries and ensure that an identity of viewpoint concerning the essential problems of the African revolution develops.

The fundamental objectives of Revolutionary Pan-Africanism today differ from those of the 1950s and 1960s. To ignore this fact is to run the risk of misleading the people and lapsing into opportunism. As our Party already pointed out ten years ago, and as reality has increasingly confirmed ever since:

> It is now quite clear that the African revolution, as it could be defined up until the fall of President Nkrumah, with its three component elements, namely progressive independent states, movements struggling against the old colonialism and movements struggling against the neo-colonialist regimes, has ceased to exist as a single and fraternal current. Demagogy cannot hide this truth from the African people for ever.[22]

Conclusions

Today, and indeed it has been true for several decades, Pan-Africanism and African unity are rooted in objective class interests. Hence, Pan-Africanism has two variants, each expressing the interests of one of the two groups of classes which clash in contemporary Africa. Revolutionary Pan-Africanism expresses the interests of the working class and the poor peasantry, allied to the other exploited classes of Africa. Pan-African demagogy expresses the interests of the ruling African bourgeoisie, their allies and their masters — the imperialists and world reaction.

It is crucial that African revolutionaries today and in the future no longer let themselves be misled by the African petty-bourgeois regimes, with their so-called anti-imperialism and even more dubious revolutionary socialism. One look at their overall policy is enough to see that these regimes have sunk into Pan-African demagogy.

177

On this fundamental question, we in the U.P.C. have distanced ourselves from the opportunists and tired pseudo-Marxists, in that we adhere firmly to Revolutionary Pan-Africanism, the content of which we have outlined in this book. We are in constant struggle against a Pan-African demagogy which is constantly launching attacks against our Party. Nonetheless, the U.P.C. does not say that all African regimes should be attacked all the time, without exception. Nor do we say there is nothing progressive or anti-imperialist about the policy of a few African states. What we do say is: make sure you do not lose sight of the wood for the trees. Whilst it is true that the policy of certain African states is objectively progressive — especially in matters of foreign policy — *one should always examine the overall policy of these states, especially their domestic policy, their policy towards the African working class and poor peasantry.*

In our own country and in Africa as a whole, the revolutionary U.P.C. continues in the course set by Rueben Um Nyobe, Felix-Roland Moumie and Ernest Ouandie. We strive to educate the working masses of Cameroon and teach them the following watchwords:

Down with the national chauvinism of the bourgeoisie, and especially with the blind micro-nationalism, Pan-African demagogy and pseudo-revolutionary socialistic phraseology of certain African bourgeoisies: down with all mystifications!

We strive to make the patriots and revolutionaries of Cameroon, and all African patriots and militants, aware of one fundamental and crucial truth, which has always animated the anti-imperialist struggle of the entire continent: *Revolutionary Pan-Africanism and genuine proletarian internationalism are convergent and in no way contradictory.*

Notes

1. Samir Amin, *Unequal Development*, op.cit., p.317.
2. See also Kwame Nkrumah, *Africa Must Unite*, (London, Nelson, 1963); Cheikh Anta Diop, *L'Unite Culturelle de l'Afrique Noire*, (Paris, Presence Africaine, 1959); Cheikh Anta Diop, *Les Fondements Economiques et Culturels d'un Etat Federal d'Afrique Noire*, (Paris, Presence Africaine, 1974); Theophile Obenga, *L'Afrique dans l'Antiquite*; (Paris, Presence Africaine, 1973).
3. K. Marx and F. Engels, *Manifesto of the Communist Party*.
4. Even Ahidjo warbles on about 'the unanimously observed failure of the international development strategy'. See *Cameroun Information*, December 1973, p.4.
5. Samir Amin, *Accumulation on a World Scale*, op.cit., Vol.I, p.32.
6. Jagdish C. Saigal, 'Reflexions sur la theorie de l'Echange Inegal', in Samir Amin, *Unequal Exchange*, op.cit.
7. Paul Bairoch, 'Commerce exterieur et development economique:

Quelques enseignments de l'experience libre-echangiste de la France au
XIX siecle', *Revue Economique*, No.1, January 1970, pp.25-6. See also
Christian Palloix, *L'Economie Mondiale Capitaliste*, op.cit., Vol.I,
pp.106-107.

8.   Pedro Ferre, *Memorias del Brigadier General Pedro Ferre, Octubre de
     1821 a Diciembre de 1842*, (Buenos Aires, Editora Coni, 1921), pp.
     371-4. Also Andre Gunder-Frank, *Lumpen Bourgeoisies and Lumpen
     Development*, (New York, Monthly Review). Far be it from our own
     'Brigadier-General' Pedro Semengue to express such views.

9.   P. Santos Martinez, *Historia Economica de Mendoza durrante el
     Virreinato 1775-1810*, (Madrid, Universidad Nacional del Cuyo, 1961),
     p.61. Cf. Andre Gunder-Frank, op.cit., p.61. Are the American
     imperialists brazen enough to deny their own history? Africa will
     laugh them out of court if they do.

10. Samir Amin, *Accumulation on a World Scale*, op.cit., Vol.I, p.289.

11. There are many examples: the Bulus in Cameroon, the Fang in Gabon,
     the Bakongo in Zaire and Congo-Brazzaville, the Mandiako in Mali,
     Mauritania and Senegal, the Mandigue in Mali and Guinea.

12. One only has to consider the extraordinary attraction Nigeria exercises
     over Togo, Benin, etc.

13. See Woungly Massaga, *L'Afrique Bloquee: l'Exemple du Kamerun*,
     (CIML, C.P.90, 1211 Geneve 7, Switzerland, 1971), p.119.

14. S. Amin, *Accumulation on a World Scale*, op.cit., Vol.II, p.377.

15. Christian Palloix, *L'Economie Mondiale Capitaliste*, op.cit., Vol.II,
     p.12.

16. 'Given that the salary differentials between the centre and periphery
     are proportionately greater than the differences in productivity between
     the two regions, unequal exchange will result whatever the type of
     products (capital goods or consumer goods) the countries of the
     periphery choose to specialize in. There is thus little basis for the
     argument which recurs so often in the classical economic literature,
     according to which the less developed countries suffer a deterioration
     in the terms of exchange simply because they are specialized in the
     production of certain goods (namely raw materials and consumer
     goods) for which the world demand is inelastic and the import of
     which is restricted in the developed countries.' Jagish C. Saigal, op.cit.,
     pp.118-19.
         Even if an African country specializes in the manufacture of
     'smart' shirts for export, part of its surplus labour will end up in 'its
     metrppole' simply because of the appallingly low salaries paid to the
     workers.

17. *Le Monde*, 30 March 1974, p.35. In 1972, General Motors, the world's
     largest capitalist company, made 'only' $2,100 million net profit. In
     1973, the year when the dominated countries were supposed to have
     seized 'a terrible weapon', Aramco's profits soared to $3,200 million.

18. See *Le Monde*, 7 February 1975, p.31.

19. See *L'Humanite*, 9 May 1974, p.5.

20. See *Le Monde*, 13 February 1979, p.18.

21. One of these mechanisms is the freedom to transfer capital. The French
     bourgeoisie's point of view was clearly expressed by President Pompidou

in late 1973, showing the importance of the issue. 'He [Pompidou] effectively told the African states: "I understand why, given the evolution of your developing economies, you wish to take entirely into your own hands the means of your development and notably your currency. You wish this currency to be an efficacious, practical and reliable instrument for your international and domestic affairs, and for your trade within the Franc Zone. I agree entirely. You may fix for yourselves the parity of your currency. You may dispose of up to 35% of your assets abroad, as you see fit. Even more, since you wish to create a regional development bank, I am prepared to help it get going. You want to borrow on the international market? In many cases I will give you my backing.

You are completely free, but the guarantee for your currencies I will willingly provide is dependent on two simple conditions: freedom of movement for capital within the Franc Zone and a fixed currency parity." The African states agreed and consequently their relations with our country are now much freer.' *Marches Tropicaux . . .*, 28 December 1973, p.3,883, formerly called *Marches Coloniaux*, the journal of the French neo-colonial lobby.

22. Woungly Massaga, 'Sur quelques problemes de l'heure', *Resistance*, (U.P.C., October 1971), p.15.

5. The Bankruptcy of the O.A.U.: Its Significance for Africa

Evaluation of the O.A.U.: Three Main Currents of Thought

The 15th anniversary of the Organization of African Unity, in 1978, was marked by an interesting debate. Critics and enthusiasts of every kind sought to assess what had been achieved in terms of African unity during those 15 years, and what could be envisaged for the future.

As early as mid-1977, we in the U.P.C. had sought to draw up a balance sheet for the O.A.U.'s activities in relation to various political forces within and outside Africa.

> Is the O.A.U. now completely bankrupt? This is one of the crucial questions for present-day Pan-Africanism.
>
> The O.A.U. continues to serve its purpose for the neo-colonial and reactionary bourgeois regimes in Africa. Many erratic progressive African governments still argue that bankruptcy is far too strong a word and warn against extremist viewpoints.
>
> Certain progressive forces outside Africa suggest that the question is a complex one (maybe too complex for Africans?) whilst others present the O.A.U. as 'a bastion against superpower hegemony' in Africa.
>
> This is all tragi-comic hypocrisy. The popular masses of our continent, the patriotic youth of Africa and all the revolutionary African militants will not be duped.[1]

The debate on the achievements of the O.A.U. after 15 years of existence effectively confirmed this analysis. 1978 was an important year in terms of the problems faced by African unity. It was a year full of major political events requiring a response from the O.A.U. These events endowed the 15th anniversary with a certain solemnity. Above all, they enabled the different viewpoints, representing various African political forces of different strength, to be expressed in sufficient detail for an analysis to be made of them.

Three main currents of thought have emerged, corresponding to the positions of the various social classes in Africa. The three currents of thought represent the three essential forces in a capitalist society, which is what Africa is today. Before going any further, it is worth summarizing these three currents.

(1) *The conservative current*, represented by the African neo-colonial bourgeoisie, expresses imperialism's position.[2] This current sees the O.A.U. as ideally suited to bring about African unity and considers the balance sheet after 15 years to be broadly positive. From this point of view, if the O.A.U. did not exist, it would have to be invented.

(2) *The semi-critical current* retains its illusions and thus no longer knows what to do. It is politically lost and cannot imagine 'what can be done without the O.A.U.'. This current expresses the positions of an intellectual petty bourgeoisie which is sometimes, if not always, sincerely patriotic and democratic. It is implicitly backed by many political forces outside Africa. Some of these forces are powerful and are ready to admit the increasingly grotesque impotence of the O.A.U. But they remain convinced that, 'despite everything', the Addis Ababa organization is still the best that can be achieved in terms of African unity. Given this, some argue that 'the O.A.U. should not be attacked', that 'it should be saved, redynamized and equipped with efficient means to serve the peoples'. Others are even less in touch with reality and demand a 'return to Nkrumah'.

(3) *The revolutionary current* expresses the aspirations and interests of the workers and poor peasants of Africa, and expresses the deep aspirations of patriotic radical African youth. The distinctive feature of this current is that it is aware that the historical role of the progressive petty-bourgeois regimes of the early 1960s is over. The African revolution has now entered a new phase, the struggle of the workers and peasants for social liberation, for true popular democracy and a transition to socialism. For this current, the balance sheet after 15 years of the O.A.U. is plainly negative: *The O.A.U. is bankrupt. We need a permanent Revolutionary Pan-African Organization.* This does not mean that, under the present conditions, the few genuinely progressive African regimes should pull out of the O.A.U. The important thing is that they should not allow the reactionaries to tie their hands and that they should beware lest they too sink into Pan-African demagogy. It is important to remember that the reactionary states are informally grouped under the imperialist baton. Consequently, the progressive states must also concert their efforts, and elaborate and follow a common anti-imperialist strategy, so that they may stand up to the reactionaries in the O.A.U. and advance the unification of Africa, by relying on the popular masses who are the only force capable of effecting this process and who have the most to gain from it. Finally, the revolutionary current, in accordance with the essential theses of Pan-Africanism ever since the Pan-African Congresses between World Wars I and II, maintains that African unity without *political unification* can only be a lie and a trap.

All the honest democrats, revolutionary militants and anti-imperialist youth of Africa, along with every true friend of Africa throughout the world, should remember that *these three currents already existed long before the creation of the O.A.U. in Addis Ababa in 1963*, even if in those days their respective positions were formulated slightly differently and in less clear-cut terms.

The present conservative current was already the conservative current in 1961-63. It was then called the Monrovia Group, and its members were much the same as today: Houphouet-Boigny, Senghor, Ahidjo, Bourguiba, etc. Of course, Haile Selassie, Tafewa Balewa (Nigeria) and Leon Mba (Gabon) may have vanished from the scene, but they have fitting successors in Sadat, Mobutu, Bongo, Hassan II and Bokassa. It was this Monrovia Group which adopted a course dictated by world imperialism and which did everything in its power to ensure that conservative and neo-colonial positions carried the day within the O.A.U. – all in the name of 'African Wisdom', of course. Their argument was childishly simple and boiled down to the assertion that, since the political unification of Africa was manifestly utopian, what was required was 'co-operation' through an O.A.U. set up to serve as a sort of heads of state trade union.

It is no coincidence that the second current, the semi-critical petty-bourgeois current, calls for both a 'return to Nkrumah' and a 'redynamized O.A.U.', the 'hope of the African peoples'. This semi-critical current is the worthy heir of the petty-bourgeois Pan-Africanism of 1961-63 (see Chapter One). According to this stratum's conceptions, African unity can and will be established through 'diplomatic channels'. The blatantly reactionary lackeys of imperialism who dominate many regimes in Africa can and will be persuaded to accept revolutionary (and hence political) unity, all through the good offices of the O.A.U. But, even the petty-bourgeoisie, whose opposition to neo-colonialism is so vague, is now forced to recognize the increasingly grotesque impotence of the O.A.U. But this class shrinks from drawing the political conclusions which flow from this recognition. They dare not admit that the U.P.C. and others were correct when they warned against the very idea of the O.A.U., as early as 1962. They prefer to scramble around desperately searching for some way of 'patching things up'. As for the so-called 'Communist Parties of Tropical and Southern Africa', they anathemize all those who threaten to 'destroy the O.A.U.'.

The contemporary revolutionary tendency is, in contrast, concerned with the development and extension of the positions outlined at the Conference of Popular African Anti-Imperialist Organizations at Accra in May 1962, by our Party and others.[3] This position is now shared by revolutionaries in many other African countries and cannot fail to attract wider and wider support.

The core of the problem is, therefore, the same as it was 15 years ago. The only difference is that the various political forces involved have had 15 years in which to learn from experience. What happened in 1963 could conceivably be called a mistake, today, given all that is generally known about neo-colonialism and the O.A.U., no such excuse is admissible. It is a matter of deliberate and conscious choice for everybody who is involved.

The Present Overall Context in Africa

1975 in Africa was marked by three events of major importance, for the continent in general and for the O.A.U. in particular.

First, the major Portuguese colonies, Angola and Mozambique, won their independence. Second, there were significant changes in Madagascar and an anti-feudal and anti-imperialist revolution emerged in Ethiopia. Third, the Spanish colonialists withdrew from the Western Sahara – to the amazement of everybody, they did so in such a way as to allow the reactionary regimes of Morocco and Mauritania to launch a cowardly aggression on the Sahraoui people and their leadership, the Polisario Front. In doing so, Mauritania and Morocco obviously managed to 'forget' their differences of the 1960s.

Mozambique and Angola were important victories, and not just because they put an end to nearly 500 years of inhuman Portuguese colonial domination. By 1975, neo-colonialism had had 15 years to prove itself. The peoples of Africa had seen what it could and could not do. The revolutionary forces in Angola and Mozambique were able to draw the appropriate conclusions from the experience of the petty-bourgeois progressive regimes of the early 60s. How deeply the lesson has sunk in remains to be seen. They surely cannot have failed to observe the gradual transformation of the surviving petty-bourgeois regimes into bourgeois neo-colonial regimes. Consequently, Angola and Mozambique have now proclaimed an orientation based on a *transition to socialism guided by the theory of scientific socialism, Marxism-Leninism*. This is one of the reasons why, in March 1977, the U.P.C. declared that, 'with the independence of Angola and Mozambique, a new era has begun in Africa, the era of the socialist revolutions'.[4]

Angola: The Duplicity of the O.A.U.

The victory in Angola and the circumstances which attended it highlighted the duplicity which underlay the consensus established in the O.A.U. between the bourgeois neo-colonial reactionaries and the politically exhausted semi-nationalist petty-bourgeois current. For the first time in many years, the O.A.U. was forced to choose between neo-colonialism and the transition to socialism. The Angolan affair demonstrated that the struggle in Africa had changed its nature. The choice was now between neo-colonialism and socialism. There could be no fudging of the issues by invoking ideas of African Socialism or Senghor's *Negritude*. As a result, the O.A.U. divided into two camps, curiously of equal numeric strength, during its January 1976 Special Summit Conference in Addis Ababa.[5] The MPLA was (and still is) the true voice of the African people of Angola and the bearer, in that country, of everything which is revolutionary, progressive or even honest in Africa. With the support of the socialist countries and of progressive Africa, the MPLA won the day against the FNLA-UNITA-FLEC coalition (a heterogeneous collection of puppet movements financed from way back by the C.I.A. and the French imperialists, openly backed by nazi South Africa, and at whose side the African people were astonished to discover the eclectic China of the Three Worlds theory – a more ungodly and perverse alliance would be difficult to imagine).

When the Angolan affair came to a head in 1975-76, a curious phenomenon emerged. Faced with a choice between the interests of the African peoples and those of imperialism, many African governments did not hesitate to join a coalition which included the South African devotees of apartheid, despite all the O.A.U. condemnations of that regime. The South African ruler was John Balthazar Vorster, one-time militant in the Nazi organization *Ossewa Brandwag* (he was imprisoned for his activities during the Second World War) and since then boon companion of the imperialist 'defenders of human rights'. Vorster later admitted to the press that, before invading Angola from the south, he had sought and obtained the assent not only of the American war criminal Henry Kissinger, but also of at least six black African heads of state! It would, therefore, seem that from now on, whenever there is a major problem which calls for a choice between socialism or neo-colonialism, the O.A.U. will find itself split right down the middle and quite incapable of taking any serious decision.

African public opinion was reminded of this fact in 1978, during the O.A.U. Khartoum Summit called to discuss the problem of armed imperialist intervention in Africa. The African reactionaries, grouped around Senghor and his constant accomplice in crimes against Africa, Houphouet-Boigny, attempted to put up an enormous smokescreen by equating the constant interventions of the imperialists with the Cuban people's internationalist support for struggles against neo-colonialism. Once again the O.A.U. split into two equal camps and proved incapable of either adopting a clear position against the neo-colonialists or condemning the insolent imperialist forays into our continent.[6] The Conference ended up by recognizing each government's right to call in whoever it felt like calling in.

The political bankruptcy of the O.A.U. was never so sickeningly apparent as during the crisis in the Western Sahara. Not only has the O.A.U. shown itself incapable of taking a decision on the subject, it has studiously avoided calling a special summit to even discuss the matter. Every year since 1976, the O.A.U. has voted to hold a Special Extraordinary Summit on the Western Sahara, yet it has never done so. This charade has gone on year by year, and over half of the governments of the member countries seem quite content to let it continue. In fact, the 1981 Nairobi Summit decided still not to admit the Democratic Sahraoui Arab Republic despite its recognition by 26 of the 50 member states!

To those who have really analysed the basis and purpose of O.A.U. policy, all this is not as surprising as it might seem. Indeed, the real question is why such events have only occurred recently rather than in the past.

The Class Content of the O.A.U.
We have stressed the great importance of a class analysis of African society after nearly 20 years of neo-colonialism. This analysis brings out why the

contradictions within the O.A.U. are now so intense. These contradictions are essentially a reflection of the class contradictions in African society. They have developed over 20 years of neo-colonial capitalist penetration. During the first 15 years of the O.A.U., it was a mix of ultra-reactionary neo-colonial regimes co-existing with inconsistently progressive governments who refused any political confrontation with the forces of reaction. This form of co-existence suited the reactionaries perfectly. However, since 1975, regimes with a straightforwardly revolutionary orientation have emerged; this has both encouraged some of the inconsistently progressive regimes and forced everybody involved to show their true colours.

The O.A.U. is not a U.N. on a smaller scale. It has a different legal character. The O.A.U. Charter contains certain absurd political principles such as the 'inviolability of the colonial frontiers', while at the same time stating quite clearly that one of the organization's purposes is the struggle against colonialism and racism in Africa. Of course, no honest person would claim that one could struggle against colonialism in contemporary Africa without also struggling against neo-colonialism. The hitch is that at least three-quarters of the present regimes are neo-colonial. Even many relatively progressive regimes remain neo-colonial in their economic foundations, for all their often sincere aspirations to join the fight against neo-colonialism. For people who do not use the term as a reactionary mystification or as camouflage for a condescending paternalism, truly revolutionary regimes in Africa are very few — almost certainly less than ten. But these are the reason why the O.A.U. has entered a phase in which it will be constantly undermined by its own contradictions, providing each group remains consistent, of course. Those who bewail the divisions within the O.A.U. are wilfully blind to the scandalous poverty of the workers and block their ears to the cries of anguish and anger of the African people. In practice, they help demobilize the African workers.

This is the real context in which the O.A.U. should be seen. The O.A.U. has now entered a phase in which its unimpressive and indeed broadly negative record will increasingly raise the question of what purpose, if any, does it serve. It is thus of great importance for African revolutionaries to assess that record.

The O.A.U. Record: Its Economic and Social Measures to Promote African Unity

When the O.A.U. was created in 1963, as a 'realistic' means of proceeding 'gradually' towards the unity 'to which we all aspire', as Houphouet, Ahidjo and the rest of the reactionary clique put it, the blatantly neo-colonial regimes argued that 'economic liberation' was a necessary first step. To the surprise of the African peoples at the Addis Ababa Constituent Summit, 'Brother Ahmed', the champion of the African social-verbalists, backed this approach and declared:

The creation of an African Common Market, the industrialization of Africa, the sharing of our resources, the harmonization and rationalization of our activities in order to avoid duplicating efforts, are the natural consequences of the fact that our countries have made identical choices, choices which call for an honest and realistic approach.[7]

Yet Kwame Nkrumah had previously pointed out: 'African unity is, above all, a political goal, which can be won only by political means. The economic and social development of Africa will proceed from this political achievement, not the other way round.'[8] Sekou Toure, speaking after Nkrumah, must have known that he was answering the Ghanaian's point.

Right from the start, economistic theses concerning the liberation and unity of Africa prevailed within the O.A.U. This is not surprising, since it was the African neo-colonial bourgeoisie which was calling the tune in the organization. Economism is simply a bourgeois subterfuge which occasionally infiltrates the thinking of the revolutionary movement.

Progress Towards Economic Liberation and Unification?

Ten years later, an O.A.U. Ministerial Conference was held in Accra from 19 to 23 February 1973. At the Conference, an expert report was submitted to the ministers. The report stressed the need to create the basis for capitalist development of Africa. It spoke of co-operation between African states, of a common energy and mining policy, of promoting African national or multi-national business, of the need to do everything possible in order to be able to process minerals on the spot, etc., etc.[9] Three months later, in May, the 10th O.A.U. Summit was held in Addis Ababa. Houphouet-Boigny spoke of the pressing need for 'ever more structured and fraternal common economic fronts' to unite Africa. 'The era of the great African economic units' was supposedly upon us.[10] It was one way of recognizing that, in ten years, the O.A.U. had achieved very little. In 1978 at the 15th Summit, in Khartoum, Sekou Toure once again called for an African Common Market. Which all goes to show that, *after 15 eventful years, the O.A.U. had achieved nothing towards even a genuine economic unification of Africa.* The African bourgeoisie continues to believe that endless repetition of slogans is the best way to set up an African Common Market. For example:

> *The Ivory Coast Minister of Trade Predicts [sic] an African Common Market:* On 6 November 1978, in Abidjan, during meetings between Ivory Coast leaders and businessmen from Mali and Mauritania, who were attending an exhibition of their countries' products, Ivory Coast's Minister of Trade, Mr. Maurice Seri Gnoleba, expressed his hope that the project of creating a vast West African Common Market would soon be put into effect. 'There is every reason to be hopeful', he said 'since the political will is there, in all the countries concerned . . . . The faith of our heads of state in the institutions they have set up, for instance, C.E.D.E.A.O. and C.E.A.O., gives us good grounds for

believing that a vast West African Common Market will soon become a
reality. It is up to the businessmen of the region to make sure that
it does.[11]

So what has the O.A.U. to show for 15 years of economic activity?
     The O.A.U. has at best contributed to the development of an embryonic
inter-African road and communications network. Apart from the creation
of the African Development Bank, that is the sum total of the organization's
achievements. The O.A.U. was powerless to prevent the disintegration of the
East African Community's Free Trade Zone which had integrated Kenya,
Uganda and Tanzania. Bodies such as the Organization of Senegal River
States remain as insignificant as ever. The Community of Great Lake River
States (Zaire, Burundi, Rwanda) is just a joke. Associations such as the
West African Economic Community (C.E.A.O.) and the Central African
Customs Union (U.D.E.A.C.) do exist but, as everybody knows, they are
firmly in the hands of the French imperialists. The Economic Community of
West African States (ECOWAS) – in French C.E.D.E.A.O. – not to be confused
with the C.E.A.O., brings together nearly all the West African states,
including Nigeria (C.E.A.O. has only six members), but it has only just been
set up. One can already safely predict that it will be closely linked, not to say
subordinate, to the E.E.C. This is particularly obvious when one considers
that the overwhelming majority of African states decided to play the Western
European imperialists' game five years ago by signing the Lome Convention.
When the agreement came up for renewal in 1979, it illustrated the close
anti-African complicity between the African neo-colonial bourgeoisies and
their imperialist counterparts. As the European neo-colonialists themselves
pointed out about the ministerial-level conference held at Freeport (Bahamas)
on 22-24 March 1979:

> The general philosophy of the negotiations was expressed . . . by
> Mr. Michael Anchouey when he declared that all the participants had
> 'striven to find solutions acceptable to both sides, so as to give the world
> an example of successful co-operation before the United Nations
> Conference on Trade and Development (UNCTAD) was held in Manilla
> in May'.
>   The new Convention will be very similar to the old one. There
> will be no major departures from the text of the first Lome Convention,
> just a few improvements.[12]

So much for the 'Common Markets' and other 'economic fronts'
vaunted by Houphouet and Sekou Toure.
     In the meantime, the African states continue to become increasingly
endebted to neo-colonialist countries and bodies. For instance, in recent
months, several African governments have contracted major debts. In every
case, the governments concerned were on the verge of economic bankruptcy.
     The foreign debt of Gabon, a little country endowed with exceptional

The Bankruptcy of the O.A.U.

natural resources, is currently put at around $3,800 million. According to American estimates, the July 1977 O.A.U. Summit in Libreville cost the country over $1,000 million. Sadat's Egypt, Kaunda's Zambia, and Congo-Kinshasa (renamed Zaire by the murderer Joseph Mobutu) have each contracted debts of the same order of magnitude. By 1978, Mobutu already owed $3,000 million. Ghana and the Sudan are expected to be the next victims of such 'aid'. The conditions under which the imperialists grant this 'aid' to Zaire have disastrous consequences for the already much-mortgaged independence of Lumumba's country. Even the imperialist press speaks of the 'humiliation' of the country upon which these same exploiters imposed Mobutu as head of state. This did not stop 'Brother Ahmed' from planning a visit to Kinshasa in late 1978 in order to congratulate his 'companion in arms in the anti-imperialist camp', Joseph Mobutu. The visit was cancelled for as yet unknown reasons.

Guinea-Conakry's Revolutionary Pretensions Exposed

What really motivates the Conakry regime? Recently, there has been a 'fraternal reconciliation' between Conakry, Dakar and Abidjan. 'Brother Ahmed' has attended the O.A.U. Summit in Khartoum and trotted out his economistic platitudes about an African Common Market independent of imperialism, and so on, and so on. The underlying reality is illuminating.

The Guinean foreign debt is now estimated at over $1,000 million. Somehow, it has to be repaid. The regime's economic plans for the period up to 1983 concentrate mainly on the development of the aluminium industry. Guinean bauxite exports rose from 2.6 million tonnes in 1972 to more than 10 million tonnes in 1977. They are expected to reach 35 million tonnes by 1983. 42 million tonnes of alumina and 150,000 tonnes of aluminium are also forecast.[13] The 'Revolutionary Democratic Republic' of Guinea-Conakry will then be the world's largest producer and exporter of bauxite. It will occupy a dominant position in the sector, especially as the country is supposed to hold around two-thirds of the world's known bauxite reserves. The complex infrastructure required for this development (a port at Kamsor, 150 kms of railroad, a mining complex, etc.) will cost around $300 million. As it happens an American financial consortium with World Bank backing has accepted to advance the necessary funds. The immediate consequence is that most of the big aluminium multinationals (which the regime of course combats 'with the utmost energy' at the U.N.!) are associated with the project. They include Alcan, Alcoa, Harvey, Pechiney, Aluminium Werke and Montecatini. With such a battery of multinationals involved, one does not need to look very far to find the instigators of the Guinean regime's recent open move to the right, including the reconciliation with Houphouet and Senghor:

The principal actor in this manoeuvre was Andre Lewin, the French Ambassador in Conakry. Lewin convinced Senghor and Houphouet-Boigny, as well as [the then] French President Giscard d'Estaing and U.N. Secretary-General Kurt Waldheim, that Sekou Toure was ready

189

to end his long feud with the West. Lewin also persuaded M. Claude Cheysson ([then] Commissioner for Economic Development in the European Economic Community) and Robert McNamara, President of the World Bank, to meet Sekou Toure.

Observers believe that it was Cheysson who convinced Sekou Toure to edge away from the Soviet Union and move perceptibly towards the West. Guinea had been selling the bulk of its bauxite at a low price to the Russians, in lieu of cash payments for imports, and Cheysson offered a higher E.E.C. price.

McNamara is said to have specifically requested Sekou Toure to cease his war of words against Ivory Coast and Senegal and to liberalize his regime.[14]

So where are the 'economic fronts' and other 'African Common Markets'? Guinea has clearly opted for total dependency upon the imperialist coalition.

Obviously, the Guinean planners could not just overlook such a glaring contradiction. But what solution did they come up with? They simply brought in a consortium of Arab countries such as Iraq and Saudi Arabia — doubtless all in the context of a great 'Arabo-African policy' with 'the ultimate goal of integrating Black Africa in the Arab Nation', and in keeping with 'Islamic solidarity'.

The same policy was adopted when it came to exploiting the iron ore deposits near the Liberian border. Those involved in the project include European and Japanese companies, as well as countries such as Algeria, Sadat's Egypt, Liberia, Libya, Nigeria and, of course, Saudi Arabia. As the spokesman of the French neo-colonialists put it:

> The Mount Nimba iron ore deposits in South-eastern Guinea are a major asset, which has already attracted the American giant, U.S. Steel. Certain seams contain exceptionally high-grade ore. If U.S. Steel does go ahead, it will join the Nigerian, Libyan, Algerian, Japanese (Nichimen), Spanish (Ini, Sierra Minerai, Cofei), French (Solmer and Usinor) and Liberian interests already associated with Guinea in the consortium.
>
> Oil exploration is already well under way. The Guinean Oil Company, in partnership with Buttes (U.S.), Naftagas (Yugoslavia) and C.F.P.-Total (France), began drilling operations in 1977 on its 44,000 square kilometre offshore concession.
>
> The Konkoure River Complex has been set up in the north-east of the country to treat bauxite from the 500 million tonne deposits in Ayekoye. Six Arab countries (Egypt, Iraq, Kuwait, Saudi Arabia, United Arab Emirates and Libya) joined the scheme in 1976, in partnership with Guinea. Also, Algeria, Nigeria and Reynolds (U.S.A.) might join Yugoslavia and Guinea in a project to produce 5 million tonnes of bauxite and a million tonnes of alumina every year at Dabola,

in the centre of the country.

In the meantime, the Friguia factory (2,000 employees, 1960 of them Guinean), founded in 1959 some 150 kilometres away from Conakry with the participation of Olin-Mathieson (U.S.A.) and Pechiney-Ugine (France), has just celebrated its 10 millionth tonne of alumina.[15]

Comparing the number of African countries involved in the important Guinean projects listed above with the number of imperialist companies and reactionary Arab regimes who are extending their neo-colonialist activities in Guinea, it seems obvious that Brother Ahmed's slogans about an African Common Market are simply camouflage for his own sense of futility. It is no coincidence that the U.S. State Department went so far as to congratulate the Guinean Government for its 'positive contribution' to the 1978 O.A.U. Summit. As the reader can see, there was nothing particularly surprising, then, about the Guinean Assembly President's recent visit to Morocco, during which he told Hassan II that 'Guinea stands side by side with Morocco in every circumstance'.

Is there any hope that Conakry will abandon this increasingly right-wing orientation in the short or middle term? It does not seem likely, especially when one knows that, according to the forecasts, more than 90% of Guinean exports will depend on the aluminium industry by 1985. Even the *New African*, a journal which no one would describe as socialist, wrote in its May 1978 issue:

> In spite of President Toure's incessant claims of 'strict and exhaustive socialist planning', the danger looms strong that Guinea's nationalist and socialist orientation could be increasingly restricted to internal and rhetorical uses.

We now know why Guinea, Senegal, Ivory Coast, Sadat's Egypt, Morocco, Mobutu's Zaire, etc. will increasingly be 'firmly linked to the Western world' — in other words to imperialism. We now know why the 'well-loved leader of the African revolution', as the Cameroonian opportunists call him, was expected in Kinshasa as Mobutu's guest in late 1978: birds of a feather . . . . *We now know why Brother Ahmed's proclamations on the revolution, along with the rest of his anti-imperialist whimsy, will continue to be an endless stream of empty words.*

Consequences of Failure: Position of the African Peoples Today

And what about the African peoples? Can they expect a measure of social progress from this projected integration of Africa with the imperialist West and its reactionary Arab partners? The facts speak for themselves.

In late 1978, the relevant international specialist organizations estimated the number of unemployed in Africa at around 60 million. Even this enormous figure is probably very conservative. Estimates suggest that 150 million new jobs will be needed by 1985. Yet nothing is being done to

191

meet this need. We have already outlined the poverty and unemployment which prevails in the model 'Francophone' countries. If we turn to a country such as Kenya (under Anglo-American tutelage), we find that around 40% of the population of working age in the capital, Nairobi, are out of work; the town's parks are full of the unemployed. It is thus hardly surprising that the crime rate has gone up by 50% in the five years from 1971 to 1976. Furthermore:

> From December 1976 to December 1977, the consumer price indexes for middle and low incomes rose by 13.5% and 21% respectively. The rises continued throughout the first quarter of 1978, representing increases of 3.7% and 5.2%.
>
> Increases in the price of foodstuffs were an important element, especially for the lower income bracket. Foodstuffs rose by 17.2% in 1977 and by 6.6% in the first three months of this year (1978).
>
> In 1976, the average salary rose by 12.2% in the private sector and by 20.2% in the public sector. The gap between the two sectors narrowed slightly in 1977, but remains considerable. (*Marches Tropicaux*, 10.11.1978)

Some 600,000 citizens of Upper Volta work outside the country. In the 'Arab Islamic Republic' of Djibouti, 85% of the population is out of work. The criminal reactionaries of Saudi Arabia and other Gulf countries, who have no hesitation about entertaining cordial relations with the Pretoria nazis or financing anti-African aggressions to save puppet dictators like Mobutu, have not yet felt the need to finance the industrialization of Djibouti to provide work for their 'Arab brothers'. Finally, it is well known that the reason there are so many Senegalese workers in France is because of unemployment in Senegal, and that in Cameroon, out of a population of about nine million, there are something like two million young unemployed people of working age under 30. In the face of this kind of social situation, most African countries have opted for state terrorism on a massive scale, as a supposed miracle cure. Not surprisingly, Cameroon, the one time so-called Central African Empire and Kenya have all opted for similar legislations concerning armed robbery: the death penalty is now standard. In all these countries, theft and armed robbery are increasingly frequent phenomena.

For almost ten years, the African Sahel has been afflicted by drought. Hundreds of thousands of cattle have died, leaving tens of thousands of peasants and herdsmen destitute. One might have expected the O.A.U. to adopt a more responsible attitude to this African calamity. Given that many African countries import foodstuffs, even though 80% of their population is made up of peasants, the southwards advance of the desert should surely be a major preoccupation for an organization like the O.A.U.

Even by its own economistic standards, the O.A.U. is an economic failure.

The Question of an African Language of Communication

Has the O.A.U. any cultural achievements to its credit? The May 1978 issue of the Senegalese democratic opposition journal, *Ande Sopi*, contains a commemorative article analysing 15 years of O.A.U. activity:

> It is quite aberrant that, 15 years after the foundation of the O.A.U., non-African bodies are still handling the planning, co-ordination and implementation of policy in social and cultural matters which should be the province of the specialized commissions of the continental organization. However, on the credit side, the organization of the first Pan-African Cultural Festival in Algiers in 1969 was an opportunity for Africa and the world to evaluate the authenticity, wealth and resplendency of Africa's cultural heritage. The symposium's achievement was to discredit completely the irrantional cultural concepts of the African neo-racists and to draw up a bold far-reaching cultural Charter. It is regrettable that nearly 10 years later, this cultural programme has still not been fully implemented by governments (always the same) who continue to declare their support for the emancipation of the people. [What a pity that the comrades of *Ande Sopi* are not more specific as to the governments they have in mind. The African people have a right to know! − E.M.]

It would seem that, when a progressive decision cannot be forestalled, the simplest solution is simply to make sure that it is not implemented. This tactic is current, both on the cultural level and in politics, as is amply borne out by the case of the Western Sahara − a special O.A.U. Summit on the subject has been approved three times, but has never been called. How long can one deliberately blind oneself to the fact that this is the result of the deliberate policy of the African neo-colonial bourgeoisie?

Twenty years after independence and 15 years after the foundation of a so-called Organization of African Unity, there has still not been a single serious political attempt to establish an African language of communication. Indeed, although Swahili is spoken by some 100 million men and women in Africa − in other words much more widely than Arabic, *this great African language is not even one of the O.A.U.'s official languages*. Since the best way of promoting a language is still to speak it, this is a staggering omission. With a few exceptions which owe nothing to the O.A.U., the problem of teaching African languages and teaching in those languages has not been seriously tackled anywhere. As for Senghor, who is so proud of his ability to write to the Pope in Latin, he is quite incapable of learning anything from the many and sometimes masterly studies of African languages by African linguists, some of them from Senegal. He is obviously far too busy protecting the purity of the French language.

At least half all African youth are without work. Yet everywhere there are more and more mosques and cathedrals. This massive inflow of imported superstition highlights the acculturation of most African neo-colonial bourgeois

193

regimes, who are quite incapable of adopting a genuinely African cultural stance. It also reveals the monstrous hypocrisy which prevails within the O.A.U. on the subject of neo-colonialist cultural penetration by European and Arab-Islamic reaction.[16] With characteristic duplicity, Bongo, Bokassa, Mobutu, etc. suddenly decide to change their names and call themselves El Hadj Omar Bongo Albert, Al Sayed Al Ahmed Bokassa Jean-Bedel, Anouar Al Mobutu and so on. Genuine and healthy Afro-Arab co-operation is an altogether different matter. It should be based on mutual respect for the personality of each people and should start by exposing and finding a solution to the shameful fact that, in 1970, there are still black slaves in certain reactionary Arab Middle Eastern states. There can be no real friendship in the midst of lies. Any Arab progressives who find this presentation too blunt should look to their conscience.

The Political Activity of the O.A.U.

The Liberation of the Countries Still Under Colonial Domination

In April 1977, in an article entitled *L'O.U.A. et l'Afrique Australe*, published in the *Cahiers Upecistes*, we stated:

> For almost two years, the five front-line states — Angola, Botswana, Mozambique, Tanzania and Zambia — have assumed almost the entire burden of supporting the people of Southern Africa's struggle against the racist settlers. The so-called Organization of African Unity has been conspicuous only by its absence.
>
> The present position of the Addis Ababa trade union on the question of Southern Africa is a shameful collapse and wide-ranging bankruptcy, amounting to an historic failure of Pan-African dimensions.

Since then, the O.A.U. has been put right out of the running over the Namibian question. The major imperialist countries in Europe and America (the U.S., Canada, Germany, Britain and France) have quite simply bypassed the O.A.U. over an issue which is of major importance for the whole future of Africa. Why on earth this should be more a matter for the imperialists than for the O.A.U., which officially represents all Africa, remains a mystery. The imperialist powers have even put themselves above the U.N., which is supposedly responsible for Namibia. In doing so, these countries clearly had two main aims: 1) to avoid what they are wont to call 'automatic majorities' voting in the U.N.; 2) to preclude any eventual intervention by the socialist countries. And what has the O.A.U. been doing in the meantime? Nothing. The imperialist countries, who in principle have no direct administrative responsibilities in Namibia, have suddenly assumed the role of mediator, in an attempt to protect their large-scale economic interests — in other words, the wealth they have been able to accumulate during a hundred years of exploitation of the African people of Namibia. The O.A.U.'s failure to take any significant part in the whole affair cannot be simply dismissed as a result of the mediocrity of its Cameroonian pachanga-dancer Secretary — General Eteki Mboumoua, whose election in 1974 merely confirmed the Organization's impotence.

The O.A.U. and the French Government made an interesting spectacle of themselves in 1978 over the African island of La Reunion. The O.A.U. Liberation Committee met and declared that, in accordance with the aims set down in the O.A.U.'s Charter, they were calling for the decolonization of La Reunion. Black patriots from Guyana then quite rightly called on the O.A.U. to support their struggle to free themselves from the hypocritical colonialism of the French. A tragi-comedy in two acts ensued. First, Mr. Raymond Barre, then France's Prime Minister, who just happened to be the son of La Reunion settlers, launched into an exhaustive analysis and brought out a myriad of complex factors aiming to show that La Reunion was undoubtedly 101% part of France. Mr. Barre thus resoundingly confirmed the generally held suspicion that our French friends' knowledge of geography is somewhat shaky (every people is entitled to its little weaknesses, after all). The French Premier advanced the idea that 'geographically speaking'(!) La Reunion was French and had nothing to do with Africa.[17] Michel Debre, who was elected to the Chamber of Deputies by the inhabitants of La Reunion's cemeteries, then intervened, threatening to cut off French 'aid' to various African regimes if they persisted in demanding independence for La Reunion. After all, if La Reunion became independent, Mr. Debre would probably lose his seat. Act two opened a few weeks later, when the O.A.U. Council of Ministers declared that the subject was closed and that there was to be no further mention of the liberation of La Reunion, that totally unknown island whose population was so uncultured and unpolitical that they had not even been able to engender a liberation movement of their own. The 1978 O.A.U. Summit in Khartoum ratified this scandalous position: so the O.A.U. now officially refuses to talk about the liberation of an African territory which is still under direct colonial domination.

During this same Khartoum meeting, the O.A.U. Summit, like the Council of Ministers before it, decided not to recognize a delegation from the Comoro Archipelago in the Indian Ocean. Earlier, in July 1977, the Libreville Summit, which elected Bongo Albert Omar, an obvious French neo-colonialist puppet, as O.A.U. President, had been at pains to avoid the question of the liberation of Mayotte, an island in the Indian Ocean occupied by France and used as a military base. The only support the Libreville Summit would give the occasionally progressive and nationalist regime which controlled the Comoros at the time was to call on Bongo to 'reason' with France, ask that the imperialists 'leave the Comoros in peace' and hand back Mayotte. In retrospect, the joke seems in poor taste.[18] The events which followed have all the features of a piece of well planned skullduggery. Not only did Bongo do nothing about Mayotte, but while Bongo was still President of the O.A.U., France cynically fomented a mercenary aggression, led by the gangster Bob Denard, which overthrew the Comoros Government, murdered Ali Soilih, the Comoros President (during an 'escape attempt', a favourite method of killing political opponents in France's African neo-colonies), and installed a bunch of pro-French sheep as the new Government. The O.A.U. may well find that the Comoros will soon be putting in an official request for the O.A.U. to disengage from the Mayotte affair; this would hardly be surprising since Bob Denard, the mercenary, was for a while a member of the Directory, which took over and ruled the country after the French 'dirty tricks' brigade was let loose. The fact that Denard later quit the Directory makes little difference. Soon after the February 1979 O.A.U. Council of Ministers Meeting in Nairobi decided to re-admit the Comoros, under the puppet Ahmed Abdullah, the French neo-colonial lobby was crowing about the 'full resumption of *co-operation* between France and the Comoros'.

The U.P.C. has long been aware that Bongo's entourage is crawling with French and other mercenaries like Denard. Gabon has become a centre for this kind of activitiy in Central Africa. In January 1977, a plane crammed with mercenaries took off from Gabon and headed for Benin, where the aim was to conduct a putsch. This operation, however, ended in complete fiasco. In late August 1978, a French DC3 disappeared off Italy. Amongst its passengers were Roland Raucoules, Michel Winter and Philippe Toutu. The following quote from *Le Monde* sheds some light on ex-O.A.U. President Bongo's 'merciless struggle against mercenaries in Africa'.

> The ex-O.A.S. activist Roland Raucoules (codename 'Sebastopol') and Biafra veteran who spent some time as Mr. Omar Bongo's private pilot is better known as a *baroudeur* [mercenary soldier] than as a pilot. The 'professional career' of Mr. Michel Winter is more hazy. He served with the colonial Parachute Regiment and is noted as an ex-activist by the *Renseignements Generaux*; he also spent some time in Biafra and . . . in Cameroon, as a *co-operant*.
>
> It is generally believed that the missing DC3, which was bought for 500,000 francs, cash down, on 21 July last year, was not intended merely for gun-running. It was more probably meant to serve as a troop carrier, bearing a commando operating under cover of a foreign intelligence service, with the mission of assassinating several prominent Chadian personalities.[19]

A few months later, bloody confrontation between government factions broke out in Chad.

In Zimbabwe, considerable efforts were made to impose a neo-colonial solution on the African freedom fighters. The O.A.U. bears a considerable responsibility in the matter. In November, 1965, when Ian Smith and his racist clique proclaimed U.D.I., an emergency session of the O.A.U. Council of Ministers voted to break off diplomatic relations with Britain, the racists' accomplice. To the amazement of all Africa, the next O.A.U. Summit reversed this decision and only a handful of countries implemented the break. The imperialists drew considerable comfort from this 'realistic and wise decision', and proceeded to indulge in the usual hypocritical manoeuvrings, quietly supporting the racist clique while endlessly churning out lies about the effectiveness of sanctions against the Salisbury racists. For instance, on the subject of arms shipments:

> The International Institute of Strategic Studies in London has, for example, reported that in 1978 the Rhodesian Air Force increased the number of its *Alouette* helicopters to 66, as against 16 in 1976. There was no need for the French government to deliver these very effective anti-guerrilla weapons directly, since the South Africans have an unlimited licence to manufacture *Alouette II* and *Alouette III* helicopters. This is an excellent illustration of the real meaning of the French decision not to sell any more arms to South Africa and the embargo on arms for South Africa agreed to by the Western countries. As for Rhodesia, the embargo was repeatedly violated last year [1978]: 18 F-337 Cessna planes manufactured under licence in Reims and 11 Bell 205A helicopters were delivered. They now form the backbone of the Rhodesian Army's aerial anti-guerrilla strike force, which has conducted repeated bloody raids into Zambia and Mozambique.
>
> Western mercenaries have flocked to reinforce the hard-pressed Rhodesian Army, in what is probably one of the longest and best organized mercenary operations in recent history. It is generally estimated that about 20% of the Rhodesian Army's 10,000 soldiers are mercenaries, whose recruitment and transport would not be possible without the tacit connivance of the Western governments.
>
> The South Africans [recruit] directly. A discreet and specialized service within the Paris Embassy on the Quai d'Orsay deals with the matter. They have close links with European far right movements and with ex-marine or ex-paratrooper associations in the United States.[20]

Not only did the O.A.U. fail to prevent the imperialist countries from engaging in such disgraceful manoeuvres, but certain O.A.U. members actually provided the white Rhodesians with active support by helping their black puppets to wage war on the national liberation movement — the Patriotic Front — in the midst of its struggle against the settlers. Supporters of the Muzorewa and Sithole factions are being trained secretly in Zaire, Uganda, Libya and the Sudan. French intelligence circles have confirmed that President Mobutu of Zaire and Chief Chirau met in February 1978 in Europe.[21]

The fact that many African countries are well known to maintain economic and political relations with South Africa itself does not prevent the O.A.U. from 'energetically condemning' the Vorster clique. Ivory Coast, Gabon, the so-called Central African Empire, Zaire, Malawi and others who, unlike Mozambique, are not compelled by circumstances inherited from the days of colonialism, continue to deal extensively with the Pretoria Nazis.

Houphouet-Boigny openly preaches the need for 'dialogue' with the supporters of apartheid and meets them as and when he sees fit, without any official authorization from the O.A.U., which has not even condemned his actions. Bongo receives millions of dollars from South African funds, thanks to which he gets himself elected President of the O.A.U., by a Summit meeting which 'condemned South Africa with the utmost energy'.

So much for the Organization of African Unity's disgraceful record in terms of support for the liberation of African peoples still under direct colonial domination.

The Problem of Nationalities and the Colonial Frontiers
We have already mentioned the arbitrary nature of the present frontiers in Africa. Everybody, even the slave traders who drew them up in the first place, has finally recognized that the frontiers were decided in terms of imperialist rivalries and interests. The outcome was that many African peoples speaking one language and living in a coherent territory were split up to suit the imperialist pirates.

Unless it is argued that a people can speak one language and live in a coherent territory without sharing a mode of production and a way of life, in other words, without a distinctive economy and culture, it seems fair to say that *the peoples of Africa formed nations before the arrival of the colonialists*. It is high time that the Africans got over the intellectual barriers placed in their way by dubious Western sociological authorities, many of whom turn out to be vulgar paternalists the moment it comes to Africa. We have to admit that one of the major imperialist successes to date has been to convince African intellectuals (including some anti-imperialist militants) trained in the Western mould, and incapable of breaking out of it, that the problem of the contemporary African states is simply 'a problem of tribes which are constantly at one another's throats' (and the aim, therefore, must now be to 'build a nation out of this multiplicity of tribes') rather than a problem of nationalities. It is striking to observe the complex intellectual contortions certain African progressives will put themselves through rather than speak of *nationalities*, for fear of losing the 'good Marxist' label granted to them by their European Marxist friends and comrades.

In the modern states which had developed in Africa long before the European imperialists invaded, the phenomenon of tribalism, as we know it today, had almost vanished. This affirmation may seem paradoxical. But Cheikh Anta Diop notes that:

> In the days of the Ghanaian and Malian empires, detribalization was already widespread throughout the territory of these great empires, as is borne out by the testimony of Ibn Khaldoun and Tarikh on Sudan. It seems reasonable to assume that in agglomerations such as Ghana, which was amongst the largest in the world from the 10th Century onwards, tribal organization had been completely displaced by the requirements of urban life. In any case, the transmission of individual

names and of inherited property practised under the Malian Empire, as described by Ibn Batuta, confirms that the tribal system had effectively disappeared from the region by 1352.[22]

The problem of the frontiers inherited from colonialism does not correspond exactly to the problem of nationalities in Africa. But the problem of the nationalities lies just below the surface. Up to now, the O.A.U. has been quite incapable of providing any solution whatsoever to a single one of these problems, which are so crucial to the future of our continent. The following list details the major frontier conflicts and other bloody clashes which have occurred between African countries since the O.A.U. was founded.

(1) Algeria and Morocco fought in the Tindouf region in 1964; (2) Morocco clashed repeatedly with Mauritania during the 1960s, claiming all that nation's territory. From time to time the French puppet, Senghor, lets it be known that he might lay claim to that part of Mauritania populated by blacks; (3) Morocco and Mauritania, now allies, have engaged in overt aggression against the Sahraoui Democratic Arab Republic since 1975, following a series of Franco-American manoeuvrings which Spain was dragged into; (4) Libya and Chad are in open conflict over the Aozou Strip, an area of Chad's territory occupied by Libya; (5) Somalia and Ethiopia are at war over the Ogaden, which is at present Ethiopian territory; (6) Somalia lays claim to part of Kenya's territory; (7) there is considerable tension between Sudan and Ethiopia over both politics and territory; (8) Cameroon and Gabon have already clashed militarily over frontier issues, although the matter was kept relatively secret; (9) Cameroon and Nigeria have also clashed repeatedly, for the same reasons and with equal discretion; (10) Ghana and Togo quarrelled extensively over ex-British Togoland; (11) Mali and Upper Volta recently engaged in military confrontation over a border dispute; (12) the traitor, Mobutu Joseph, made insane claims on oil-rich Cabinda in Angola, claims which were also made on their own account by certain more or less official circles in Brazzaville; (13) to the amazement of everybody, the clownish and bloody dictator, Idi Amin Dada, was so confident of the O.A.U.'s impotence – he should know, given that he was its President for 1975 – that in 1978 he arrogated the right to 'adjust' Uganda's frontier with Tanzania unilaterally. He thereby provoked a war in which the silence of the O.A.U. and of most African states, on a question which is supposedly one of the keystones of the Pan-African organization, can only be described as tragic. None of these serious problems has really been resolved by the O.A.U., a fact which is itself quite eloquent.

There are at the moment three main positions in Africa on the question of frontiers and nationalities. First, there is the O.A.U. position, which consists in saying, with a semblance of wisdom, that major rectifications of the frontiers inherited from colonialism will only lead to constant fratricidal war in Africa. Imperialism explicitly supports this position and ensured that it was enshrined in the O.A.U. Charter. Of course, the O.A.U. is quite incapable of implementing its own policy, in the Western Sahara for instance.

Western pressures and the fact that there are millions of tons of phosphates in this small country have meant that the O.A.U. heads of state do not even dare to debate the Moroccan and Mauritanian aggression against the Sahraoui people. More importantly, the O.A.U. position on the inviolability of the colonial frontiers provides no answer to the following fundamental question: why should the peoples of Africa remain split into several states, created by imperialism for its own needs, merely because this or that French bandit, priest or merchant arrived in part of Africa before his British or German competitors, or vice versa?

Then there is the position, condescendingly suggested to Africans by many friends outside Africa, especially in Europe, who invoke the dangers of *Jacobin centralism* (*sic*). This position, which is implicitly or explicitly shared by more than a few African anti-imperialist militants, consists in seeking to resolve the problem of nationalities in Afrca today in exactly the same way as it was resolved in Europe in 1848. One is tempted to point out that this approach seems to express a current belief that Africans are incapable of finding an original solution to their own problems and that everything has to come from abroad, notably from Europe. But let us raise the level of debate and go straight to the heart of the matter.

The dislocation of the multinational feudal empires in 19th Century Europe and the emergence of homogenous states and European nationalities were based on two fundamental conditions which do not hold in Africa today. The first condition was that the subject European nationalities were being dominated by other European nationalities (from the same continent, and usually a neighbour) or by piratical feudal European families. The second condition was that the national problem coincided with the will of the bourgeoisies of the various nationalities to liberate themselves from the feudal yoke and attain their own class maturity. *Indeed the core of the national problem in 19th-Century Europe was the problem of the liberation of each nationality's bourgeoisie.*

In Africa, the situation is completely different. No African nationality has really dominated another. At a pinch, one might mention the case of Eritrea, but even then it is the exception which proves the rule. Even the 'rivalries between tribes which are constantly at one another's throats' in Africa cannot be equated with the domination exercised over certain European nationalities in the 19th Century, any more than the constant rivalry between the Walloons and the Flemish in Belgium can be assimilated to Portugal's one-time domination over Brazil. *For over a hundred years the main form of domination in Africa has been that exercised by European imperialism. There is no need to invent imaginary dominations to cover up the real one.* The fact that it is non-African imperialists who have dominated the African countries and that there is thus no serious contention between neighbouring African peoples is an objective historical factor. It means that African unity is not encumbered by the ball and chain of warlike rivalries and hatred accumulated over centuries, as in Europe. But, equally, it does not mean that African unity will be served up to us on a plate.

Unlike the European bourgeoisie, which liberated itself when capitalism was on the ascendant and when the bourgeoisie was still an historically progressive force, *the African bourgeoisie emerged at a time when the historically progressive role of the bourgeoisie was already over*. It emerged under imperialism, and what is more, under the declining rotten imperialism of neo-colonialism, the imperialism which Kwame Nkrumah rightly described as in its last stage. Consequently, the neo-colonial African bourgeoisie begins where the European bourgeoisie ends, and incorporates all that is reactionary, petty and disgraceful about the latter. The African bourgeoisie is fundamentally incapable and historically unsuited to play a truly progressive role in the present neo-colonial era.

The truth is that, if one wanted to apply the 19th-Century European solution to the national problem in contemporary Africa, one would have to create not 20 states in Nigeria, but several hundred. In Cameroon, there would have to be over 100 different states. Most states would have around 100,000 inhabitants, and very few would have more than one or two million, if they were to form a homogenous nationality in the strictest sense of the term. What good would such a fragmentation of the peoples of Africa do in an era when capitalism has already integrated the entire world? Only to cast the Africans, bound hand and foot, straight into the maw of imperialism's 20th-Century sharks. A national policy inspired by this 'struggle against Jacobin centralism' would in fact be an anti-national policy, because no real national independence would be possible in such a framework. The micro-countries which would result would have even less independence than the small states of today. No argument can justify campaigns by African revolutionaries at the end of the 20th Century to bring about the fragmentation of existing countries, which are already too small for the historical task of development which faces them.

On the other hand, this argument should not be taken to justify annexationist policies such as Morocco (and Mauritania until recently) are attempting in the Sahara. It is one thing to reject the fragmentation of Africa into thousands of tiny republics which would inevitably become easy prey to foreign domination, and quite another to say that any means are acceptable to achieve that end. Annexation is totally unacceptable, in that it involves the incorporation of a country into a state *against the will of its population*, usually by force but sometimes by trickery and deceit. In the Western Sahara, force was used. But our Party has also denounced 'peaceful annexations'. For instance, in May 1972, the Ahidjo regime conducted a 'lightning referendum' (completed some 15 days after it was first announced) and proceeded to annex Western Cameroon, through what amounted to a *coup d'etat*. The underlying reason for this piratical operation was the desire of French neo-colonialism and its agent, Ahidjo, to displace British imperialism and seize control of Western Cameroon's oil reserves.

The third position on the problem of nationalities and colonial frontiers in Africa is as follows. *Only a revolutionary political unification of Africa into a Union of African Socialist Republics, freely accepted by all its peoples, can truly resolve the problem.*

The first implication of this revolutionary position is that the present frontiers would cease to have any serious meaning. It is worth recalling that the boundaries of the various states which originally made up the Federation of Nigeria were recently extensively recast with little or no problem. In the context of a revolutionary national policy – in other words, a policy in keeping with the interests and aspirations of the people – there is no reason why the Fang-Beti people, for instance, should not be regrouped into a single national entity within a Union of African Socialist Republics, rather than being torn between Cameroon and Gabon as at present. In other words, we believe that it is perfectly possible to regroup ethnic nationalities into more coherent units, but this time it would be done by Africa itself, in the interests of the African peoples, not by slave traders in order to satisfy the imperialists' thirst for profits and pillage.

The formation of such a Union of African Socialist Republics is the essential task which the O.A.U. should have undertaken. The revolutionary militants of Africa, and notably the U.P.C. in Cameroon, predicted as long ago as May 1962 that the O.A.U. would be incapable of assuming this great task which is so essential to the genuine liberation of our continent. We based ourselves on the facts, on the very conditions which led to the birth of the O.A.U., and on the nature of its midwives, Haile Selassie, Houphouet-Boigny, Senghor, Tafewa Balewa, Fulbert Youlou, Tsiranana, Ahidjo etc. – imperialist lackeys all. Unlike the U.P.C., many Africans, including great patriots such as Kwame Nkrumah, believed that, 'despite everything', the O.A.U. could achieve this political unity of Africa. The judgement of the past 15 years is conclusive: *the O.A.U. is bankrupt and everybody can see it now.*

The Bankruptcy of the O.A.U. Is Now Complete

The grotesque inadequacy of the O.A.U. hardly needs further documentation. Recent examples include events in the Sahara and the war between Ethiopia and Somalia, which started in 1978, over the Ethiopian province of Ogaden. Shortly after Ethiopian forces, with the help of a Cuban contingent, had retaken the strategic town of Jijiga, the Somali army was forced to withdraw and evacuate the Ogaden, which it had infiltrated under the banner of the Western Somalia Liberation Front. The war was temporarily over, but the fundamental problem remained. Any thinking African patriot cannot but be sickened by this war and by the way the O.A.U. reacted. Several progressive regimes, notably Madagascar, have sought a real solution to the problem, but as for the O.A.U., it stooped to a new low. It was no coincidence that the Somali regime managed to inform first of all the American imperialists of its decision to withdraw from the Ogaden. The fact that it was President Carter, in Washington, who announced the evacuation of the Somali troops, although there existed an Organization of African Unity which supposedly enjoyed official moral and political authority over all Africa, was not only sad, it was profoundly significant.

Contrary to what many outsiders and most politically ignorant African technocratic intellectuals imagine, the African people are not incapable of understanding what is going on and will not have missed the political significance of these events.

For instance, in Douala (Cameroon), apart from the government newspaper, the *Cameroon Tribune*, which never says anything serious or honest, there is also another little paper which, while it is not really free and not in the least revolutionary, is at least formally independent of Ahidjo's U.N.C. In February 1978, this newspaper, the weekly *Gazette*, published a long article on the war in the Ogaden. The Ethiopian counter-offensive was just beginning. The article, written by the paper's editor, Abodel Karimu, alias Akafricus, was entitled 'In the face of Africa's powerlessness to impose arbitration, Mengistu goes on to the offensive', and reflected the growing awareness of the African people, even if expressed in petty-bourgeois terms. Contrary to the cant in the imperialist press about the 'Russian-Cuban menace in Africa', Abodel Karimu wrote:

> The truth of the matter is that the danger which threatens Africa once again is not so much the backing given by this or that foreign power to one or another of the belligerents, as *Africa's refusal to face up to its own responsibilities.* The responsibilities at issue, enshrined in the O.A.U. Charter, are to find and impose a solution which does not come from Moscow, Washington, Paris or London.
>
> The political vacuum created by the procrastinations of an Africa weakened by petty squabbles was an open invitation to the great powers to step in, and they did so without a moment's hesitation.

Abodel Karimu's analysis is not without its weaknesses, but he put his finger on the fundamental issue, even if he could not or did not dare provide a satisfactory answer.

It is quite clear that the O.A.U. – not Africa – has refused to face up to its responsibilities over the problem of frontiers and nationalities. It is clear that the O.A.U. – not Africa as a whole – prefers to procrastinate, over the Sahara, over the Uganda-Tanzania frontier, over any serious issue, in the hope that a miracle will release it from the need to make a decision. What our compatriot Abodel Karimu calls 'the vacuum created by the procrastinations of an Africa weakened by petty squabbles' is in fact the bankruptcy of a neo-colonial bourgeoisie which is powerless to solve any serious problem because of its connivance with international high finance. The responsibility for this shameful treason lies with the O.A.U., the neo-colonial African bourgeoisie and the nationalist petty bourgeoisie of the 1950s, which since then has engaged in the worst kind of opportunist collaboration with the bourgeoisie and imperialism, disguised as Pan-African demagogy. They are to blame, not Africa.

Let us look at concrete instances, for example the Western Sahara.

Who has refused to face up to their responsibilities there? Who else but the O.A.U.? Let us assume, for the sake of argument, that the parties to the conflict in the Sahara could state their case and explain their positions to Africa as a whole. Let us then assume that all the peoples of Africa (and not just the Sahraoui people, which would be far more logical and just) were asked to decide the issue. Does anybody doubt that 99% of the vote would confirm a people's right to self-determination? Is it not the O.A.U. which should compel Morocco (backed by the U.S. and France, who covet the Sahara's phosphate wealth) to allow the Sahraoui people to choose their own fate freely, without outside pressure?[23] Why has the O.A.U. effectively refused to debate the subject at a special Summit? Is this refusal not an implicit recognition by the O.A.U. that it is politically bankrupt and reduced to praying for miracles?[24] Why do so many people wish to hide this simple truth?

In July 1976, the O.A.U. Summit in Mauritius agreed to call a special Summit on the Western Sahara during the following year. The project was openly sabotaged by Eteki Mboumoua, then O.A.U. Secretary-General and by Sewoosagur Rangoolam, Prime Minister of Mauritius and President-Elect of the O.A.U., whose pockets were jingling with South African rands. In the following year, during the 1977 Libreville Summit, Bongo and Hassan failed to have 'the dossier on the Sahara declared closed', and once again it was decided to call a special Summit to deal with the question. The date and the place were set: Lusaka, October 1977. Just a few weeks before the appointed date, the Zambian Government announced that it could not guarantee the safety of the delegates because of Rhodesian bombardments. Throughout the following year, El Hadj Omar Albert Bongo, who had by then been elected President of the O.A.U., manoeuvred endlessly to prevent the special conference on the Western Sahara being held, much to the delight of his French masters. The decision to hold the conference was confirmed once again at the Khartoum Summit in 1978. The question now is whether the revolutionary and progressive forces within the O.A.U. will stand by and allow Bongo and the other French puppets to carry on with this kind of political gangsterism, aimed at officially choking a worthy African people 'in the name of all Africa', simply because a few thieves in France and America and a few bourgeois Africans want to make more money for themselves.

Who will court ridicule and claim that this example of the O.A.U.'s impotence is unique in Africa? For several years now, Libya has blatantly disregarded the O.A.U. Charter by occupying part of Chad. Both Chad and Libya are members of the O.A.U., an organization which demands that the colonial frontiers be respected. What has the O.A.U. done? Nothing. In late 1978, Idi Amin Dada decided to 'readjust' his borders, at Tanzania's expense. This amounted to a gross violation of the principle which the O.A.U. holds so dear, yet what did the Organization do? Instead of condemning the Kampala clown, it offered itself as 'mediator'. Can this really be interpreted as something other than impotence?

Our Party predicted all this long ago, as we have repeatedly pointed out.

We would have preferred not to have been proved right, we would have preferred the freedom of the African people to have been advanced by the O.A.U. As it is, we do not claim clairvoyance. Um Nyobe, founder and Secretary-General of our Party, put it quite simply in 1957: 'There are no prophets in politics; but if one is constantly guilty of having been right first, one draws a certain moral satisfaction from reviewing past events.'

Abodel Karimu's inability to come up with a clear answer to the problem, or even to pose it correctly, has wider implications. The failure is not his personally. It expresses the conceptions of an entire African class, the conceptions of the African petty bourgeoisie. The form of expression may vary, but the basic idea is the same: the O.A.U. is still worthwhile, it can be renovated; '*despite everything*', it can still bring about African unity, the real African unity the African peoples dream about. Indeed, let us go on.

In the middle of June 1978, when the insolent imperialist interventions in Zaire to save the decaying regime of Anouar El Mobutu were at their height, the total ineffectiveness of the O.A.U. led various political forces and currents of opinion in Africa at last to give the matter some thought. It is more difficult to cheat intellectually during a political crisis. Indeed, at such times, each social class tends to express its own position as clearly as possible (sometimes by keeping silence, of course). Everybody is seized by an uncontrollable political excitement; everybody demands the right to speak.

Can the O.A.U. Be Revived?
On 15 June 1978, an African sociologist called Yahya Diallo published an article entitled 'Back to Nkrumah' in the French daily, *Le Monde*. It is worth quoting extensively from this article, which so clearly expresses the author's class viewpoint.

> When Kwame Nkrumah presented his project for continental unity to the inaugural session of the Organization of African Unity in 1963, it seemed utopian. Yet it was a programme which was well suited to the needs of the peoples of Africa, who were still hostages, under the tutelage of others and lacking the coherent strategy which would enable them to achieve independence and liberation.
>
> Nkrumah's project, which had both a military and an economic dimension, and which defined a strategy geared to establish the political foundations of African unity, ran into all sorts of obstacles, many of them due to personal rivalries. Today, however, it is clear that the one and only way of protecting the future of the peoples of Africa, which has already been mortgaged by men who care little for the happiness of their fellows, is to set up an economic body on a regional, national and inter-African basis. [The informed reader will note that Diallo glosses over the third dimension of African unity, the political dimension, which Nkrumah saw as the essential starting point. E.M.]
>
> Having failed to adopt a coherent political strategy, the O.A.U. now finds that its very existence is under threat from a programme of

destablization elaborated following imperialism's reverses in Asia . . . .

South Africa can relax. North America, Western Europe and now China are moving towards a coalition. The natural alliances are reforming . . . .

How can one claim to defend somebody when one sells arms to their enemy? Who supplies South Africa and Ian Smith with weapons? Who arms and recruits the mercenaries?

So far, despite our reservations, Diallo emerges as a sincere African patriot. But, after affirming that only Africans can resolve Africa's problems, the sociologist calls on 'all Africans' to:

> agree on the preconditions of their common independence. For a start, we must revive the O.A.U. and endow it with a Defence and Security Council, backed by an Organization and Co-ordination Committee. We should set up a permanent control and security body for the region which stretches from the Red Sea to Southern Africa. Analogous bodies could be created later, to cover the other regions of Africa where armed conflict has broken out.
>
> The resolution of inter-African conflicts must be the responsibility of the African states themselves, irrespective of any ideological, confessional or religious considerations. Nkrumah was right when he said, 'As long as we remain Balkanized, regionally or territorially, we will be at the mercy of colonialism and imperialism'.

Diallo's sincerity here gives way to a whole series of considerations which completely debar him from resolving the problem he sets out to tackle.

First, he seems to forget that, even in 1963, the O.A.U. was a compromise between those who agreed with Nkrumah and the others, who thought his project utopian. In other words, the O.A.U. only existed in the first place because, unlike the U.P.C., Kwame Nkrumah and the nationalist petty bourgeoisie of his day agreed to reach an understanding 'on the preconditions of their common independence' with the reactionaries. Diallo himself recognizes that this compromise amounted to adopting an incoherent strategy or no strategy at all. And on this point at least, he is right. But his conclusion is that the O.A.U. has to be revived. At which point, we get completely lost.

Second, Diallo proposes that one way of reviving this Organization, which has gone 15 years 'without a coherent strategy', would be to endow it with a Defence and Security Council. Diallo cannot be unaware that his project can have only one of two contents. Either it is equivalent to Nkrumah's 1963 proposal for an African High Command responsible for a common defence system, which was rejected. In which case, why should those who rejected the proposal in 1963 accept it now? Or else, his proposal differs very little from the *existing* Defence Council of the O.A.U., presided over by the Defence Minister of Guinea-Conakry! Of course, nobody has ever heard of this body, except once. In late 1975, when the imperialists sensed that 'their nurselings in the FNLA and UNITA were on the brink of defeat in Angola, they sought to call in 'African' troops. Their idea was to provide themselves with an argument against the presence of the internationalist Cuban troops who had been called in by MPLA to help eject the invading South African army. Eteki Mboumoua, roused from his slumbers, declared that, 'if things do not sort themselves out quickly, the O.A.U. Defence Council could well decide to send Pan-African troops into Angola'. Then nothing; complete silence.

In fact, the real problem, which Diallo's proposal does not deal with, is what his Defence and Security Council would be good for. The present one is no use at all, never has been and probably never will be. As for Diallo's proposal, everybody knows that Houphouet-Boigny wants nothing to do with a Pan-African Force which could help our brothers in Southern Africa get rid of the Pretoria Nazis. On the other hand, Houphoet and Senghor were quite willing to co-operate with French imperialism by creating an 'inter-African police force' to rescue dictators whose rule is threatened by their own people. With the characteristic cowardice of the colonial bourgeoisie, Houphouet claims that in any war with the South African racists 'the rear-guard of the South African Army would be in Abidjan before the first Ivory Coast soldier had had time to kit up'.

So what purpose would Yahya Diallo's Defence Council serve? Could it be used to send troops to act as buffers between two African armies? One only has to look at the recent history of Africa to see why it could not. The O.A.U. and its Defence Council seems to have vanished from the face of the earth during the war between Idi Amin Dada and Tanzania and during Nigeria's intervention in the conflict in Chad. Indeed, the moment a problem becomes serious, the African states behave as if the O.A.U. simply did not exist. Luxurious summits and fooling the African people seem to be its only real purpose.

Third, what would the other organs of a renovated O.A.U. that Diallo proposes be good for? He himself does not specify. Perhaps he has not thought about it in any great detail. Intellectuals generally — and not just in Africa — have a tendency to indulge in superficial reflection on serious issues. Unfortunately, it takes more than an academic title and the co-operation of a major imperialist newspaper to make a real analytical contribution.

Finally, Diallo suggests that the African states can resolve all inter-African conflicts, 'irrespective of any ideological, confessional or religious considerations'. What does this really mean? Surely it is a pious dream. How does Diallo imagine that people can reach agreement, 'irrespective of any *ideological* considerations', in an African society which is increasingly divided into social classes with opposed and contradictory interests and aspirations? For instance, what sort of solution does he see to the conflict that involves on one side the revolutionary Angolan state led by the MPLA rooted in the masses and, on the other, the neo-colonial state led by Senghor Leopold Germanicus, who supports Savimbi, an ally of the Pretoria Nazis? Dreamers dream, and capitalist penetration of Africa continues.

As for the phrase 'irrespective of any confessional or religious considerations', this makes one wonder whether Yahya Diallo is himself a member of
some religious or confessional group. We can, of course, grant that first names
do not necessarily always mean very much. But it is an irrefutable fact that
religious affinities are a distinct element in a great many of the relationships
which are presently being established amongst or with reactionaries in Africa.
If Yahya Diallo is really an honest African patriot, he must know that, right
up to the overthrow of the criminal regime led by Reza Pahlavi in Iran, it
was no secret that:

> Iran works in close co-operation with South Africa in matters of oil.
> Despite Iran's condemnation of apartheid, there was no question of
> the Shah stopping oil supplies to South Africa's Sasolburg refinery —
> in which Iran has a 17% stake . . . . According to South African
> officials, Iran exports 50,000 barrels of oil daily — worth $220 million
> a year — to South Africa. In return, Iran spends only $103 million in
> South Africa. Iran's trade balance with South Africa and with a number
> of African countries is thus exceptionally favourable to Tehran.
>   The second important consideration for Iran in building bridges
> with African countries is the Islamic religion. [!] There are more than
> 100 million Muslims in Africa — about a quarter of the continent's
> total population; Iranian officials themselves admitted that they were
> sympathetic to Somalia because it is an Islamic Republic, which
> Ethiopia has never been despite its much larger Muslim population.[25]

Given this context, how are we to take Yahya Diallo's proposition?
The question becomes even more legitimate when one knows that *Le Monde*'s
sociologist goes on to say:

> Neither Cuba nor the U.S.S.R., nor the United States, nor any of their
> allies[26] can substitute themselves for the Africans. Only the Africans,
> in co-operation with their friends from the Arab world and other
> continents [*sic*!], can agree the conditions of their common indepen-
> dence; they will do so on the basis of their profound solidarity.

This 'Afro-Arab co-operation on the basis of a profound solidarity' is clearly
dear to Yahya Diallo's heart; especially as he envisages the 'ultimate goal of
integrating Black Africa within the Arab Nation'.

Since the question seems to be so important to Arab reactionaries that
they bother to engage the services of African intellectuals and encourage
them to develop 'theories' which will 'get the merchandise moving', we might
as well make sure that there is no possibility of a misunderstanding.

No serious Arab (or African) progressive can accuse the U.P.C. of being
in the slightest bit tainted by anti-Arab chauvinism. On the contrary, in 30
years of activity, our Party's revolutionary solidarity with the struggles of

the Arab *peoples* has always been clear, especially when the Arab reactionaries (bourgeois or feudal) were filthily betraying the struggles of the Arab populations themselves. So we have no qualms about stating our views bluntly: if certain Arab or Muslim pseudo-progressives care to indulge in the usual petty-bourgeois gymnastics and ally themselves with African and Arab reactionaries, with the downright hypocritical aim of inducing the African workers and peasants to believe in some Afro-Arab so-called 'profound solidarity' which transcends social class, that is their own affair. But nobody can expect the U.P.C. to endorse a 'deep solidarity' between the feudalists of Saudi Arabia, Morocco and the Arab Emirates, the neo-colonial bourgeoisie of Egypt and elsewhere, as well as the most reactionary regimes in Africa. Genuine Arab and African progressives are not so easily fooled by reactionary Pan Islamism and would obviously have a very different definition of 'the preconditions of our common independence'. After all, it is difficult to see what the princes of the Ibn Saud family in Arabia could possibly have in common with the workers and peasants of Cameroon, Senegal, Zambia, Uganda, Nigeria, Algeria, Morocco, Kenya or the 'Fraternal Arab Republic' of Djibouti. Perhaps it is worth adding that taking all black Africans for idiots shows a certain lack of political intelligence. We are unlikely to embrace co-operation with the bourgeois in the Arab world so long as Arab reaction is operating as imperialism's spearhead against Africa and cynically manipulates Pan Islamism, to consolidate totally corrupt and discredited dictatorships throughout the continent. This kind of 'integration of Black Africa within the Arab Nation, is certainly not *our* 'ultimate goal'.

The stunning cynicism, arrogance and political blindness with which Libya, Iraq and – if the press is to be believed – some Palestinians intervened on the side of the grotesque regime of Idi Amin Dada in Uganda exposes the present policy of the Arab League towards Africa for what it is: rampant neo-colonialism, on the part of Arab reactionary and pseudo-revolutionary regimes alike. This intervention in Uganda, in particular, highlighted the tragi-comic quality which attaches to the efforts of contemporary 'progressive' charlatans to mislead black people. Here was a dictator who came to power in 1971, thanks to a *coup d'etat* cobbled together by the British neo-colonialists, with a little help from Israel. Just because, in one of his countless bouts of delirium, this lunatic declared that 'Hitler was right to massacre the Jews', he immediately became the darling of several 'revolutionary' Arab governments. They soon came to prefer this ally – who was generally considered an embarrassment, even by the imperialists – over any democratic change in Uganda, thereby showing how little they really cared for the fate of the African people of that country. Of course, all this will be 'forgotten' at the next O.A.U. Summit, where everyone will welcome the fraternal delegate from the 'General Secretariat of the General People's Congress of the Libyan Popular and Socialist Arab Jamahiriya'. As for Senghor and his crew, they are keeping quiet for the moment, like frightened toads, and do not even dare remind Iraq of the great principle of 'Africa for the Africans'.

Diallo in his article calls for a return to Nkrumah. Does he mean to put the clock back by 15 years? In 1963, Nkrumah was undoubtedly the most advanced Pan-Africanist amongst the heads of state. But we now know, and Diallo recognizes, that Nkrumah was mistaken about the O.A.U.'s ability to bring about the political unity of Africa, without which we will remain at the mercy of colonialism and imperialism. His mistake was forgiveable and we can now explain it. At the time, militant Africa as a whole had little experience of neo-colonialism and the shameful venality of the African neo-colonial bourgeoisie. Today, we have had at least 15 years in which to observe the work of the O.A.U. and the activities of the African bourgeoisie, a class which is compared with the colonialist settlers what the plague is to cholera. What was an understandable error on Nkrumah's part in 1963 became a serious and quite unacceptable misunderstanding on the part of Diallo and all African patriots in 1978-79. It amounts to cynically misleading the African peoples instead of mobilizing them. How can one expect an organization which has done nothing of value in 15 years to be 'revived' in any meaningful sense?

Nkrumah's position had two main facets. *He was entirely right to argue for the need for a Continental Government.* In doing so, he was at least ten years in advance of any other African head of state and earned his place in history. *But he was mistaken in his belief that this political unity could be achieved by a heads of state trade union.* He neglected the fact that at least 80% of these heads of state came from a class which had no interest in such unity.[27] After two decades of neo-colonialism, we must redress Nkrumah's position, keep what was good but cut out the bad, however painful that may be to some. We must preserve the correct thesis, which points to the need for political unification, but we must also admit that the O.A.U. cannot bring such unification about, that it is an inappropriate instrument which has in no way advanced unification in the 15 years of its existence. This is the only real way of going 'back to Nkrumah', and it is a course which he himself would doubtless have adopted had he lived, as is clear from his last writings.

The positions expressed by Yahya Diallo and Abodel Karimu have a wider import, as can be seen from the writings of certain political friends of Mamadou Dia, ex-President of the Council in Senegal, who was ousted by Senghor's 1962 neo-colonial and pro-France *coup* and is co-founder of *Ande Sopi*, a Senegalese opposition journal. Mamadou Dia's friends effectively express the interests, aspirations and opinions of broad sections of the petty-bourgeoisie in Africa, especially when it comes to the question of the O.A.U. and African unity. In an article published in June 1978 under the title 'The O.A.U., an Anniversary: The Hope of the African peoples?', *Ande Sopi* presented a very critical survey of the O.A.U.'s activities. Unfortunately, the essay articulates certain rather superficial points of view:

> The Organization of African Unity, founded in May 1963 by the Summit Conference of African Governments and Heads of State, originally aroused high hopes among the Peoples of the entire continent [Not

quite: the U.P.C. had no such hopes, even in 1962, E.M.] .... Those militant regimes present ensured that concrete and lucid proposals were made with a view to endowing Africa with an efficient and committed executive body capable of tackling both immediate and long-term problems. Because of the uneven level of consciousness of the heads of state, not to mention imperialism's success in misleading all too many African governments, the structures adopted were timorous ones, defending non-operational programmes which would, in any case, not have hampered neo-colonialism's freedom of action in Africa. Wisdom or laziness? The fact remains that political regroupment, the mobilizatory slogan of the anti-colonialist forces, had ceased to be the main goal.

Let us be clear. If we are talking about Nkrumah's project, it is not correct to talk about 'those militant regimes present' making propositions. History records that, when it came to the vote, Nkrumah found himself *alone* in supporting the political unification of the continent. This is quite clear from the speeches by heads of delegations published after the May 1963 Conference. Furthermore, what the Senegalese journal calls 'the uneven level of consciousness of the heads of state' was in fact the way that the different class interests each entailed a different class consciousness. It was not the 'uneven level of consciousness of the heads of state' or even imperialist efforts which 'misguided so many African governments'. *The reactionary governments simply took advantage of the nationalist petty-bourgeois governments' naivety.*

In 1979, it is surely about time that African revolutionaries stopped playing into the hands of the neo-colonial African bourgeoisies and accepting the easy excuse that these bourgeoisies are not conscious of the harmful consequences of their policies. These people are perfectly aware of what they are doing, usually more so than the African 'democrats' are!

The *Ande Sopi* article goes on to denounce the 'inefficiency of governments' and the fact that unjustifiable 'conflicts between independent states are multiplying'. One is tempted to answer that the real point is not whether these conflicts are in any way justifiable but that, given the present Balkanization of Africa, such wars are almost inevitable. The author then reminds us that 'in terms of culture the artificial boundaries established by the foreign powers in their zones of influence in Africa still prevail.' He continues as follows.

What can the Pan-African Organization do to remedy this unpromising picture? Not much.

The O.A.U. is not endowed with any real executive power to engage in the decisive actions which the masses so obviously wish to see.

Absolutely nothing of any significance has been achieved in this domain [of the consolidation and application of the Organization's principles. E.M.] No independent African state has voluntarily accepted to transfer any part of its sovereignty to a Pan-African or regional executive.

On the economic level, we are still very far from any practical implementation of the African Common Market envisaged in 1963. [Let us recall that Nkrumah foresaw this failure in 1963, as his speech quoted at the beginning of this chapter shows. E.M.]. Under the pretext of the need for pragmatic progressive measures, regional economic unions were set up, but they are now stagnating, immobilized by national sectarianism and constant attack from the multinational companies. Forms of economic co-operation which could at least have served as a model, for instance the East African Community, disappear as if by magic, to be replaced by a notion of Euro-African co-operation which turns our continent into a periphery of the centres of world capitalism.

Although *Ande Sopi* does not say so in so many words, it would seem that we are no longer alone in having recognized the obvious, namely that *the O.A.U. is bankrupt and incapable of doing anything serious to advance the real unity of Africa*! But what is to be done? The Senegalese journal's solution is as follows:

A Peoples' O.A.U.
Now that the Pan-African organization has been almost entirely taken over by retrograde forces, especially given the recent succession of unfortunate presidencies, the issue is how to save the O.A.U., to redynamize it and endow it with efficacious means of serving the Peoples of Africa [Incredible but true! E.M.].

Its responsibilities in the domains of sovereignty, diplomacy and security should be enlarged [Remember Yahya Diallo and his Defence and Security Council. E.M.]. The O.A.U. must also strengthen its representativeness by opening itself up to include the democratic organizations of women, workers and young people. The participation of popular movements in the formulation and implementation of its projects would be salutary for the Organization. The O.A.U. must cease to be a trade union geared to ensure the survival of anti-popular regimes. Without popular control, heads of state will always go back on the commitments made at the previous Summit and the O.A.U. will stagnate, killing all the hopes of the African peoples.

The 'recent succession of unfortunate presidencies' is obviously not the core of the matter. We would argue that it is the political collapse of the O.A.U. which explains why people like Idi Amin Dada (1975), Sewoosagur Ramgolam (1976) and Albert Bongo (1977) have become President. The fact that a man as unsuitable as Eteki Mboumoua could be appointed as Secretary-General of the O.A.U. in 1974, on the express recommendations of Joseph Mobutu, gives some indication of how low the organization had sunk. When El Hadj Omar Albert Bongo was elected O.A.U. President by his peers, everybody knew that the 'young wolf' of Libreville was accepting finance from the Pretoria Nazis for various economic projects, and that he maintained regular trading links with Ian Smith's despicable clique. None of this prevented the O.A.U. Summit from appointing Bongo to the Presidency for a year. When Eteki Mboumoua was elected Secretary-General, after ten indecisive ballots, it was common knowledge that the man was an indolent sybarite. Appropriately enough, he was fast asleep throughout the memorable session which elected him to the top job in the O.A.U. apparatus, where he replaced his colleague and compatriot, Ekah Ngaky, who was so deeply involved in various manoeuvres mounted by 'Tiny' Rowland, the neo-colonialist boss of Lonrho. It will also not have escaped the African people's attention that neither the revolutionary states nor even the slightly progressive ones seem at all keen to assume either the annual Presidency or the post of Secretary-General.

By reiterating the idea of an executive body with more responsibilities in matters of sovereignty, diplomacy and security than the present General Secretariat, *Ande Sopi* (timidly) seeks to revive the 'spectre of Nkrumah'. But as long as the O.A.U. remains the O.A.U. of today, none of this can happen. That is not what it was set up for. It is easy to imagine Houphouet-Boigny's riposte to any such proposal: 'Perhaps what you have in mind is another Organization altogether?', he would say, to applause from Senghor, Bokassa, Bongo, Sadat, Hassan, Bourguiba, Ahidjo and, no doubt, his 'companion in arms in the world anti-imperialist camp', the 'Great Strategist and pillar of the African Democratic Revolution' (Sekou Toure). The other proposal, to 'open out the O.A.U. so as to include the popular organizations of women, workers and young people', would no doubt also create a great furore. But which women's organizations does the author have in mind? The N.C.U.'s camp followers in Cameroon, the W.O.N.C.U. (Women's Organization of the N.C.U.), for example? And which workers' organizations? Gangster trade unions like Ahidjo's own N.U.C.W. (so-called National Union of Cameroonian Workers) which stands 100% behind Ahidjo's fascist N.C.U. and is always ready to denounce workers to Ahidjo's political police? And which youth organizations? Perhaps the author was thinking of our Y.O.N.C.U. (Youth Organization of the N.C.U.), into which a few informers, tormented by hunger, dragoon young Cameroonians, with a little help from SEDOC (Ahidjo's political police), of course.

It is quite astounding that a democratic opposition paper like *Ande Sopi* should suggest that popular movements should, or even could, participate in the formulation and implementation of O.A.U. projects. Can *Ande Sopi* really imagine a Senegalese delegation to the O.A.U. which would include Senghor's clique as well as representatives of *Ande Sopi*, of COSU, of the R.N.D., of the Majhmout P.A.I. and the underground P.A.I., of Wade's Democratic Party — not to mention the anti-imperialist students of Senegal, side by side with the Germanicus clique, the great poet's agents and his trade

213

unions, etc. etc.? Or who but a fool could envisage a Cameroonian delegation to the O.A.U. made up of a clown like Ahidjo, his indescribably corrupt government, his fascist N.C.U., his Y.O.N.C.U., his W.O.N.C.U. and his N.U.C.W., alongside our Party (the U.P.C.), the MANIDEM Movement and the newly emerging National Union of Socialist Students of Kamerun (NUSSK)?

This nightmare prospect is the direct outcome of one fact: certain sincerely patriotic Africans will not or cannot draw the right conclusion from their own observations — that the O.A.U. has shamefully collapsed. They therefore desperately try to wrap the O.A.U. in soap bubble lifejackets, to prevent it sinking for good. But you cannot save what is already dead. Politically, the O.A.U. is well and truly dead. The most you can say for it is that the only people who could save it would be the imperialists, who probably want to keep it going as a way of fooling the African people. In other words, its only possible saviour is the devil himself. Yet the comrades from *Ande Sopi* ask the African people to keep this instrument of the imperialists in working order.

Since it is a matter for dreaming, let us dream. Suppose that tomorrow the revolutionary and truly progressive regimes in Africa decide to do away with today's charade. Suppose they manage to acquire the strength (and above all, the political will) to transform fundamentally the Organization's political machinery and *the hypocritical principles on which it is based:* non-interference, absolute sovereignty of states, inviolability of colonial frontiers, and other nonsense. *If all this happened, there would be no more O.A.U.!* The whole content of the O.A.U. would be different and the problem would no longer be the same. This comes down to what our Party has been saying for years: *The present O.A.U. is bankrupt! We need a Revolutionary Pan-African Organization! We must now struggle straightforwardly for a Union of African Socialist Republics!*

We Have Come to a Great Historial Turning-Point

We have come to a great historical turning-point for our continent. The Organization which has represented our continent until now has failed completely. We are passing or have already passed from the era dominated by national liberation struggles to the era of acute class struggle in Africa. In 20 years, neo-colonialism has had plenty of time to carry out its purpose. The African neo-colonial bourgeoisies have developed substantially, in alliance with imperialism. With very few exceptions, wherever the nationalist petty bourgeoisies of 1958-62 have won power and succeeded in retaining it, they have become neo-colonial bureaucratic bourgeoisies. In any African countries where genuinely progressive regimes come to power, imperialism and African reaction will do all in their power to overthrow the Government, isolate the new revolutionary regime or simply put the clock back.

We must be very careful never to forget that the whole basis for the evolution undergone by the African bourgeoisie and the nationalist petty bourgeoisie of 1958-62 lies in the socio-economic conditions of neo-colonialism.

The crucial point is not the 'nastiness' of this or that individual, this or that African President, although some are considerably nastier than others. We face a much more serious challenge, comparable, in terms of its historical importance, to the Slave Trade, the 19th-Century imperialist invasion, and the renaissance of the African national movement after the Second World War. When people say that Africa is changing, mutating, that is really what it means.

Under these circumstances every serious African revolutionary now has a duty to analyse what has happened and what is still happening in order to draw the long-term conclusions for Pan-Africanism. We should not let ourselves be misled by the various African and non-African political forces who argue, from their own interests, that we are only confronted with the failure of a few individuals − or with the failure of 'the whole of Africa'. Nor should we be daunted by those who warn us that it is 'a complex question'. Every social question is complex, but that has never stopped men and women searching for a solution to their problems. Finally, we should not let ourselves be undermined by those who are frightened of everything great and who proclaim that the political unity of Africa is a 'utopia', in order to justify their own renunciation of a purpose without which no African people can ever be truly liberated.

A number of questions require honest answers. For instance, is the notorious and quite blatant bankruptcy of the O.A.U. entirely the fault of a few folklore Presidents and Emperor El Bokassa? Is the French neo-colonialists' puppet, Omar Albert Bongo, the only one to blame? Or is the guilty party that blood-spattered clown, Idi Amin Dada? Is 'Africa as a whole' responsible for the impotence and cowardice of the O.A.U. in the face of so many problems, as is claimed with breathtaking ingenuousness by a few petty-bourgeois Africans who are quite incapable of understanding and mastering the movement of history?

Do we really 'weaken Africa with petty quarrels' when we say that the reason the O.A.U. has proved it is incapable of bringing about African unity (true unity, in other words, political unity) is simply that the continent is being paralysed by a few reactionaries like Houphouet, Senghor, Ahidjo, Hassan II, Bongo, Bokassa, Mobutu, Sadat, Bourguiba and all the other lackeys?

Were we to allow such theoretically inconsistent and politically aberrant ideas to penetrate unhindered into the minds of the masses and youth of Africa, we would be failing in our political duty and taking a giant step backwards. In effect, we would be pretending there was no class struggle in Africa and that the O.A.U. had not collapsed.

Those who seek to 'save', 'redynamize' or 'recapture' the O.A.U., and who, in doing so, mislead the African peoples who have been reduced to slavery for over 500 years, are not bad men. Their aim is to console the African people, with stories of how the same O.A.U. which killed their hopes can be saved and revived. But whoever consoles slaves for their condition, instead of calling on them to revolt, is, in fact, helping the slave-owner.

History has confirmed this truth again and again, throughout the millenia.

There is also the special case of those who present themselves as African Communists and claim to have been constantly at the forefront of the African peoples' struggles (a notion which could do with a bit of — shall we say — proving). The 'Historic Document' in which these comrades gave their views displays an alarming condescension towards other revolutionaries in Africa, who are labelled 'middle-class revolutionary democrats', barely good enough for the 'National Democratic Revolution, the only one on the agenda in Africa today' [*sic*!], but who should leave the socialist revolution to the only competent authority, the 'international communist movement'. This 'Historic Document' is less self-assertive when it comes to the central issue here, the problem of African unity and the analysis of what the O.A.U. stands for today. On that subject, it is content with a few bizarre ideological exercises, political noises and a display of servility towards this or that socialist country. The African masses will soon grow tired of African revolutionaries who are so willing to disqualify themselves for their proper task.

The alternative is to tell the African workers, poor peasants and patriotic youth of Africa the truth. The O.A.U. is an organization which allows neo-colonialist African reaction to paralyse the revolutionary regimes, even if the latter do manage to get a few progressive but 'voluntary' policies through. Within the O.A.U., the reactionaries actually prevent the progressive regimes from envisaging the future of African unity. For many people, African unity thus becomes merely a series of ritual meetings, instead of a bold quest for that political unification which is the precondition for Africa's freedom and sovereignty. It was no coincidence that, before 'withdrawing', the French colonialists took good care to dismantle the old federations of French West Africa and French Equatorial Africa. The O.A.U. will never be able to create genuine unity.

There is no shortage of people who say that those who proclaim the bankruptcy of the O.A.U. and call for a Revolutionary Pan-African Organization are campaigning for a utopia. Hence, the prevalent fear of stating the obvious amongst many Africans, including some revolutionaries. The fact is that the war in Uganda, for example, has torn apart the O.A.U.'s veil of hypocrisy. Instead of neutralizing Ugandan opposition forces based in Tanzania, the Tanzanian Government supported them and helped to overthrow Amin's regime. In some senses, this set a major historical precedent in Africa. If, in the face of all this, our African Communist comrades prefer to hide their heads in the sand and to proclaim their 'unfailing but critical support for the O.A.U.', while castigating those who 'seek to destroy this Organization', we can only feel sorry for them and suggest that the future will show who is right.

Those who pour sarcasm on the African militants who say, like the U.P.C., that only the political unity of Africa will enable us to resolve the enormous problems we face today, generally also claim that there is nothing to gain from a politically united and socialist Africa, or even from the exposure of the O.A.U.'s bankruptcy. But nothing would ever have happened in history if the oppressed classes had always waited for everybody's approval before acting. In a different context, who but a minority of conscious revolutionaries is prepared to state that the women of Africa must and will surely be liberated? And who is willing to declare that this liberation will come from women's own revolutionary struggle, not from the speeches of the fat bourgeois who have been lying to our mothers and sisters for over 20 years? Who in the bourgeoisie or petty bourgeoisie is prepared to state this truth, at a time when women themselves (including some so-called liberated intellectuals) are still wondering 'whether we will ever manage to abolish polygamy, dowries and all the traditions which reduce us to the level of cattle' — and even whether they should be abolished?

In Africa today, a minimum of political courage is essential. We have to be prepared to 'swim against the tide' if need be. We need courage if we are to overcome the venality and careerism which prevails amongst African intellectuals and the fear which inhibits the oppressed working people. In all the African neo-colonies, there is still a spirit of 'every man for himself', 'looking after No. 1', etc., especially when it comes to revolution and the need to analyse social problems in a clear, precise and revolutionary way, both in theory and in practice. This fear, which paralyses so many people on a national level, cannot but have consequences on a continental level, on the problems of African unity and the African revolution.

Who is it who calls the advocates of a Union of African Socialist Republics utopians? Is it not the same people who consider the workers' and peasants' revolution in each African country a utopia, and who pay African militants to fill the heads of the African people with fundamentally counter-revolutionary and eclectic theories in order to prove that 'a transition to socialism is impossible in contemporary Africa'? It makes little difference whether the pretext used is that the African peoples are too backward and the bourgeois neo-colonial regimes too firmly entrenched, or that 'the stage of national liberation is not yet complete and Africa is not yet ripe for the socialist revolution'. The masses have been crushed by years of bloody repression and do not always even believe in the possibility of liberation; it takes courage to announce that one day, far sooner than is usually thought, the African workers will be free, as a result of their own efforts.

As Lenin said.

It is not difficult to be a revolutionary when the Revolution has already broken out and is in full swing, when everybody is jumping on the bandwagon, to follow the fashion or even in pursuit of a career. It is much more difficult — and far more vital — to act as a revolutionary when the situation still precludes direct, open, massive and truly revolutionary struggle, to know how to defend the interests of the Revolution (by propaganda, agitation, organization) in a non-revolutionary atmosphere, when the masses are still incapable of immediately grasping the need to adopt a revolutionary course of action.

Yes, the O.A.U. has collapsed. It is a major historical event for Africa. But the failure and impotence of the O.A.U. cannot be laid at Africa's door. They are the failure and impotence of the neo-colonial bourgeoisie and the petty bourgeoisie of 20 years ago. This is the central reason why the workers, poor peasants, present-day radical petty bourgeoisie and all true African patriots and revolutionaries should not waste their time 'reviving' the O.A.U. On the contrary, *it is time to prepare the workers and young people for the struggle to establish a Revolutionary Pan-African Organization and a Union of African Socialist Republics.*

Notes

1. See *La Voix du Kamerun*, No. 9, May-June 1977, p.24.
2. This current now includes the People's Republic of China, ever since the appallingly anti-Marxist and counter-revolutionary Three Worlds theory was launched. The reasons are becoming increasingly apparent.
3. See Chapter 1 of this book.
4. See 'l'O.U.A. et l'Afrique Australe' in *Cahiers Upecistes*, No. 10, April 1977.
5. At this conference 22 countries voted for the MPLA and 22 against. Ahidjo was the first of the 'antis' to admit defeat and recognize the People's Republic of Angola shortly afterwards.
6. Senghor's dishonest neo-colonial motion was defeated by 21 votes to 20 with 7 abstentions. Reliable sources who covered the Conference said that Sekou Toure voted for Senghor.
7. See *Addis-Abeba, Mai 1963 . . .*, op.cit., p.118.
8. Ibid., p.94.
9. See *Marches Tropicaux et Mediteraneens*, 4 May 1973, p.1,241.
10. Ibid., 1 June 1973, p.1,485.
11. Ibid., 17 November 1978, p.3,032.
12. Ibid., 30 March 1979, pp.789, 790.
13. See *New African*, May 1978, p.14.
14. Ibid., p.14.
15. *Marches Tropicaux . . .*, 17 November 1978, p.3,030.
16. Colonel Gadaffi's support for Idi Amin Dada speaks volumes.
17. See *Le Monde*, 30 June 1978.
18. See *La Voix du Kamerun*, the U.P.C. organ, No. 10, August-September 1977, p.26.
19. *Le Monde*, 14 September 1978.
20. *Le Monde Diplomatique*, March 1979, p.12.
21. *The Guardian*, 17 February 1978; *The Citizen* (South Africa), 10 February 1978.
22. Cheikh Anta Diop, *L'Afrique Noire Precoloniale*, (Paris, Presence Africaine, 1960).
23. One can only deplore the fact that the traditional Moroccan Left, along with the Istiqlal bourgeoisie, supports Hassan II's chauvinistic policies.
24. In 1978 Houphouet and the French made an enormous fuss about a

so-called 'peace in the Sahara'.
25. *New African*, May 1978, p.5.
26. Why does Diallo not mention France? Self-censorship perhaps?
27. The African bourgeoisies try to hide behind the excuse that 'Africa is too big to form a single state'. What they really mean is that, in a unified Africa, there would not be room for all their multifarious bourgeois cliques.

Appendix

We have already outlined the U.P.C.'s position on Pan Africanism, as of 1962.
Essentially, it can be summarized as follows: no unity with the reactionary
camp in Africa, no false unity. Instead, what is called for is a clear demarcation between the progressive tendency, as originally represented by the
Casablanca Group, and the 'reformist', in other words reactionary, tendency
controlled by imperialism. The U.P.C. also called on the anti-imperialist states
to reinforce the Casablanca Group.[1] By May 1962, our Party had shown that
two conceptions of Pan Africanism were already confronting each other. In
fact, we could have talked of three conceptions, since even within the anti-
imperialist camp, there were some supporters of the 'diplomatic approach',
notably the great patriot Kwame Nkrumah.

By then, the U.P.C. had already pointed out that there was an ineluctable
contradiction between the reactionary (demagogic) and anti-imperialist
positions. Our Party outspokenly rejected any form of organizational or political unity with the demagogues of Pan-Africanist reaction. We pointed out
that such unity could only serve reaction and imperialism. All this was in
May 1962, long before the 'emergence' of the U.P.C. Revolutionary Committee, to use the phrase of the Cameroonian opportunists.[2] In 1972-75, more
than ten years later, a few opportunists and pseudo-Marxists notable only for
their servility vis-a-vis foreign parties and governments, began to proclaim that
the notion of a necessary demarcation on this issue had been invented either
by the Revolutionary Committee or by our comrade Massaga alone. This gross
falsification of history amounts to an effort to sabotage our Party and the
struggle of our people. Every serious Cameroonian patriot should be ready to
refute it.

As early as May 1962, the U.P.C. stated that: 'The road to true African
Unity does not take us towards a fusion of the Brazzaville, Monrovia, Lagos
and Casablanca groups. That would be a serious mistake, which would benefit
only neo-colonialism and imperialism. African leaders would find they were
being pushed to relegate the struggle against neo-colonialism into the background.[3] In May 1963, in Addis Ababa, the fusion described above did
nonetheless take place: the O.A.U. was born.

From that point onwards, the actions, political basis and ideology of the
O.A.U. have consistently demonstrated the correctness of the U.P.C.'s

predictions. The fundamental problem of the struggle against neo-colonialism has been struck off the agenda altogether. Indeed the O.A.U. has to some extent proved incapable of truly confronting the equally fundamental problem of the struggle against classical colonialism as practised by Spain, France and the racist settlers of South Africa, Namibia and Zimbabwe. Even worse, the O.A.U. has shown itself to be a mere bag of wind whenever it is faced with a real issue, such as the need to break off diplomatic relations with Britain when the racist settlers implemented their U.D.I. in Zimbabwe, or the drought which has prevailed for over 10 years in the Sahel. The O.A.U. has revealed itself as a head of state's trade union, a tool of repression, an instrument of the African neo-colonial bourgeoisies in their continental counter-revolutionary crusade.

In 1972-73, a small group of Cameroonian opportunists decided to announce that 'all this stuff is just nonsense', that imperialism has done nothing at all in Africa since 1962, had played no part in what happened at Addis Ababa in 1963 and has generally been politically irrelevant. They also suggested that the present African governments, for example those headed by Sekou Toure, Ahidjo or Mobutu, have not been up to anything very serious.

In short, the Cameroonian opportunists led by Njem declared their position as follows:

> Concerning the special bonds which link the various detachments of the African anti-imperialist movement, the U.P.C. reaffirms its support for the progressive states of Africa, and especially for the governments of the People's Democratic Republic of Algeria, the Republics of Guinea, Nigeria (sic!) and Congo-Brazzaville, the Arab Republic of Egypt, Tanzania and Equatorial Guinea. The U.P.C. endorses their actions and their policy of fighting against imperialism, colonialism and neo-colonialism. It denounces any action which might discourage or hold up the progressive evolution of these countries or weaken them by leading them away from Revolutionary Pan Africanism . . . .
>
> [The U.P.C.] remains convinced that these governments will manage to foil the imperialist plans aimed at creating a kind of inter-governmental Holy Alliance of African countries against the democratic and individual rights of the African Peoples, notably against their right to fight the puppets of neo-colonialism.[4]

If one thing emerges clearly from all this muddle, it is that the clique centred on the opportunist, Njiawue, and the little traitor, Njem (Bona Claude, Pierre Pondy, etc.) are suffering from acute amnesia.

It has to be stated as firmly as possible: the U.P.C., and all true Cameroonian revolutionaries, have no time for such nonsense; we saw through it back in May 1962, at the latest! And we would like to ask our little opportunists whether the regimes they described as anti-imperialist in 1972-75 have or have not embraced what the 'African communist' Njiawue would describe as 'the most blatant puppet regimes'? Please remember, little opportunists, that

221

in 1962, our Party, which was then also yours, clearly warned that the O.A.U. would amount only to 'unity within the camp of counter-revolution'. If our little saboteurs had genuinely tried to work out what Revolutionary Pan Africanism consists of nowadays, they would undoubtedly have reached the conclusion that, to varying extents, all the governments they mention have engaged in actions which not only 'might' but quite obviously do 'hold up the progressive evolution' of the existing states and of all Africa. Furthermore they would have realized that some of these governments do not just 'hold up' this evolution, but actually do everything in their power to break whatever progressive tendencies exist. Some of the governments have drifted further and further away from their original Revolutionary Pan Africanism, even if, from time to time, they still take objectively anti-imperialist decisions. This is the fundamental difference which our opportunists cannot (or will not?) grasp. The essential point is precisely to explain this *qualitative transformation* which has turned regimes which were once progressive (on balance and despite the occasional mistake) into reactionary regimes which merely happen to take the occasional anti-imperialist decision. And there is absolutely no way of explaining that, or of understanding anything about it, if one decides, like our Cameroonian opportunists and pseudo-Marxists, to ignore the history of the last 20 years of neo-colonialism in Africa.

In the policy document they published in late 1978 for the 'Conference of Communist Parties of Tropical and Southern Africa',[5] the 'African communists' of the Senegalese African Independence Party, the Sudanese Communist Party and the South African Communist Party put forward a point of view which completely avoids the question of 'the real evolution of the progressive states of the period 1958-62'.

Indeed these comrades reduce the obvious qualitative transformation detailed in this study to a simple matter of 'persisting difficulties and negative manifestations in the countries oriented towards socialism'; the countries in question are not, of course, exhaustively listed and it is suggested that 'their number is steadily growing'. The text goes on to say:

> The difficulties and occasional negative manifestations which exist in the countries oriented towards socialism cannot obscure the fundamental and qualitative difference between the socialist path to social development and the capitalist path. In the countries oriented towards socialism, efforts are made to consolidate national independence and the position of the working class. What problems there are should not be taken as a reason for passivity or systematic condemnation. [Not for the first time, revolutionaries are accused of 'systematically attacking everybody'. Where have we heard *that* before? E.M.] Such condemnations can disorient the revolutionary forces in Africa. Communists and all conscientious patriots take a firm stand alongside these progressive states in their struggle against imperialism and African reaction.[6]

Despite the occasional phrase about 'the internal balance of class forces', the above quoted thesis amounts to a refusal to make an honest assessment of the experience of the petty-bourgeois nationalist regimes which emerged during the early years of Africa's regained independence. In launching the concept of revolutionary democracy onto the political scene, our 'African communist' comrades seem to be responding mainly to the requirements of a 'His Master's Voice' policy. Certainly their slogan has much in common with equally dubious concepts launched in the 1960s such as the 'national democratic state' and the 'non-capitalist road to development'. In any case, they have certainly provided the 'Pillar, Great Strategist and beloved leader of the African Revolution', 'Brother Ahmed', with a new idea; he immediately reclassified his country as a 'Revolutionary Democratic State'.

Given that the U.P.C.'s position on this subject was clearly laid down in 1962, and given the declarations made by the Njem-Njiawue opportunist clique at a time when Pan-African demagogy is rife throughout the continent, *the U.P.C. and all other serious Cameroonian patriots can only conclude that these people are acting as renegades* who have no right whatsoever to use the name of the U.P.C., and only get away with doing so thanks to the complicity of their few allies abroad. In our article 'La Question de l'Unite de l'UPC' which appeared in Issue No. 1 of *Cahiers Upecistes* (November 1973), Njiawue's opportunism in terms of organization and general strategy was fully exposed. We now discover that his stance on Pan Africanism amounts to a denial of other Upecist theses. Indeed, even Nicanor's theses on the important question of the armed struggle are a betrayal of the positions of the U.P.C. over the last 20 years. Since no major change has occurred to justify such a departure, we can only suggest that these new theses have been introduced to please the opportunist's masters. It is high time Njiawue and friends are shown up for what they are — systematic contradicters of what they themselves were saying and writing not so long ago, despite the fact that there has been no major change to justify such a reversal of positions.

For instance, on 30 September 1959, the President of the U.P.C., Comrade Felix-Roland Moumie, published a declaration which the Party later issued as a pamphlet entitled *La Revolution Kamerunaise et la Lutte des Peuples Africains*. As it happens, the preface to the pamphlet was written by Njiawue:

> Will the Cameroonian people's aspirations to genuine freedom and reunification ever be satisfied? What means can be used to break the oppressive regime and finally impose respect for the popular will? These are the questions that this brochure seeks to answer.
>
> My intention here is not to comment upon the fundamental ideas developed by the author. They are very clearly expressed and stand up on their own. I will only try to throw a little light on the circumstances in which our Party reached these major decisions and which influenced our people's clearly expressed choice to intensify the armed struggle as a means of completing our Revolution.

It is an undeniable fact that the Cameroonian people today have no choice but to engage in violent confrontation in order to win their freedom by meeting the sword with the sword.

Obviously, those whose sordid interests lead them to band together against the emancipation of the African peoples will not hesitate to tell the most outrageous lies and suggest that the Cameroonian people have chosen this path without having exhausted every peaceful method of making their demands.[7]

Today ... the uprising of the Cameroonian people is far from being a simple armed insurrection; it is a well thought out revolutionary action.[8]

I dare hope that this appeal, launched by one of the most authoritative voices of the Cameroonian National Revolution, will be heard and that the Cameroonian people will soon enjoy the support they need from friendly and fraternal peoples, in order to pursue thier action and to achieve, as quickly as possible, the essential goals of their revolutionary war.[9]

Compare that to the sophistry and verbal acrobatics of Njiawue's tract, the real content of which is 'How to eliminate the U.P.C. and disarm the Cameroonian proletariat by depriving them of their means of struggle', although he has called it 'How to eliminate opportunism and arm the Cameroonian proletariat with its means of struggle', and you will understand just how far Nicanor has gone in reneging on the U.P.C.'s positions just to please his friends and masters.

Let us trace his itinerary. September 1959: Njiawue, at the time still an Upecist, writes the preface to a text by the President of the Party dealing with the essential problems of our revolutionary struggle. In the text, the Party leadership explores some fundamental issues such as 'what means can be used to break the oppressive regime and finally impose respect for the popular will?' Njiawue recognizes that 'the fundamental ideas are very clearly expressed and can stand up on their own'. He accepts that our Party's decision to intensify the armed struggle corresponds to the 'clearly expressed choice' of our people. He even goes on to add that the Cameroonian people were constrained to take up arms and had exhausted the possibilities of non-violent struggle. He specifies that all those who suggested the contrary — obviously he foresaw that such people would emerge — would be acting to safeguard their own 'sordid interests', would tell 'the most outrageous lies' and would be clubbing together 'against the emancipation of the African peoples'.

To do him justice, Njiawue, in 1959, was capable of writing well and accurately. He had learnt how the leaders of our struggle tackled problems; they always expressed their ideas 'very clearly'.

June 1972: The leaders of 1959 have fallen heroically, but no new events have emerged to justify any fundamental revision of our Party's position on the revolutionary struggle in Cameroon. However, the struggle is running into certain difficulties. It is a period when the militants and the popular masses expect the new leaders to come up with some clear ideas. Njiawue, who in the meantime has become a pseudo-Upecist, nonetheless presents himself as a Party leader (he claims to be a member of the U.P.C.'s Revolutionary Committee). He takes up his pen, but instead of elucidating a question such as that of the armed struggle in Cameroon today, when neo-colonialism is triumphant, when there is no Parliament worth the name, when even the children know that the ballot boxes are rigged by the agents of Ahidjo Birawandu's bloody dictatorship, he chooses to confuse the issue completely. His twenty tightly written pages entitled 'How to eliminate opportunism and arm the Cameroonian proletariat' never deal explicitly with the methods of struggle. In September 1959, Comrade Moumie wrote:

> Violence or non-violence? That is the false dichotomy through which the imperialists and their ideologues seek to stifle the liberation struggle of the African peoples.
> Fortunately, we do not have to choose between violence and non-violence; we have to combine different forms of struggle, legal and illegal, peaceful and violent, according to the balance of internal and external forces at each given phase.[10]

For a long time now, and throughout the last ten years as well, this position, which stresses the need to combine all the various forms of struggle, has been presented explicitly in the U.P.C.'s publications.[11] But when Njiawue or his friends and masters tackle the question, they either studiously avoid the real issue or content themselves with insults addressed to some hypothetical 'left militarists', without ever proposing a coherent and practical alternative strategy. Nicanor's idiotic ramblings are geared only to one thing: to destroy our Party. His project of creating an 'Independent Proletarian Marxist-Leninist Party' is a mere diversion. Above all, he wants to avoid having to give a clear answer to the question of whether or not revolutionary violence should be a part of our methods of struggle. He needs to hide the fact that he is now opposed to armed struggle and has reneged on his earlier commitments, simply in order to please those who have long sought to use him as a political agent within our party and as a means to manipulate us.

In April 1960 the leadership of the U.P.C. published a pamphlet entitled *Le Kamerun sous un regime de dictature fasciste* (Cameroon under fascist dictatorship). The pamphlet contains a Declaration by the Party Leadership dated 16 March 1960 and a text, 'Coup d'oeil sur la Republique Neo-Colonialiste d'Ahidjo', dated 9 April 1960. The pamphlet is signed jointly by Felix Moumie, at the time U.P.C. President, Ernest Ouandie and Abel Kingue, the then Vice-Presidents. Once again, the preface is by Nicanor, who, in 1960, was writing:

> The Cameroonian people is getting stronger and stronger and continues to draw a rich harvest of lessons from daily events. It is more and more

confident in its abilities; awareness of its material poverty has not sapped its morale vis-a-vis the ruling butchers, who are armed to the teeth with the most modern weapons. Now that the Party has been cleansed of *undesirable elements who nearly caused it to disintegrate by professing opportunist and revisionist theses based on non-violence*, it is infused with a new vigour. [My emphasis, E.M.] [12]

Today, Njiawue has himself adopted these same 'opportunist and revisionist' theses, but he has done so hypocritically, secretly. He has become one of those 'undesirable elements' he spoke of and whose exclusion from the Party he welcomed. It would seem that it is time we cleansed our party of such elements once more.

The present position of our opportunists on the subject of the African Revolution is not only inconsistent, it involves deliberately closing one's eyes to everything that has happened in Africa over the last twenty years, to the entire evolution of neo-colonialism. But it is also a *renegade's* position since, as we have seen, these 'comrades' are now reneging on what they supported in 1962, although events have constantly confirmed the correctness of our Party's original theses.

But perhaps the Cameroonian opportunists have simply decided to lose their memories in order to gain a better understanding of the present? Let us consider this hypothesis and see where it takes us.

In May 1962, in Accra, before an assembly of nearly all the anti-imperialist organizations in Africa, our Party declared that there was no way to reach genuine African Unity by means of fusing the various groups of existing states, each with their different orientations. The Party put forward its own very clear alternative: to draw a sharp dividing line between the potential partisans of Revolution (the Casablanca Group) and the supporters of counter-revolution (the U.A.M., the Monrovia, Lagos and Brazzaville groups and all their accolytes). Our Party warned against imperialist plots — real plots, not the 'uninterrupted series of plots' described by Njem and Co. — and added that: 'These plots are all the more difficult to detect since most of the plotters do not hesitate to indulge in the worst forms of revolutionary verbiage.' [13]

The U.P.C.'s alternative was to 'form popular associations to provide dynamic support for the Casablanca Charter'. Given the period, and the anti-imperialist camp's general lack of experience of neo-colonialism, this approach constituted a far-seeing way of defining Revolutionary Pan Africanism, as opposed to the verbiage of Pan-African Demagogy. The idea of popular associations to provide support for the Casablanca Charter (a specific programme) rather than for an assortment of Heads of State was already an effective way of countering the Heads of State trade unionism which has characterized the O.A.U. The Tanzanian, Mohammed Babu, was later (1964) to pick up this idea, but in a deformed version, namely O.A.U. National Support Committees.

Ten years later, in 1972, with the benefit of all the experience of neo-colonialism in Africa, in Cameroon, in Zaire, in Mali, in Ghana, etc., the Cameroonian opportunists come up with a definition of Revolutionary

Pan Africanism which is scientifically and politically far inferior to the one put forward on the basis of far less experience by our Party in 1962. The definition offered by these 'comrades' boils down to the following platitude: 'Revolutionary Pan Africanism conjoins in a single process the struggles against imperialism, colonialism and neo-colonialism.'[14]

This definition, which in fact defines nothing at all, remains sufficiently vague to allow all sorts of accommodations and agreements with an opportunistic Pan African Demagogy. We are talking about agreements on important questions, not just the inevitable tactical understandings of limited importance which in no way throw the fundamental political line into question. This definition provides the basis on which the opportunists can put out 'non-exhaustive' lists of the 'anti-imperialist and revolutionary countries in Africa'. The opportunists' texts, published and written in Conakry, often contain statements like this one:

> Today we are witnessing an attempt to eliminate the very spirit of the U.P.C., to cut the present off from the past, to distort the nature of our Party and the noble cause it defends; efforts are being made to steer it away from its internationalist course, to cut it off from its natural allies.[15]

The reader who has familiarized himself with the positions of the revolutionary Upecists, as expressed in this volume and other publications, can easily decide who really wants to 'cut the present off from the past', the revolutionary Upecists or the isolated, neutralized opportunist renegades who stubbornly and dishonestly claim allegiance to our Party.

The main failing of these saboteurs is their implicit or explicit determination to deny the existence of class struggle between Africans in contemporary neo-colonialist Africa. Or, if they are forced to recognize the existence of this class struggle (as the Cameroonian pseudo-Marxists are), they simply refuse to adopt the only course neo-colonialism leaves open to African revolutionaries committed to the class struggle.

Any Cameroonian patriot, especially one who supports the U.P.C. and who takes the trouble to work out what the U.P.C.'s 'fundamental line' should be and who asks himself who can or should be the U.P.C.'s natural allies, will of course frame the question differently. Unlike our 'African communist' comrades, he will be concerned with the present phase of neo-colonialism in Africa, rather than with some imaginary historical period during which 'in most African countries it is the national democratic revolution, not the socialist revolution which is on the agenda'. (Come to think of it, is it not precisely this 'national democratic' revolution our African communist comrades condescendingly delegate to mere 'revolutionary democrats'?)

The genuine Cameroonian patriot will in fact want to know what is the precise content of the U.P.C.'s struggle during such a phase. He will point out that, in terms of revolution, there are no such things as 'natural allies' divorced from their socio-historical context. He will be led to conclude that, given the

227

present neo-colonialist conditions, the Cameroonian people's struggle — which has been led by the U.P.C. for over 30 years — is now not only a national liberation struggle but has become and will increasingly be a class struggle between the Cameroonian workers and the fat-bellied neo-colonial bureaucratic bourgeoisie. *The U.P.C. is fighting for the country's real independence, for a form of independence which will benefit the workers, for independence within socialism.* The neo-colonial bourgeoisie will never deliver that form of independence, indeed it cannot even begin to pursue it. The present ruling bourgeoisie is the ally and lackey of imperialism (predominantly French and British imperialism at the moment) and is in perfect accord with its masters when it comes to living off the backs of the Cameroonian workers. The independence the U.P.C. is fighting for can only be won by the workers and poor peasants through struggle. The U.P.C. thus must and can only be the organization of the working class and poor peasants, the organized vanguard of those classes. It accepts within its ranks individuals from other classes only on the condition that such individuals commit themselves firmly to the political position of the two revolutionary classes. The 'natural allies' of the U.P.C. are thus the workers and poor peasants of Africa and the world, and the organizations of these classes, or at least those amongst these organizations which are genuinely revolutionary rather than revolutionary or 'marxist' in name and verbiage alone. In practical terms, our patriot will ask himself whether or not there are any African states today which are led by such organizations, which are genuinely under the control of the workers and poor peasants of Africa. And he will be forced to conclude that there are *none*. He may add the rider that there are two African states in which such organizations are being built and where one can therefore say that the path to workers and peasants' power has been opened up: those two countries are Angola and Mozambique. As for the other African countries, there may be a few that are engaged in a revolutionary process, but none can truly be described as in transition to workers' and peasants' power. Even Njiawue would not dispute this point. The conclusion is that there is a tiny handful of African countries where, since 1975, the true natural allies of the U.P.C. are in power, or more precisely are in the process of establishing their power. Only opportunist demagogues and unprincipled lackeys would dare to deny a fact which is so amply confirmed by the practice and experience of the 'anti-imperialist revolutionary and socialist governments of Africa'. Those who do deny it do so simply to please their masters, whose interests are best served by treating the African people like idiots and insisting that African revolutionaries accept that numerous 'socialist and revolutionary governments' already exist throughout our continent.

What do our opportunists think when confronted with little gems such as this one:

A Congolese delegation led by M. Charles Ngouoto, Minister of Agriculture, and including M. Charles David Ganao and Maurice Sianard, respectively Minister for Foreign Affairs and Minister of the Interior, was received on 13 September (1973) by President Ahidjo, to whom they transmitted a message from President Marien Ngouabi.

The visit is one element within the overall framework of co-operation instituted between the two countries.[16]

What on earth is the Minister of the Interior, the big boss of 'Marxist-Leninist' Congo's police force, doing with Barbatoura Birawandu Ahmadou Ahidjo, the fascist? Furthermore I seem to remember that 'comrade' Ngouoto is a member of the Political Bureau of the Central Committee of the 'Marxist-Leninist' Parti Congolais du Travail (Congolese Workers Party). What relations could possibly exist between the P.C.T. and Ahidjo's fascist U.N.C.? After all, the P.C.T., in its capacity as a 'fraternal party', has been represented at almost every U.N.C. congress since 1968.

But I digress. The facts which confront our Cameroonian patriot are not that difficult to grasp: in some (very few) African countries, the prevailing socio-historic conditions have meant that the power of the one-time nationalist petty bourgeoisie is not yet consolidated. Furthermore, in those particular countries, the popular masses are quite politically conscious. As a result, official policy often includes elements which are genuinely anti-imperialist – even if these elements are often responses to contradictions between the various strata in power and their imperialist masters; no marriage can be completely without conflict, after all.

Our Cameroonian opportunists have studiously avowed to specify the present real political content of their Pan Africanism. They have not bothered to describe neo-colonialism with any analytic precision or to consider its effects in any but the most general terms. Our little saboteurs have contented themselves with boldly stating that neo-colonialism exists, as if we were still back in 1960. Then they go on to suggest that, although neo-colonialism exists, it has no bearing on the 'anti-imperialist and revolutionary states of Africa'. All that then remains for them to do is to draw up a list ('non-exhaustive', naturally) of these states, adding new names to it as the occasion arises, for instance Nigeria, Equatorial Guinea, etc.

The opportunists' procedure is thus quite coherent. As far as the U.P.C. is concerned, they have called for a return to unity 'as in the period before 1962'. Obviously they hold that nothing has happened since that time, apart from a few 'uninterrupted series of imperialist plots' against the U.P.C. They believe that everybody can be put in the same bag. The only 'selection' criteria they suggest are the speeches people make claiming adherence to the U.P.C. So much for their position on the unity of the U.P.C.[17] Their attitude to Pan Africanism is very similar; everybody should 'come together' on the basis of speeches and proclamations, as it was in the days before 1962. The renegade Njiawue and the little traitor, Njem – alias Bona Claude alias Pierre Pondy, the same Pierre Pondy who scurrilously attributed the signature of a warrant for Bishop Ndongmo to President Ouandie of the U.P.C.'s Revolutionary Committee – are well matched. They do not and will not concern themselves with what all these 'revolutionary and anti-imperialist' heads of state do in practice.

Our Cameroonian pseudo-Marxists and opportunists could fairly be described as 'romantics', in the sense in which the term was used amongst Russian revolutionaries some 80 years ago.[18] What do such people really believe?

Either they remain committed to the struggle during this neo-colonial last quarter of the 20th Century, in which case their dream of going back to the 'U.P.C. of before 1962' and to the Pan Africanism of before 1962 — of before the O.A.U., in fact — is an indication of gross disregard for political realities and suggests a romantic petty-bourgeois utopianism. Or else their real commitment is to the U.P.C. of before 1962 and to the Pan Africanism of before 1962. If so, they must also take the whole of Africa back with them to those days of over 15 years ago, a project which is not only obviously utopian but actually reactionary in the historical sense of the term, since they simply want to turn the clock back.

By giving such a hollow and watered down definition of Revolutionary Pan Africanism, the Cameroonian opportunists have objectively — and perhaps consciously — put themselves in the service of continental opportunism, in other words of the most blatant reaction. In exchange, they may hope for good relations with states ranging from the 'Marxist-Leninist' Congo to 'anti-neo-colonialist' Chad, and not excluding 'revolutionary' Nigeria or, if the mood takes them, Equatorial Guinea. In fact, the pseudo-Marxist Njiawue has defined nothing at all. He is happy playing with his non-exhaustive list; if he wakes up in the morning with an urge to add all the countries beginning with P to his list, he can do so at will. And if he decides to include Malawi and Ivory Coast amongst those 'anti-imperialist and revolutionary' African states, all he has to do is pick up his pen.

When Ahidjo went to Algiers in October 1971 on an official visit, the Algerian paper *El Moudjahid* gave an account of Cameroonian history beginning in 1960-61, so as not to have to disclose what Ahidjo was doing in the 1950s, for instance in 1958, when he was a companion in arms of Aujoulat, the Algerian *pied-noir* settler who fought against the U.P.C. and the very idea of independence and reunification for Cameroon. When Ahidjo went to China in 1973, Chou-en-Lai also treated Cameroonian history as beginning in 1960-61, for the same obvious reasons.[19] There are many similar examples of this curious form of amnesia, which our Cameroonian opportunists extend to key aspects of our revolutionary struggle — questions which affect the life of thousands upon thousands of men and women — whilst pretending to hold the secret of the unity of Cameroon's patriots and revolutionaries.

The political and ideological inconsistency of the pseudo-Marxist Njem who seeks to build a 'model independent working-class Marxist-Leninist Party, fighting for the purity of Marxism-Leninism' is particularly clear when one considers what Lenin was saying on the subject some 60 years ago.

> There has been a certain rapprochement between the bourgeoisie of the exploiting countries and that of the colonial countries, so that in many and perhaps even most cases, the bourgeoisie of the oppressed countries,

while supporting national movements, is at the same time in accord with the imperialist bourgeoisie and fights alongside the latter against the revolutionary movements and the revolutionary classes.[20]

This analysis of the situation in the colonial countries and of the political approach of the bourgeoisie in those countries was originally approved by the Second Congress of the Communist International in 1920! What Lenin and the congress of the entire vanguard of the world working class said 60 years ago can easily be applied to the world today; for instance, one can say that the putrid neo-colonial bourgeoisie of the African countries, while proclaiming itself nationalist and engaging in the occasional nationalization, is, at the same time, in accord with the imperialist bourgeoisie and will struggle alongside the latter against all revolutionary movements who oppose neo-colonialism, in other words against any organization which is fighting for workers' and poor peasants' power. Naturally, no serious progressive African (let alone a revolutionary, not to mention a Marxist-Leninist) will contest the truth of the above.

So what does our self-proclaimed strict Marxist, Njiawue, think about it all? What is his opinion of Lenin's thesis? In theory at least, he entirely agrees. For instance, in one of his pamphlets on the independent states of Africa and the parties that rule those states, this is what he had to say:

> During the 1960s, most of these parties managed to prevail over colonialism and win political power. But which class still holds the reins of power in the countries where these victories were achieved? . . . The economic and political weakness of the ruling classes and class fractions has led them to throw themselves into the wide-open arms of monopoly capitalism. Today they exploit the working masses jointly with the capitalists, who had no sooner been kicked out than they returned under the neo-colonialist formula. The African ruling classes have, on the whole, established their class solidarity with the bourgeoisies of Europe and America. Furthermore, fear of the masses and the spectre of communism led them to link arms with the most blatant puppet regimes and create the holy alliance known as the O.A.U.[21]

It is worth noting that Nicanor Njiawue is referring to regimes whose present ruling parties are petty-bourgeois, or were petty-bourgeois in the 1960s. When Nicanor inveighs against the regimes which ended up linking arms 'with the most blatant puppet regimes' to 'create the Holy Alliance known as the O.A.U.', he surely cannot be excluding countries such as Guinea and Algeria, for example, or Congo-Brazzaville. He cannot have been taken in by the claims of the party which rules in Brazzaville to be a true workers' party, even if it does genuinely aspire to become one. As a good Marxist, Njiawue must be fully aware that the Algerian F.L.N. is not a Communist Party. He must know that 'Brother Ahmed's' constant self-proclamation as the 'Great Strategist of the African Democratic Revolution' and his demands that the Cameroonian opportunists recognize him as the 'Beloved leader of the African Revolution' are in themselves sufficient proof that the Guinean Democratic Party is not a Communist Party and that in this particular case the 'revolution' has been reduced to a mass of verbiage. Njiawue knows that, over the last ten years at least, explosive political struggles have regularly broken out between the divergent wings of the P.C.T. Our 'convinced Marxist' cannot be unaware that 'French imperialism controls everything in the Congo', in the words of the ex-President of the Marxist-Leninist P.C.T.'s Central Committee, or that, according to the same orator, it is nonetheless the smooth operation of the state-owned enterprises which really matters. Njiawue knows that all these revolutionary heads of state never miss an opportunity to join in the repression of revolutionary militants, in Cameroon or in other African countries. Nobody has forgotten what happened to Mulele. And what is all this in aid of? Simply to win the favour of men like Ahidjo or Mobutu, who are the authentic representatives of the most openly reactionary forces in Africa. Nicanor clearly knows all this since he says and writes it, as his previously quoted text shows. In short, Njiawue knows that nearly all the African regimes, and notably those he and his opportunist friends, Njem and Co., classify as anti-imperialist, are in fact *acting out of bourgeois class solidarity* when they link up with blatant puppet regimes to sustain the new Holy Alliance known as the O.A.U.

A revolutionary Marxist could conclude that

> We, as Communists, should and will support bourgeois liberation movements in the colonies only when they are genuinely revolutionary, and when their exponents do not hinder our work of educating and organizing in a revolutionary spirit the peasantry and the masses of the exploited. If these conditions do not exist, the Communists in these countries must combat the reformist bourgeoisie.[22]

Even from the point of view expressed by Njiawue himself, it should be perfectly clear that what Lenin, with extraordinary foresight, described in 1920 as 'bourgeois liberation movements in the colonies' is precisely what we in 1979 would call 'bourgeois movements, bourgeois or petty-bourgeois states in the colonial or neo-colonial countries' in the regions dominated by foreign imperialism. This seems quite obvious, and indeed not even Njiawue would deny it.

A pseudo-Marxist, on the other hand, would say that one has to endorse opportunism, amnesia and wilful blindness, that one has to prevent revolutionaries from fighting against the reformist bourgeoisie. He would also endlessly moan about the difficulties that the struggle against the African reformist bourgeoisie (a struggle which is in any case supposedly reactionary and counter-revolutionary given the present neo-colonial conditions in Africa) is going to pose for revolutionary militants in exile.[23]

In 1916 international Social Democracy was in crisis. The opportunists provoked an unparalleled defeat in the history of socialism. Lenin, as a revolutionary Marxist, wrote:

> The bourgeoisie of the oppressed nations [a description which applies
> exactly to the present neo-colonial African bourgeoisies. E.M.] con-
> stantly turned the slogan of national liberation into a way of mystifying
> the workers: in domestic affairs, the bourgeoisie uses these slogans to
> conclude reactionary agreements with the bourgeoisies of the dominant
> nations.[24]

Today, 60 years later, Pan Africanism is in crisis. The nationalist petty
bourgeoisie of the 1958-1960 period has become a neo-colonial bureaucratic
bourgeoisie, and has thereby provoked an unparalleled defeat in the history
of Pan Africanism. It is clear, for instance, that the supposed nationalizations
of the wealth that was once pillaged by colonialism is a giant fraud, a mystification conducted by the neo-colonial bourgeoisie, since those nationalizations
consist mainly in transferring the wealth involved to the ruling African
bourgeois classes.

In 1916, Lenin had already concluded that, faced with such a situation,
the communists should fight against the reformist bourgeoisie in the dominated countries. Today, ever since 1972, the African 'Leninist' Njiawue has
concluded that to struggle against the African bourgeoisie which is perpetra-
ting such an appalling mystification of the workers is to deliberately complicate
the life of revolutionary militants in exile. Perhaps Njiawue's knowledge of
history has let him down, or has he just forgotten that, in 1916, Lenin was
also still in exile?

The usual argument runs that just because somebody did something in a
particular way at a given moment does not mean that we should mechanically
do the same thing 50 years later, without taking the new situation into
account. This truism is, however, quite inapplicable to the present situation.

In Njiawue's 'revolutionary countries', the ruling bourgeoisie has refused
to allow the Communist Party to conduct any activities whatsoever; in other
words, any true Marxist-Leninist, as our Nicanor claims to be, would conclude
that, since the bourgeoisie hinders (the communists') work of educating and
organizing the peasantry and the masses of the exploited, the communists
must struggle against the reformist boureoisie. But what Njiawue actually
concludes is that one must not attack the ruling bourgeoisie so as not to
cause oneself problems in exile. In the Sudan, for example, the bourgeoisie
has decapitated the Sudanese Communist Party in an attempt to ensure that
the Sudanese workers will not be organized and trained in a revolutionary
spirit. Given Njiawue's past record, it is puzzling that Sudan does not yet
figure on the list of 'Tropical and Southern African countries which have
chosen a socialist orientation in recent years', as our 'African communist'
comrades put it in their Historic Document.

We are now in a position to give a full characterization of Njiawue's
Marxism, which we might as well call 'Marxism'-Njiawueyism. It is an opportunist current marked by: (1) a Marxist phraseology; (2) dilettante positions

on organizations; (3) a covert opposition to the use of violence in the revolution and notably to armed struggle; (4) total flunkeyism and class collaboration in international policy, notably in terms of Pan Africanism. In short it is a betrayal of everything the U.P.C. stands for.

All this shows why the Cameroonian opportunists fear any mention of texts such as 'African Unity or Neo-Colonialism', published by the U.P.C. over fifteen years ago. The opportunists and their stablemates, the pseudo-Marxists, would like to pretend that such texts never existed; the texts provide an instant refutation of all the sophistry put forward today by renegades who have opted for a despicable servility. The mere mention of such texts is enough to stump the opportunists completely, by showing that one must be half-blind and utterly without memory to even advance theses like those of our little saboteurs.

The Cameroonian opportunists have dodged the decisive question of how to define late 20th Century Revolutionary Pan Africanism in terms of its basic principles and explicit political content. Instead, they indulge in a cretinous enumeration of 'anti-imperialist and revolutionary' countries, on an *ad-hoc* basis devoid of any serious objective general criteria. They have thus sunk into pure subjectivism and fallen into step with Pan African Demagogy, in other words with neo-colonial African reaction. In the process, they have lost all contact with the question of how to define African Unity for the Cameroonian revolutionaries of our time, the question which, as Njiawue the renegade once said, 'so fascinates Cameroonian revolutionaries today'. They are utterly bankrupt.

Notes

1. See Chapter 1 Section 4 of this volume.
2. The U.P.C. Revolutionary Committee elected as the Party leadership by the Popular Assembly which met clandestinely on 13 September 1962 and which elected Ernest Ouandie as its President.
3. See *Unite Africaine ou Neo-Colonialisme?*, U.P.C., 1962, p. 11.
4. See 'Declaration-Programme . . .', the pamphlet published in late 1972-early 1973 by the opportunist saboteurs. The pamphlet was written in Conakry at the instigation of Jean Claude Njem, alias Pierre Pondy, the Pondy of the Yaounde 1970 'trial'. It is well known that, at this 'trial', Bishop Ndongmo mentioned a warrant handed to him by Njiawue and Pierre Pondy, a warrant the authorship of which the latter had attributed to President Ouandie, who denied having any connection with it. The reader will find a detailed critique of the pamphlet in *Cahiers Upecistes*, No. 1, November 1973, in an article entitled 'La Question de l'unite de l'UPC'. The various projects outlined by the saboteurs in the pamphlet have all subsequently disappeared like clouds of smoke before the breeze.

5. 'Pour la liberte, l'independence, le renouvau national et le progres social des peuples d'Afrique tropicale', published in *Bulletin d'Information*, Editions Internationales Paix et Socialisme, Prague 1978, No. 16-17.

6. *Op. cit.*, pp. 27-28.

7. Nicanor Njiawue, Preface to *La Revolution Kamerunaise et la lutte des Peuples Africains*, by Felix Roland Moumie, U.P.C., 1959, p. 1.

8. *Ibid.*, p. 5.

9. *Ibid.*, p. 6.

10. *Ibid.*, p. 7.

11. See for example Woungly-Massaga, *l'Afrique bloquee . . .*, 1971. Also 'La Question de l'Unite de l'UPC', *op. cit.*, p. 52.

12. *Le Kamerun sous un regime de dictature fasciste*, U.P.C., 1960.

13. *Unite Africaine ou Neo-Colonialisme, op. cit.*, p. 16.

14. *Declaration-Programme*, the opportunists' pamphlet, p. 6.

15. *Ibid.*, p. 3.

16. *Marches Tropicaux*, 28 December 1973, 9. 3915.

17. *Cahiers Upecistes*, No. 1, November 1973.

18. Lenin, *A Characterization of Economic Romanticism, op. cit.*

19. Such bouts of amnesia are becoming generalized whenever it comes to the history of Cameroon over the last 30 years, especially when it is taught to young Cameroonians who did not themselves live through the period of the anti-colonialist struggle. Let us begin by repeating that the U.P.C. never considered Christians as such as its opponents, although many fascist Baptist pastors in the pay of the regime sought to assault our People and make fools of them by canonizing the dictator, Ahidjo. However we cannot avoid noticing that in his *Histoire du Cameroun*, an abridged version of which serves as the country's official history textbook at the moment, Abbe Mueng Engelbert seems to have been more concerned to show himself a 'true believer' than a serious historian of that part of our history from 1945 to the present day. The book is a monument to amnesia.
    Outright falsification is prevalent in almost every domain the present neo-colonial Cameroonian bourgeoisie touches. Everything is done to please El Hadj His Excellency, especially in the social sciences, where, as Friedrich Engels put it: 'The old intransigent spirit has completely disappeared (. . .), and has made way for an empty eclecticism, motivated only by the grossest careerism and financial self-interest, by the most vulgar *arrivisme*. The official representatives of this science have become the declared ideologues of the bourgeoisie and the present state . . ., at a time when both are in open opposition to the working class [and the poor peasantry, the overwhelming majority of our people. E.M.]. (This intransigent spirit) . . . it is only the poor working people who will never give it up: they have no concern with career, profits or benevolent protection from above. Friedrich Engels, *Ludwig Feuerbach and the End of Classical German Philosophy*, Editions Sociales, 1966, p. 85. Every Cameroonian will have recognized the intellectual and bureaucratic petty bourgeoisie of our country in this description.

20. Lenin, *Second Congress of the Communist International (19 July-7 August 1920): Report to the National and Colonial Commission (26 July)*, Complete Works, various edns.

21. Nicanor Njiawue, *Liquider l'opportunisme . . .*, pamphlet, p. 15.
22. Lenin, *op. cit.*
23. This is, it seems, Njiawue's view; he rejects the U.P.C. Revolutionary Committee's view of the 'revolutionary countries of Africa'. Speaking of Massaga, Njiawue writes: 'In his information bulletins and his open letters, he has systematically sought to sabotage the relations between our Party, on the one hand, the socialist states and the anti-imperialist countries of Africa, such as Guinea, Congo-B and Algeria on the other. In doing so, he has added to the woes of our militants living abroad. (See *Eliminating opportunism . . .*, p. 3.)
24. Lenin, *The Socialist Revolution and the right of nations to self-determination*, Complete Works, various edns.

Other Books Available from Zed Press

On Africa

Robert Archer & Antoine Bouillon
The South African Game
Sport and Non-racialism in South Africa
Hb and Pb

Mohamed Babu
African Socialism or Socialist Africa?
Hb and Pb

Faarax M.J. Cawl
Ignorance is the Enemy of Love
(Trans. from Somali by Dr. G. Andrzejewski)
Pb

Basil Davidson
No Fist is Big Enough to Hide The Sky
The Liberation of Guinea and Cape Verde:
Aspects of an African Revolution
Hb

Aquino de Branganca and Immanuel Wallerstein (eds.)
The African Liberation Reader
Documents of the National Liberation Movements of Southern Africa
Hb

Ronald Graham
Monopoly Capital and African Development
The Political Economy of the World Aluminium Industry
Hb

E. Madunagu
Problems of Socialism: The Nigerian Challenge
Pb

Dan W. Nabudere
The Political Economy of Imperialism
Hb and Pb

Dan W. Nabudere
Imperialism in East Africa
Volume 1: Imperialism and Exploitation
Volume 2: Imperialism and Integration
Hb

Okwudiba Nnoli
Path to Nigerian Development
Pb